PAWN POWER IN CHESS

PAWN POWER
IN CHESS

by

Hans Kmoch

DAVID McKAY COMPANY, INC.

New York

10   9   8

ISBN: 0–679–14028–X

Kmoch, Hans.   Pawn power in chess.   New York, D. McKay Co. [c1958]
    304 p.   illus.   21 cm.   I. Pawn   (Chess)   GV1451.5.P3K57   794.1
    58–12250 ‡   Library of Congress

MANUFACTURED IN THE UNITED STATES OF AMERICA

To My Wife Trudy

PREFACE

The proper use of pawns, which is of paramount importance in chess strategy, sometimes puzzles even experienced players. Existing theory apparently offers insufficient guidance in certain respects. In the present work we have tried to facilitate the understanding of pawn play by isolating its elements and elaborating on their various aspects.

Our treatise on this subject was first published in German two years ago. However, PAWN POWER IN CHESS is an English treatment of the same subject rather than a direct translation of *Die Kunst der Bauernfuehrung*.

New York   HANS KMOCH

We wish to express our gratitude to Dr. Walter Meiden of the Department of Romance Languages of the Ohio State University for his careful reading of the English manuscript and for his numerous suggestions both as to subject matter and to style.

CONTENTS

Part One

THE ELEMENTS OF PAWN PLAY

Part Two

PAWNS AND PIECES

Part Three

PAWN POWER IN THE GAME

ADDENDA

Page *51*, after line 3:

But 2 ... B–B3 is actually the decisive error, as pointed out by Nathaniel Cohan; the correct continuation, sufficient for equality, is 2 ... N–B1!, followed by 3 ... N–N3 and 4 ... B–R5.

Page *265*, continuing first paragraph:

By way of exception, however, the exchange method (8PxP! etc.) offers chances here, as was later demonstrated by Benko in one game of his match against Reshevsky.

Page *268*, continuing first paragraph:

Also ... P–QB3, preceding ... P–K4, is usually played and with some success. Yet, Black's task remains difficult.

Part One

THE ELEMENTS OF PAWN PLAY

Pawns, unlike pieces, move only in one direction: forward. They move little by little and usually at long intervals. The march of a pawn is limited to six advances, but in most cases it ends earlier or does not start at all. Most games are over before all the pawns have come into action, and many of them end before any pawn has reached the eighth rank.

The pawn formation as a whole changes very gradually, thereby lending to the general situation characteristics of a more or less permanent nature which offer clues in the search for reasonable moves and strategic plans.

The critical examination of a position requires a consideration of many factors, but those concerning the pawn structure usually deserve priority.

In discussing the details of any given position it is convenient to refer to them with technical terms of basic significance. Such terms are also useful inasmuch as concepts with names make a deeper impression on the mind than concepts without names. But in the field of pawn play there are many terminological lacunae; some of them we were obliged to fill in with original suggestions.

While our technical terms such as *duo, lever,* and *span* are necessary, at least for the purpose of this book, we use certain new expressions simply for the sake of brevity, for instance *twin* instead of *double pawn.*

The classification of the elements of pawn play, some of which are almost inseparably intertwined, offers a formidable problem. We have nevertheless attempted such a classification.

CHAPTER I

THE ELEMENTS IN REVIEW

The initial pawn formation is perfect; neither side can obtain any tangible advantage by force. Disturbances of the balance are caused by errors. Only errors committed by one side enable the other side to obtain the upper hand, although recognizing the errors and taking advantage of them may require real ingenuity.

Pawns in general have the function of acting as a vanguard for the pieces. At the outset their only guiding factor is the position of the two Kings. Further indications as to play arise however almost move by move, particularly with every alteration of the pawn structure. Every such change has some elementary significance, the knowledge of which offers important hints in practical chessplay.

There follows a review of the qualities and duties of the pawns, both initially and in elementary formations.

I–§1: Location

A pawn's location is defined by its distance from the four rims, the sum of which forms the *pawn-cross* (*Diagram 1*).

The horizontal beams of the pawn-cross are uneven and unalterable; we refer to them as *lee* and *luff*, calling the shorter side *lee* as it frequently offers better shelter to the King. A change in lee and luff by means of capture has radical consequences, for the pawn disappears and emerges as a new pawn with a different denomination. For instance, if PQN2 carries out a capture on QB3, White virtually loses his QN-pawn but gains a QB-pawn.

The vertical beams, while never even, change with every advance of the pawn but do not alter the pawn's denomination. We call the vertical distances from the rims *spans*, distinguishing be-

3

tween *frontspan* and *rearspan* (and referring to the vertical distance between two opposing pawns as *interspan*).

The lengthening of the rearspan is often favorable, inasmuch as the expansion of territory behind the pawn increases the freedom of the pieces. By the same token, the shortening of the frontspan limits the freedom of the opposing pieces.

<table>
<tr><td>

DIAGRAM 1

The pawn-cross

Horizontally: lee and luff
Vertically: frontspan and
rearspan

</td><td>

DIAGRAM 2

Innerpawns and rimpawns

The rimpawn has no lee

</td></tr>
</table>

Lee and luff taken as a measure, we have what we call *innerpawns* and *rimpawns* (*Diagram 2*). A rimpawn, ordinarily called Rook pawn, has no lee side, covers only one square instead of two, and is consequently inferior to an innerpawn.

The lack of the lee side is a disadvantage which often shows up in the end game, in that a rimpawn draws where an innerpawn would win. Examples to the contrary are exceptions.

Another distinction between pawns, involving their spans, results from their location and subsequent duties with respect to both Kings (*Diagram 3*).

Pawns facing the front sector of the opposing King should advance in order to attack, while pawns covering the front sector of their own King should remain stationary for the sake of safety.

Consequently, only the *center pawns* (Q-pawn and K-pawn) are entitled to advance in any case; the duties of the *wing pawns* become definite after both sides have castled.

The wing pawns are divided on the one hand into those of the *Queen side* (QR-pawn, QN-pawn, QB-pawn) and on the other hand those of the *King side* (KB-pawn, KN-pawn, KR-pawn).

It is usual to maintain the terms Q-side and K-side throughout the game, but they virtually fail to make sense when castling on the Q-side has occurred. We therefore use the alternate terms of *home side* for the *castled side* and *ranger side* for the *uncastled side*, distinguishing accordingly between *home pawns* and *rangers*.

DIAGRAM 3

Distinction according to duty

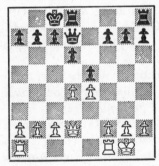

Center pawns Q4, K4 vs Q3, K4
Home pawns KB2, KN2, KR2 vs QB2, QN2, QR2
Rangers QR2, QN2, QB2 vs KB2, KN2, KR2

The center pawns should advance with caution, the rangers with gusto, but the home pawns not at all.

Somewhat exceptional is the position of the Bishop pawns, which belong to the wings but are also closely related to the center pawns; they may often advance before the question of castling is settled. This is particularly true of the QB-pawn.

I–§2: On the road to promotion

The promotion of a pawn depends basically only on the obstruction by opposing pawns. There are two types of obstruction, mechanical and dynamical.

Most hampering is the mechanical obstruction offered by the pawn's *counterpawn,* e.g. PQ2 vs PQ2. Every pawn is pawn and counterpawn at the same time; it depends on the observer's point of view.

Originally every pawn is *unfree* owing to mechanical obstruction. Removal of its counterpawn makes a pawn *half-free.*

The half-free pawn meets dynamical obstruction on the part of its opposing neighbors whom we call *sentries;* normally an inner-pawn faces two of them, a rimpawn only one. The sentries may both guard the same square or two different squares. The sentries of White's Q-pawn, for instance, are Black's QB-pawn and K-pawn; in case of PQ4 vs PQB3, PK3 they both guard against P–Q5, while in case of PQ4 vs PQB2, PK3 one guards against P–Q5, the other against P–Q6.

Dynamical obstruction is not absolute; the half-free pawn may march through, and is therefore called a *candidate*—a candidate for full freedom and promotion.

The promotion of a candidate depends on assistance by its own neighbors whom we call *helpers.* The helpers of White's Q-pawn, for instance, are White's QB-pawn and K-pawn. In the position of PQB2, PQ2, PK2 vs PQB2, PK2 the Q-pawn's bypassing of its sentries is assured.

The operation of helping a candidate to cross the guarded square or squares should start with the advance of the candidate itself. "Candidate first" is the rule for such cases. Other initial pawn moves are basically unreliable.

Helpers and sentries neutralize each other if there is a helper for every sentry. A half-free pawn with inadequate help is no true candidate but a *faker.* In the position of PQ4 vs PK3, for instance, both pawns are fakers, each one lacking the necessary helper. The same with PQ4 in the formation of PQB2, PQ4, PK2 vs PQB2, PK2, PKB3 when PK2 is paralyzed by . . . PKB3; this helper needs a *helper's helper*, e.g. PKB2, which assures the consecutive crossing of K5 and Q6.

In other words: the passing of a candidate depends on its belonging to a majority of pawns (which may or may not be just local).

Once a candidate faces no more obstruction on the part of sentries, it is *free*, as are all pawns in the position of PQ4, PKR2 vs PQB5, PKB3. A free pawn is called a *passed pawn* or, as we prefer to call it for short, a *passer*.

DIAGRAM 4

A pawn's stages of freedom

DIAGRAM 5

Outside passer PQR5

Unfree PQR2, PK4, vs PQR3, PK3
Fakers PQB3 vs PQN4
Candidate PQ4; Passer PKN2

Superior to inside passer...
PQB4

A passer is basically superior to an unfree pawn or a candidate.

The shorter its frontspan is, the greater the value of a passer. For instance PKB5 vs PQB3 favors White.

Another factor of importance in the relative value of passers is their horizontal distance from the bulk of the pawns; the greater this distance is, the better. It constitutes the so-called *advantage of the outside passed pawn* (*Diagram 5*). The outside passer counts particularly in pawn endings, inasmuch as it forces the opposing King to stray far away from its own pawns.

There is also distinction with regard to protection. A passer protected by one or two pawns is a *protected passer* (*Diagram 6*) and superior to an ordinary passer. But it is exclusively the protection by pawns that counts.

An unfree pawn or a faker may suddenly become a passer of decisive power by means of a sacrificial combination. We call such a pawn a *sneaker*. The sneaker's outstanding quality is almost invariably its short frontspan and outside location, e.g. PQR5, PQN4, PQ5 vs PQR3, PQB2, PQ3, when the unfree PQR5 sneaks through after *1* P–N5, PxP; *2* P–R6.

DIAGRAM 6

Protected passers PQB5 vs PKN5

Stronger than ordinary passers

DIAGRAM 7

The sneaker

Most common example

In the popular example of *Diagram 7* White has two potential sneakers, one of them marching through as follows: *1* P–Q6, KPxP (or *1* ... BPxP; *2* P–K6); *2* P–B6, PxBP; *3* P–K6 and wins (assuming that no piece can interfere). Note the importance of the original span situation; if Black has the move, he correctly starts with *1* ... P–Q3 but must answer *2* KPxP with *2* ... KPxP, as *2* ... P–B3 obviously makes no sense.

I–§3: The ram

Two opposing pawns, deadlocked as fighting rams, constitute an element which we call the *ram*, e.g. PK4 vs PK4 (*Diagram 8*).

Rams cause immobility. They separate the opposing armies, thereby favoring the defender.

DIAGRAM 8

The ram

Bulwark of defense

For attacking purposes it is important to avoid rams as far as possible and strive for the dissolution of existing rams.

The struggle for or against the dissolution of a ram depends mainly on the neighboring pawns.

I–§4: Stop and telestop

All squares of a pawn's frontspan tend to weakness, as the pawn needs them one after the other but can never control them.

These squares are highly suitable for harboring enemy pieces, for a piece thus posted is protected against frontal assault; it also has a close-range activity—provided the pawn is not very far advanced. The value of such a square for an opposing piece depends on the possibilities of dislodging it; obviously, it is of great importance whether a helper of the pawn can control the critical square, and if so, what effort this will require.

We call these critical squares *stopsquares* or *stops*, distinguishing between the *stop proper*, which is the first square of the pawn's frontspan, and the *telestops* (*Diagram 9*), which are the following squares of that span.

The stop proper is of paramount significance.

The significance of the telestops diminishes as the distance from the pawn increases; it would rarely extend farther than to the second telestop.

Almost every organic weakness of a pawn formation may be explained by the weakness of one or more stopsquares.

DIAGRAM 9	DIAGRAM 10
Stop and telestop	*The duo*

S = *stops*
T = *telestops*

Top efficiency and economy

I–§5: The duo

Two pawns of the same party, placed next to each other so they mutually cover their stopsquares, constitute an element which we call the *duo*. For instance PQB4, PQ4 or ... PQB4, PQ4.

The duo is the formation in which pawns reach their top efficiency in the most economical way. Two duos are apt to control an entire rank—an effect which no other formation of pawns can match (*Diagram 10*).

Pawns should be used in such a way that they form or can form duos, and remain able to do this again and again.

The ability to produce duos is the most important measure of the value of a pawn formation.

I–§6: Headpawn and head-duo

The foremost pawn of a formation figures in our theory as the *headpawn.*

The headpawn is in command of the pawnfront, indicating what should be done in order to assure the proper activity of the pieces. The headpawn usually calls for a duo which we call the *head-duo* (*Diagram 11*).

The head-duo is most important when it involves contact with opposing pawns, e.g. PQ4, PK4 vs PQ3, PK4; or PQ4, PK4 vs PQ4, PK3; or PQB4, PQ4 vs PQ4, PK3. Then, the duo usually leads to the exchange of a pawn, which in turn increases the scope of the pieces.

It was the head-duo in particular that Philidor had in mind when he realized the significance of that sort of formation some two hundred years ago. He called it a *phalanx*—a term the exact meaning of which few people would know today. We prefer the term *duo;* for one thing, it fits better into our expanded duo theory, serving as denominator for many other terms.

DIAGRAM 11

Headpawn over the middle-line

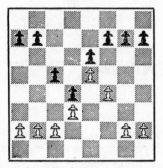

The head-duo a major problem

DIAGRAM 12

More than one headpawn

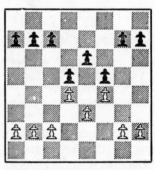

One head-duo at a time

The head of a formation would ordinarily be a center pawn placed on Q4 or K4 (... Q4 or ... K4); in such cases the forming of the head-duo offers no problems, at least not on White's part.

But once the headpawn has crossed the middle-line, the head-duo usually does offer a major problem.

Positions with more than one headpawn (*Diagram 12*) require a decision as to which one offers the better head-duo. It is wise to strive for one head-duo at a time. Much depends on the position of the Kings. Once the first head-duo has led to a satisfactory result, the second may come into play with increased effect.

Headpawns which remain after a pawn or two have been traded may have little or no commanding power.

The headpawns in *Diagram 13*, for instance, are mere puppets; they offer too little chance for any useful exchange of pawns, nor is there any need for such an exchange.

DIAGRAM 13

Remaining headpawns unex-changeable

No commanding power

DIAGRAM 14

Remaining headpawns ex-changeable

Commanding power

But the example of *Diagram 14* is different. It shows the common situation where the remaining headpawns face each other at the distance of a Knight's jump. These headpawns, because of their high degree of exchangeability, continually indicate what the plans for both sides should be. The headpawn on the fourth rank still calls for the head-duo: *1* P–QB4. Not so the headpawn on the third, for the third rank is, in general, too modest a base for a head-duo. What this pawn indicates is the elimination of the opposing headpawn by exchanging it. Black should strive for ... P–K4 or ... P–QB4.

I–§7: Types of duos

The pawns of a duo may or may not have contact with opposing pawns. Accordingly, we distinguish between *tight duos* (contact) and *loose duos* (no contact).

Apart from location, which is the distinguishing factor of any duo, tight duos are uniform in type; their axis is a ram, and they differ from each other only as far as the protection of the opposing rampawn is concerned. For instance PQB4, PQ4 vs PQB3, PQ4; or PQB4, PQ4 vs PQ4, PK3; or PQB4, PQ4 vs PQ4. But these are differences of a secondary nature.

There are more basic differences between loose duos because of their indefinite character.

With all pawns on the board, loose duos of advanced pawns ordinarily create a charged atmosphere (*Diagram 15*) because of the uncertainty as to when and where the impending contact between the pawns and subsequent start of the actual fighting may occur.

Special loose duos are the *hanging duo,* the *passer duo,* and the *buffer duo.*

The *hanging duo* (*Diagram 16*) is the optimal form of what Steinitz called the *hanging pawns:* an isolated couple of half-free pawns. This formation has distinct advantages and drawbacks. Usually involving the center pawns, or at least one of them, the hanging duo may be strong, thanks to its location and mobility, particularly so for aggressive thrusts in the middle-game. On the other hand, it is vulnerable, and its mobility may easily end after a single move.

Note that the hanging pawns in *Diagram 16* are fakers as is shown by *1* P–Q5, P–KB3! or *1* P–K5, P–QB3!. They become candidates only if the duo as a whole is allowed to reach the fifth rank, e.g. *1* P–Q5, P–QR3; *2* P–K5.

DIAGRAM 15
Loose duos

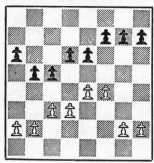

Charged atmosphere

DIAGRAM 16
The hanging duo

*Distinct advantages and
disadvantages*

The *passer duo* (*Diagram 17*) is the strongest possible formation of connected passed pawns. Its power is tremendous—so tremendous that it usually makes no difference whether these pawns have helpers or not.

DIAGRAM 17
The passer duo

Tremendous

DIAGRAM 18
The buffer duo

Bypassing

The *buffer duo* (*Diagram 18*) is a combined formation: two opposing duos facing each other with one rank between. Necessarily, one of these duos is farther advanced than the other and would normally have aggressive tendencies culminating in the desirable exchange of one of these pawns or both. However, the advance of neither of these pawns leads to an exchange by force since the other duo, working as a buffer, offers the possibility of bypassing. For instance in *Diagram 18: 1* P–N5, P–R4!; or *1* . . . P–B6; 2 P–N3!.

For the *basic duo*, which usually consists of pawns on the second rank serving to give advanced pawns duo-power, see I–§13, *Diagram 30.*

I–§8: Trio and quart

Any horizontal formation of pawns should be considered from the duo standpoint and handled accordingly. The potential duos should be preserved and utilized to the fullest extent. A *trio* contains two potential duos, a *quart* three. See *Diagram 19.* The duo possibilities in this position are QRP, QNP and QNP, QBP vs KP, KBP; KBP, KNP and KNP, KRP. These possibilities reveal the pattern in which such pawns should advance. Not for a moment should either side remain without a duo, as would be the case after *1* P–N4?, P–R5; 2 P–N5?, P–B5?. White should start with either *1* P–R4! or *1* P–B4!, then proceed accordingly,

DIAGRAM 19

Trio and quart

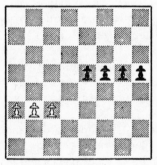

Potential duos

e.g. *1* P–R4!; *2* P–N4!; *3* P–B4!; *4* P–B5! or P–R5!. Black may start with any move but must be careful with his second as he then emerges with two duos, one duo, or none, e.g. *1* ... P–K5 followed by *2* ... P–B5!, *2* ... P–R5!?, or *2* ... P–N5?.

I–§9: The lever

The situation in which two opposing pawns can capture each other constitutes an element of pawn play which we shall call the *lever*, e.g. PK4 vs PQ4 (*Diagram 20*).

DIAGRAM 20

The lever

Power and load; tension

A lever creates tension which may or may not explode in capture. To carry out the capture frequently involves a concession. Take for instance the opening *1* P–K4, P–K3; *2* P–Q4, P–Q4; if White now captures, the position becomes completely even: *3* PxP, PxP; but if White maintains the tension by playing *3* N–QB3, and the capture is carried out by Black: *3* ... PxP, *4* NxP, the resulting pawn formation (*Diagram 14*) favors White, if only slightly.

Consequently, it usually happens that each side continues trying to induce the other to make the capture. Their mutual efforts are comparable to the stress of power and load on a lever. Hence our term.

I–§10: Types of levers

Levers, like duos, are either tight or loose.

The lever shown in *Diagram 20* is a *loose lever*, both s.
having the choice of capture and bypassing.

The *tight lever* is connected with a ram, offering the choice to
only one of the sides. For instance PQB4, PQ4 vs PQ4, PK3 when
White's leverpawn (PQB4) can either capture or advance, while
Black's leverpawn (...PQ4) can only capture. Choice in such
cases usually means initiative.

It also makes a difference whether a lever points towards the
center or towards the rim, e.g. PQB4 vs PQ4 which, since levers
are two-faced, is an *inner lever* for White and an *outer lever* for
Black. The inner lever is usually slightly superior to the outer
lever since it offers the initiative. A lever within the two center
files (*Diagram 20*) is basically neutral; we call it a *center lever*.

An innerpawn may come under simultaneous lever attack
from both sides; we then speak of a *double lever*, loose or tight,
e.g. PQB4, PQ3, PK4 vs PQB3, PQ4, PK3 (loose) or PQB4, PQ4,
PK4 vs PQB3, PQ4, PK3 (tight). The double lever doubles the
tension but is not necessarily twice as strong or advantageous as
an ordinary lever.

Viewed from the other side, the double lever presents itself
as a forking attack of one pawn against two, as e.g. in this opening: *1* P–K4, P–QB3; *2* P–QB4, P–Q4. We call this the *fork
lever* (*Diagram 21*). It depends on circumstances as to whether
the opposing features of the lever are evenly significant or not.

The fork lever may simultaneously attack a pawn and a piece,
thereby destroying a duo. In this form it has great importance in
the opening. For instance *1* P–K4, P–K4; *2* N–KB3, N–QB3;
3 B–B4, B–B4; *4* P–B3, N–B3; *5* P–Q4, PxP; *6* PxP, B–N5ch;
7 B–Q2, BxBch; *8* QNxB when *8* ...P–Q4! destroys White's
duo, keeping the chances approximately in the balance. Twists of
this type may occur in any stage of the game, as the elementary
example of *Diagram 21* demonstrates.

There are also three important levers of a combined nature,
namely the *chain lever*, the *pincer lever*, and the *cross lever*.

nsists of adjacent levers in diagonal forma-
with the farther advanced headpawn, pro-
ks the base of the opposing chain; then,
passer which, compared by the opposing
advanced, or placed more outside, or both.

DIAGRAM 22

The fork lever

The chain lever

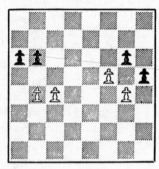

*1 P–K4ch! destroys duo and
draws*

Produces outside passer

Diagram 22 shows the chain lever PKB5, PKN4 vs PKN3, PKR4; after *1 . . . PxBP; 2 PxRP!* White emerges with the outside passer. The situation is duplicated after *1 . . . P–R4; 2 P–B5!*, which at once shows how such a chain lever arises.

The chain lever may have its full effect even if the headpawn is unfree, e.g. PKB6, PKN5 vs PKB2, PKN2, PKR3. But note that this is an outer lever for White, and an inner lever for Black, as is the lever in *Diagram 22*. Pointing to the center the lever creates an inside passer; e.g. PKN5, PKR6 vs PKB3, PKN2, PKR2 when, after *1 . . . PxRP; 2 PxBP*, Black emerges with the outside passer, and White with the farther advanced passer (which may favor either side).

The chain lever may have more than two links, e.g. PQR6, PQN5, PQB4, PQ3 vs PQR2, PQN2, PQB3, PQ4. But no matter how many links it has, the headpawn must attack the base of the opposing chain, or the chain lever lacks its characteristic effect of producing a passer. For instance PQR5, PQN4, PQB3 vs PQR2, PQN3, PQB4 when there is no passing involved. We then speak of a *mute chain lever*.

Similar to the chain lever is the *pincer lever,* consisting of two levers which convergingly attack a chain of two links, its base included, e.g. PQ5, PKN6 vs PQ3, PK3, PKB2. The main point of the pincer lever is the creation of an advanced passer, which may be superior to the outside passer it concedes to the opponent. The latter notwithstanding, passing on a more outside file may still be the issue, as is the case in *Diagram 23* after *1* ... P–R6; 2 PxRP, PxP, when Black has transferred his passer from the Q-file to the QB-file—a possibly decisive difference.

DIAGRAM 23

The pincer lever

Converging lever attack: ...
P–R6

DIAGRAM 24

The cross lever

Strong but brief tension

Finally there is the formation of *Diagram 24*, which arises from *1* P–Q4, P–Q4; 2 P–QB4, P–QB4. Is it a combination of rams? or duos? or levers? Not of rams, since it lacks the static character of a ram, and not of duos, since its symmetry is opposed to the concept of a duo. The outstanding feature of this formation are the possibilities of capture, and we therefore call it the *cross lever.*

The cross lever is likely to create a strong but brief tension.

If the pawns concerned have an uneven frontspan, the cross lever also has the ability to create an advanced passer, e.g. PQB5, PQ5 vs PQB3, PQ3.

The formation of *Diagram 24* is classifiable, in spite of its compound nature.

Not so with the formation of *Diagram 25*, which is just one example of the common case in which several elements are intertwined beyond any possibility of separation.

DIAGRAM 25

Compound formation

Ram-duo-lever intertwined

To describe and analyze such a compound formation requires emphasis on the element under consideration. Everything depends on the angle from which the formation is viewed. The diagrammed position shows a ram that might be described as *center-ram*, a duo which could be called a *center-duo, tight duo,* or *lever-duo,* and a lever which could be identified as *center-lever, tight lever,* or *duo-lever.* All this makes sense only in context. Otherwise a formation like this can be classified only as compound.

I–§11: Symmetrical and unsymmetrical exchange

The exchange of a pawn may or may not hold promise for continued tension, action, or attack. It depends on the type of the exchange, which can be either symmetrical and stabilizing, or unsymmetrical and dynamic.

The *symmetrical exchange* eliminates a pawn and its counter-pawn, e.g. *1* P–Q4, P–Q4; *2* P–QB4, P–QB3; *3* PxP, PxP (*Diagram 26*). The stabilizing effect is then due to the reduced chance for levers as well as the open file which, being basically neutral, may easily lead to the exchange of the Rooks.

<table>
<tr><td align="center">DIAGRAM 26</td><td align="center">DIAGRAM 27</td></tr>
<tr><td align="center">Symmetrical exchange and open file</td><td align="center">Unsymmetrical exchange and half-open files</td></tr>
</table>

3 PxP, PxP is stabilizing   *3 PxP, PxP is dynamic*

The *unsymmetrical exchange* is dynamic because it creates a half-free pawn and a half-open file on either side, e.g. *1* P–Q4, P–Q4; *2* P–QB4, P–K3; *3* PxP, PxP (*Diagram 27*). There is chance for new levers with new tensions, the more so since the half-open files preclude the exchange of the Rooks.

I–§12: Local majorities

An open file or a number of them may split the remaining pawns in such a way that a majority on one wing is matched by a majority on the other. These are called *local majorities*. A local majority usually amounts to an extra pawn in the status of candidate, e.g. PQR2, PQN2, PKR2 vs PQR2, PKN2, PKR2.

The majority should be handled according to the rule "candidate first" so it can produce a passer sooner or later.

In the middle-game, with the Queens on the board, local majorities have a special significance in that the extra pawn on the castled side is of less significance than the extra pawn on the uncastled side, because rangers, unlike home-pawns, can often easily advance with impunity. Then, when the end-game is reached, the majority on the uncastled side often constitutes an advantage in time, inasmuch as these pawns are farther advanced than the pawns of the other majority. This is known as the "advantage of the Queen-side majority," but it is virtually the *advantage of the majority on the uncastled side;* by stating it that way, the rule also covers those cases where the original denomination of the sides is reversed because of castling on the Queen side.

The majority on the castled side is not necessarily useless in the middle-game; it may be significant if the proportion is 4:3 so that two pawns are available for the protection of the King and two for action (*Diagram 28*).

Diagram 28

Majority on the castled side

With 4:3, useful in the middle-game

The merit of a 4:3 majority on the King side in cases similar to our *Diagram 28* has been often demonstrated by Botvinnik; he has a predilection for such positions.

I–§13: Chains

Diagonal pawn formations are called *chains;* they may be identified by the number of their links: two-linked chains, three-linked—up to six.

Two converging chains reaching into enemy territory form a *wedge* (*Diagram 29*).

Zig-zag formations we call a *saw*. The most common saw formation is the so-called Stonewall (*Diagram 30*).

DIAGRAM 29

Chain and wedge

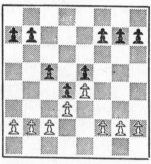

Chain PQB2, PQ3, PK4 vs wedge PQB4, PQ5, PK4

DIAGRAM 30

Most common saw formation

The Stonewall: PQB3, PQ4, PK3, PKB4

In general, diagonal formations have the dangerous quality of leaving the stopsquares of their links unprotected so that they tend to become weak.

As a rule, a diagonal formation is likely to be sound if it is based on a pawn that either belongs to a duo or is placed on the rim.

Diagram 30, for instance, shows the chain PQN2, PQB3, PQ4 with PQN2 as its *base*. Since the base is part of the duo PQR2, PQN2 (a *basic duo!*) White's chain is sound as he can create a new duo with P–QN3, and again another with P–QB4—even if Black first plays . . . P–QR4–R5.

On the K-side, the situation is somewhat different. The chain PKR2, PKN3, PKB4 needs no basic duo, as it originates from the rim; by the absence of any resistance from outside, the duo-move P–KR3 is always possible.

I–§14: Isolation—Dispersion—Distortion

Originally, the pawns form an impenetrable wall covering each other's stops. However, the advance and possible disappearance of pawns creates new situations, which have an important bearing on the balance of power.

The question of compensation left aside, the creation of unprotected stopsquares is weakening.

Unprotected stops result from the splitting of the pawn formation into parts with little or no ability to form duos. The more such parts there are, the greater the trouble they cause.

There is a splitting in vertical direction, caused by capture, and a splitting in horizontal direction, caused by the advance of pawns.

We call the vertical splitting *dispersion* (*Diagram 31*), and the horizontal splitting *distortion* (*Diagram 32*). The most usual form of dispersion is the *isolation* of one or more pawns.

DIAGRAM 31

Vertical splitting

Black suffers from dispersion, isolation

DIAGRAM 32

Horizontal splitting

White suffers from distortion

In *Diagram 31* Black has three isolated pawns of which ... PQB2 and ... PK4 are particularly disadvantageous because they can easily be assailed from the front while their central location increases the significance of their weak stopsquares.

Horizontal splitting is remediable inasmuch as the pawns, or at least some of them, retain their capacity for forming duos. However, this is an abstract point of view. A cure is sometimes possible in a case of slight distortion, but not if the formation is as thoroughly distorted as is White's pawn front in *Diagram 32*.

Distortion is usually even more damaging than dispersion, for if some of the pawns advance at random, the enemy pieces have more chance to slip through and operate from behind, meeting no opposition whatsoever from pawns.

I–§15: Backwardness

A half-free pawn, placed on the second or third rank, whose stopsquare lacks pawn protection but is controlled by a sentry, is called a *backward pawn* or, as we alternately speak of it, a *straggler*. See *Diagram 33*.

A straggler constitutes a weakness because (1) it invites enemy pieces to its stopsquare offering them a steppingstone over the middle-line with absolute cover against frontal assault (2) it hampers pieces of its own color (3) it is basically vulnerable.

There is also something which might be called *conditional backwardness*, where a pawn is backward only in certain respects.

In the position of *Diagram 34*, PQB2 is not backward since it belongs to a duo. Yet, this pawn has features of backwardness since it is located on the second rank and unable to move with impunity; and since P–QN3 might become necessary in order to prevent ... P–QN6, there is considerable danger that PQB2 will become definitely backward.

In the same diagram, there is also the conditional straggler PKN4—backward in relation to the ram PKB5 vs PKB3 and the chain PKB5, PKN4, not backward however with respect to ... PKR3 as well as to the fact that its stopsquare lies in enemy territory.

Here is a compound situation where everything depends on the circumstances.

DIAGRAM 33

Backwardness

DIAGRAM 34

Conditional backwardness

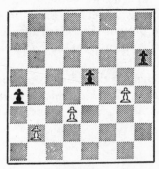

Stragglers PQN2, PQ3 vs
PKR3

PQB2 and PKN4 backward in
certain respects

I–§16: Shielding

A pawn or piece occupying a stop or telestop is protected by the opposing pawn against frontal attack. We call this *shielding*.

Shielding is most effective on the stop, e.g. KK2 vs PK6. On telestops its effect diminishes with the increasing distance from the shielder owing to increasing possibilities of frontal attack, e.g. KK2 vs PK5, KK2 vs PK4, and so on.

Pawns are originally unfree, that is to say shielded. Consequently, a weak pawn requires consideration as to whether it is still shielded, and if so, to what degree. Shielded weaknesses (*Diagrams 35, 36*) have a much lesser significance than open weaknesses.

Under certain circumstances an unshielded pawn can be artificially shielded by a piece. This we shall discuss later (*Diagrams 88, 92*).

Of the four singletons in *Diagram 35*, ... PQB4 is perfectly shielded, ... PQR4 almost so since frontal attack on it is limited to the Queen or the King, PKN2 is only lightly shielded, and **PK4** not at all.

There are five shielded stragglers in *Diagram 36,* namely PQN2, PK3, PKN3 vs PK3, PKN2.

PK3 vs PK3 neutralize each other.

PKN3 is at the same time an important lever pawn; its advance and possible exchange may essentially alter the diagrammed position in one of these ways: (1) removal of PKN3 vs PKB4, which distinctly favors White because of the resulting plain backwardness of ... PKN2 as well as the possible lever thrust P–K4 (2) removal of PKN3 vs PK3, which is dubious because of the resulting plain backwardness of PK3 vs PKN2 (3) arrival of PKN3 on KN5, whereby White attains his head-duo, thus essentially improving his position.

Also ... PKN2 has important lever power; the possible elimination of this pawn with ... P–N3, followed by ... P–R4, leads to plain backwardness of PKN3.

PQN2 is a plain liability. It has no lever power, inasmuch as the possible removal of PQN2 vs PQR5 causes plain backwardness of PQR3. Moreover, P–QN3 may easily fail against the cross lever: ... P–QN5.

DIAGRAM 35	DIAGRAM 36
Shielded isolation	*Shielded backwardness*

 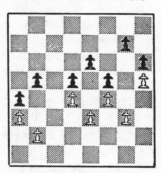

Various degrees of it	*Potential consequences*

I–§17: Siege and quartgrip

Backwardness is paralyzing. Shielded backwardness is paralyzing to a lesser extent, but it may still paralyze a whole formation of pawns. We then speak of a *siege*.

The prototype of the siege is what we call the *quartgrip*, a formation of four vs four pawns in which the shorter frontspans constitute a great advantage.

DIAGRAM 37

The quartgrip

Left: Black in the grip
Right: White in the grip

The quartgrip must be understood as containing a duo of shielded stragglers on the second rank, which virtually doubles the disadvantage of such a straggler. The attacker, having at his disposal two head-duos on the fifth rank, can create an advanced passer by force the sneaking way.

Following are a few possibilities in *Diagram 37:*

1 P–N5, P–B5 (or *1* ...PxP, *2* PxP, followed by *3* P–R6);
2 P–B5, P–B6 (*2* ...RPxP, *3* P–B6!; or *2* ...QPxP, *3* P–N6!);
3 KNPxP, KPxP; *4* P–B6 (or *4* P–N6, which creates a passer on the QB-file or Q-file); *4* ...NPxP, *5* PxRP (or *5* P–N6); *5* ... P–N5, and Black also gets an advanced passer.

After *1* P–N3, Black frees either his KR-pawn with *1* ...P–N5, or his K-pawn with *1* ... PxP; *2* PxP, P–B5. In case of *1* P–B3 the outside passer results from *1* ... PxP, while the cross lever *1* ... P–B5 frees the K-pawn.

These variations give an idea of the creative power of the quartgrip.

Although likely to occur only at an advanced stage of the game, the quartgrip is not excluded from the opening, as the following variation of the French defense shows: *1* P–K4, P–K3; *2* P–Q4, P–Q4; *3* N–QB3, B–N5; *4* P–K5, P–QB4; *5* P–QR3, BxNch; *6* PxB. If Black now proceeds immediately or soon with ... P–QB5, thus postponing the opening of lines, White is entitled to strive for the formation PK5, PKB4, PKN4, PKR5, which may lead to the quartgrip.

Needless to say, the quartgrip serves perfectly if applied against a minority, e.g. PQR5, PQN4, PQB4, PQ5 vs either PQR3, PQN2, PQ3 or PQR3, PQB2, PQ3.

Chapter II

PAWNS SINGLE FILE

Pawns are made to march abreast; when placed in front of each other by means of capture, they constitute a liability. Obviously, if two or more pawns must rely on the same frontspan or on the same sentry in order to form a lever, their fighting power diminishes.

However, the basic disadvantage of a vertical formation is not necessarily serious from the practical point of view. For one thing, it may be possible to restore the horizontal order of the pawns. Also, the vertical part of the formation may have no bearing on the pawn situation as a whole as far as the creation of passers is concerned.

Let us now discuss these questions in detail.

II–§1: The double pawn or twin

The only vertical pawn formation of importance is the vertical duo called *double pawn,* or *twin.*

The two parts of a double pawn are usually referred to as pawn (e.g. K-pawn) and foremost (K-) pawn. We call them *front-twin* and *rear-twin.*

In referring to the creation or elimination of a double pawn we speak of *doubling* or *undoubling.*

Undoubling normally requires a lever with the front-twin. Accordingly, there are three types of double pawns: sham, loose, and tight.

We speak of a *sham twin* if the undoubling is assured beforehand, e.g. *1* P–Q4, P–Q4; *2* P–QB4, P–K3; *3* N–QB3, B–N5;

4 P–QR3, BxNch; *5* PxB and *6* P–K3 (*Diagram 38*). Here, the doubling is of a transitory nature and not likely to have any detrimental effect.

If the undoubling is no fact but a possibility, we speak of a *loose twin*, e.g. *1* P–K4, P–K3; *2* P–Q4, P–Q4; *3* N–QB3, B–N5; *4* P–K5, P–QB4; *5* P–QR3, BxNch; *6* PxB (*Diagram 39*). Loose twins are most common; they usually do little or no harm.

<table>
<tr><td align="center">DIAGRAM 38</td><td align="center">DIAGRAM 39</td></tr>
<tr><td align="center">*Sham twin*</td><td align="center">*Loose twin*</td></tr>
</table>

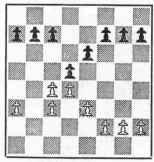

<table>
<tr><td align="center">*Undoubling lever a fact*</td><td align="center">*Undoubling lever a possibility*</td></tr>
</table>

But if undoubling by force is theoretically impossible, we speak of a *tight twin*, e.g. *1* P–Q4, N–KB3; *2* P–QB4, P–K3; *3* N–QB3, B–N5; *4* P–QR3, BxNch; *5* PxB (*Diagram 40*). Here White has no chance for a lever with the front-twin (unless ... P–Q4 or ... P–QN4 is played sooner or later, which depends on Black). The usual continuation is *5* ... P–B4 followed by ... P–QN3 and ... P–Q3 eventually leading to the so-called *Wyvill* formation: PQB3, PQB4, PQ5, PK4 vs PQB4, PQ3, PK4. Such an indissoluble double pawn is definitely a disadvantage requiring substantial compensation—which in the Wyvill case is offered by the aggressive lever PKB4 vs PK4.

Now suppose that in *Diagram 40* it were White's move and he played *1* P–B5, rightly speculating that he can exchange this pawn thanks to the inevitable ... P–Q3 or ... P–QN3. In doing so, he would only trade one disadvantage for another because after *1* ... P–QN3; *2* PxP, RPxP, his QR-pawn suffers from isolation and backwardness.

A loose twin, if immobilized in an expanded ram of the type PQB2, PQB3 vs PQB5, becomes a tight twin. See *6* ... P–B5 in *Diagram 39*.

DIAGRAM 40

Tight twin

Undoubling lever impossible

II–§2: The triad

The degree to which a twin is detrimental to the pawn formation becomes obvious when a majority thus afflicted is put to the test of producing a passer.

Most suitable for such testing is the smallest unit containing a non-isolated twin, i.e. a group of three pawns which we call a *triad*. For instance PQN2, PQN3, PQB3.

Triads, as well as formations with a double pawn in general, must be treated according to the special rule "Front-twin first" (instead of "Candidate first"). It is quite important to create space between the front-twin and the rear-twin so the latter can move. But even so, a pawn majority afflicted by doubling remains handicapped.

A triad of unfree pawns is unable to produce a passer against a duo. Neither White nor Black can get one by force in the position of *Diagram 41*. For instance *1* P–N6, PxP! or *1* P–B6, P–KN3!.

However, the defender must not allow the rear-twin to form a lever: *1* P–N6, P–B3??; *2* P–KN4!, etc. The same after *1* P–B6, PxP??; *2* PxP, etc. Accordingly, *1* P–QN4 is good, if played with the idea of capturing whenever ... P–QB4 occurs, and *1* P–B4 is also good, but then White must never capture in case of ... P–QN4.

DIAGRAM 41

Triad of unfree pawns vs duo

Creation of passer impossible

DIAGRAM 42

The twin or its helper half-free

*Left: Still no passer by force
Right: Passer, but at a high price*

The triad gains a little in creative power if the helper of the twin is half-free (*Diagram 42*, left), and still more if the twin itself is half-free (*Diagram 42*, right).

The half-free PQB2 needs a helper on QN5 in order to become a true candidate; it then could cross the guarded square QB6. Hence *1* P–QN4, threatening *2* P–N5. The attempt fails however against *1* ... P–QR3.

The half-free PKB3 is in a better situation than PQB2; in fact this front-twin is a true candidate, for its crossing of KB6 is assured, thanks to the rear-twin's acting as helper's helper. How-

ever, there is a grave concession involved inasmuch as Black's
KR-pawn queens first. Thus: *1* P–KB4, P–KR4; *2* P–N3
(*2* P–KB3??, P–R5!) *2* ... P–R3; *3* P–KB3, P–R4; *4* P–B5 (after
4 P–KN4?, P–R5, Black is two tempi ahead) *4* ... P–QN3,
5 P–KN4, P–R5, and Black queens one tempo earlier. Yes, even
in this case the doubling presents a serious handicap.

While a twin's attacking power is often reduced to the capacity
of one pawn, its defensive power usually remains unbroken. In
other words, a twin may be unable to overcome the obstruction
of a single pawn, but it is sufficient to hold two pawns. But
a triad does not necessarily prevent a trio from producing a
passer, for if one of the trio-pawns holds the twin, the two others
constitute a 2:1 majority.

DIAGRAM 43

Triad vs trio

When the trio produces a passer

In the position of *Diagram 43* Black's candidate simply marches
through: *1* ... P–R4! (*1* ... P–R3??, *2* P–B6!). The passing of
White's candidate depends on *1* P–N4, which Black, when he
has the move, can prevent with *1* ... P–KB4.

Note that in such cases the candidate cannot be a neighbor
of the twin; it would then be a faker.

II–§3: Types of doubling

Corresponding to the three types of levers according to direction there are the same three types of doubling; we call them *innerswap:* towards the center, e.g. QBPxQP, *outerswap:* towards the rim, e.g. QPxQBP, and *centerswap:* within the center, e.g. QPxKP.

Diagram 44 shows the three types of doubling.

DIAGRAM 44

Types of doubling

Innerswap: PKR2 has landed on KN3
Outerswap: PQB2 has landed on QN3
Centerswap: PQ4 has landed on K5

The outerswap is more likely to cause dispersion and be detrimental to the pawn formation than the other two types of doubling. However, there are also situations where the opposite is true.

Doubling in general often creates local majorities, particularly in the early part of the game. In such a case, the outerswap may cripple the majority. But with no majorities involved, the outerswap may be harmless or even preferable. (*Diagrams 45, 46.*)

In the position of *Diagram 45* the outerswap ... QPxB is definitely harmful, offering White a win by force in the pawn ending.

Nevertheless the outerswap is recommended in the corresponding line of the Ruy Lopez: *1* P–K4, P–K4; *2* N–KB3, N–QB3; *3* B–N5, P–QR3; *4* BxN, QPxB; *5* P–Q4, PxP; *6* QxP, QxQ; *7* NxQ; since the pawn ending is far away, Black is supposed to have a good game thanks to his pair of Bishops. This is however a question of opinion. At any rate, the crippling of Black's majority is a real disadvantage, while the compensation is questionable. May it suffice to say that of all leading masters only Emanuel Lasker repeatedly adopted this line with White, and almost invariably with success.

DIAGRAM 45   DIAGRAM 46

Majorities involved   *No majorities involved*

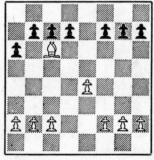 

Innerswap ... NPxB indicated   *Outerswap ... QPxB preferable*

In the same position (*Diagram 45*) the innerswap ... NPxP also has a drawback inasmuch as it causes dispersion, but this is, basically, by far the minor evil.

The situation of *Diagram 46* is different; since neither way of recapturing the Bishop creates majorities, Black has no reason to disperse his pawns with ... NPxB. Here the outerswap is preferable.

The question of local majorities is also applicable to the center-swap, which is unfavorable if it transforms e.g. PQ4, PK3 vs PQB4, PK3 into PK3, PK5 vs PQB4, PK3.

In the position of *Diagram 47* BPxN causes dispersion, yet it is preferable to KPxN which leaves White with a crippled majority. (In the latter case, Black must beware of the quartgrip. To be safe, he should avoid ... P–QR3.)

<table>
<tr><td>DIAGRAM 47</td><td>DIAGRAM 48</td></tr>
</table>

DIAGRAM 47

Centerswap and majorities

KPxN inferior to BPxN

DIAGRAM 48

Majorities without demarcation file

Innerswap BPxN preferable

The doubling may also create majorities with no open demarcation file between them. See *Diagram 48* where the centerswap KPxN concedes to Black a perfect majority on the K-side as against White's crippled one on the Q-side. For this reason the innerswap BPxN is basically preferable, dispersion notwithstanding.

II–§4: The doubled Bishop pawn

Most exposed to doubling are the B-pawns, which is due to the frequently possible exchange of a Knight on QB3 or KB3 (... QB3 or ... KB3). But while measures are usually taken to prevent the doubling of the KB-pawn, such as for the sake of castling to the K-side, the doubling of the QB-pawn is often permitted and sometimes even provoked, with the general idea that the innerswap with the QN-pawn would strengthen the center.

The doubling of one of the B-pawns is the common trait of a large family of positions. We shall confine ourselves to a few examples.

Diagram 49 shows the QB-twin in a comparatively favorable setting. Black suffers only from slight dispersion. He should maintain his duo, playing ... P–QB4 or ... P–Q4 only if there is a special reason for it such as the forced undoubling by means of KPxQP.

<table>
<tr><td>DIAGRAM 49</td><td>DIAGRAM 50</td></tr>
<tr><td>*The QB-twin within duo and triad*</td><td>*The lagging QB-twin*</td></tr>
</table>

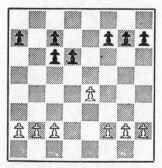

<table>
<tr><td>A slight liability</td><td>A liability</td></tr>
</table>

Diagram 50 shows a situation indicative of what happens when the rule "Front-twin first" is violated. Of course, the Q-pawn might have been on Q4 before the doubling occurred. However, the effect is the same as if White had advanced the wrong pawn of his triad. Now the triad is distorted, the twin lagging. And since ... BPxP is feasible while QPxP obviously is not, Black has the initiative.

Note that *1* ... PxP holds promise inasmuch as White emerges with hanging pawns after *2* PxP. The consequences of the un-doubling in this case are not the same as in *Diagram 49*.

While these facts favor Black, White may have adequate compensation, e.g. thanks to the lever action P–QR4–R5; he may thus shorten Black's chain on the Q-side and hit at its base; or he may have attacking chances on the K-side. But that depends on the position of the pieces. The pawn formation itself favors Black.

DIAGRAM 51

The KB-twin within duo and triad

Least detrimental to ... 0–0

The KB-twin is of special significance when combined with castling to the K-side; it then constitutes a weakness which ordinarily is serious. *Diagram 51* shows this weakness in its mildest form. The basically worst form of such a triad on the homeside is PKB2, PKB3, PK4 vs PK4 when the stopsquare of the firmly backward twin lies open to invasion. However, much depends on the tactical circumstances in each case. Generally speaking, the danger to the defender diminishes with every exchange of minor pieces. Sometimes the defender even gets the chance for a counter-attack along the KN-file. But these cases are exceptional—far more exceptional than is widely believed.

II–§5: The isolated twin

As weak stopsquares are harmful to a single pawn, how much more must they be so to a file of pawns. The mobility and safety of such pawns are gravely impaired and may cause all kinds of other damage.

Diagram 52 shows Black's Q-side in a lamentable condition, mainly because of his isolated and frontally assailable twin. White is a little better off since his twin is slightly shielded; he also has a duo but lacks, on the other hand, even the theoretical chance for a lever with his front-twin.

<table>
<tr><td align="center">DIAGRAM 52</td><td align="center">DIAGRAM 53</td></tr>
<tr><td align="center">Isolated twins</td><td align="center">The isolated and shielded
K-twin</td></tr>
</table>

<table>
<tr><td align="center">Particularly harmful</td><td align="center">Often useful</td></tr>
</table>

An exceptional case is the isolated but closely shielded twin on the K-file as shown in *Diagram 53*. This double pawn often serves well because it controls valuable squares in the central zone and is difficult to assail.

II–§6: Crossing and undoubling

A candidate's crossing into freedom and the dissolution of a double pawn may or may not be one and the same thing.

In the position of *Diagram 54*, the front-twin PQB5 is also a true candidate, becoming a passer after *1* P–B6. However, the doubling remains after *1* ... PxP as well as after *1* ... P–N3.

Black's chances for crossing and undoubling are a little different since his front-twin ... PKB5 has the status of helper. Accordingly, *1* ... P–K6 leads in case of *2* PxP to both crossing and undoubling. Not so in case of *2* P–KB3 when the subsequent *3* P–N3, PxP; *4* PxP, P–B4; *5* P–KB4 might be dangerous for Black, inasmuch as it artificially isolates and weakens his passer. If Black wants to eliminate this danger, he must first anticipate P–N3 by means of ... P–KR4–R5 and then proceed with ... P–K6.

DIAGRAM 54

Crossing and undoubling

Not necessarily the same

II–§7: Monsters

The vertical trio and the vertical quart, *triplets* and *quadruplets* as we might call them, are positional monsters, triplets a great rarity, quadruplets to all practical purposes non-existent. They obviously have the drawbacks of a twin, multiplied.

DIAGRAM 55

Triplets and quadruplets

Positional monsters

Part Two

PAWNS AND PIECES

Having explained the elements of pawn play from the theoretical angle, we now come to the more practical questions arising from the co-operation of the pawns with the pieces or types of pieces.

In discussing these questions there is little to say about the King and the Queen.

The King, owing to its vulnerability, is originally restricted to a passive rôle to be played behind a close cover of protecting pawns. Its active value increases in direct proportion to the number of pieces removed from the board, particularly the Queens, for the Queen is the only piece which the King can never attack. In the end-game, the King may even dominate the board.

The Queen, on the other hand, is too powerful to depend on the pawns; it can easily adjust itself to any formation.

With Rooks, Bishops, and Knights the situation is different. These pieces, each in its own way, depend very much on a proper co-operation with the pawns. Most important in this respect are the Bishops, since the pawn formation also has a paramount bearing on their relative value.

Chapter III

PAWNS AND BISHOPS

Of all the chessmen the Bishop alone is unalterably restricted to squares of the color of its original square. Bishops are confined to either white squares or black squares and, consequently, easily hurt by obstruction.

Most harmful to a Bishop is obstruction by its own pawns. A Bishop thus obstructed is called the *bad Bishop* as opposed to the unhampered or *good Bishop*.

The distinction between good and bad arises as soon as any pawns become immobilized, thus impairing the scope of one of the Bishops on either side. Such impairment, of which there naturally are quantitative and qualitative degrees, has substantial bearing on the relative value of the minor pieces as long as there is a Bishop on the board.

III–§1: The minor exchange

Some authorities hold that a Bishop is a little stronger than a Knight. Tarrasch called the difference the *minor exchange.*

We do not believe in the minor exchange but attribute possible fluctuations in the relative value of Bishop and Knight to later developments, particularly to changes in the pawn formation. Indeed, BxN is more often harmful than NxB, but it also is, by the nature of the game, more often possible. The possibility alone does not justify the move. Any unmotivated trade of pieces might easily do harm, and BxN often does, if played thoughtlessly.

Any trade of minor pieces ultimately depends on the question which minor pieces, if any, remain on the board and what prospects they have. The expression "minor exchange" may just as well be used to describe the superiority of a Knight against a bad Bishop.

III–§2: Bishops and rams

Bishops need open diagonals and mobile pawns; rams are a nuisance to them. But since a ram is formed in most openings, one of the Bishops of either side usually becomes obstructed very early. After 1 P–Q4, P–Q4, for instance, both Queen Bishops are bad.

The bad Bishop is of more significance than the good one. The latter, rendering adequate service, normally deserves little or no particular attention. The bad Bishop however, rendering inadequate service, constitutes a very important characteristic of the position.

Just how bad the Bishop is and how disadvantageous depends on the circumstances; there may be just one ram or several; the Bishop may be favorably placed in front of the pawn wall, where it is capable of initiating captures, or unfavorably behind the pawn wall, where it cannot initiate captures and is therefore inactive; finally the restriction may apply to only one side or to both, or to both to an unequal extent.

After 1 P–Q4, P–Q4; 2 P–K3, P–K3; 3 P–KB4, P–KB4, both Queen Bishops are not only very bad in view of the pawn formation, but also badly placed and inactive. The position is even.

After 1 P–Q4, P–Q4; 2 B–B4, B–B4; 3 P–K3, P–K3, the bad Queen Bishops are perfectly placed and active. This too is an even position.

But after 1 P–Q4, P–Q4; 2 B–B4, P–K3, the bad Queen Bishops are unequally posted, White's actively, in front of its pawns, Black's inactively, behind its pawns. White has a slight edge.

The King Bishop is often hampered by the ram PK4 vs PK4 and yet very valuable for its keeping under fire KB7, which is originally the weakest square in the neighborhood of the opposing King. As is for instance the case in the Giuoco Piano: 1 P–K4, P–K4; 2 N–KB3, N–QB3; 3 B–B4, B–B4.

The conclusion is that with ample forces on the board a single ram would ordinarily cause little if any hindrance.

The epithets "good" and "bad" may just as well refer to rams, provided there is a Bishop on the board. For instance BQ3, PQ4, PK4 vs BQ2, PQ3, PK3 when 1 P–K5! establishes a ram which is good for White's Bishop but bad for Black's Bishop, while after 1 P–Q5? it is the other way round. Consequently, 1 P–K5!, P–Q4? offers White two good rams, while after 1 P–Q5?, P–K4! he suffers from two bad rams.

The presence of several rams, especially in the central zone, leaves the bad Bishop with little chance for adequate activity. Remaining with the bad Bishop is in such cases a particular danger which either side must watch whenever considering BxN or NxB.

Too many rams may even put the good Bishop out of action, e.g. BQB2, PQN4, PQ4, PK5, PKB4, PKN3 vs BQB5, PQN4, PQ4, PK3, PKB4, PKN5 when White has no use for his Bishop. If such a condition occurs in the middle-game, the active bad Bishop may render better service than the good Bishop.

III–§3: Monochromy

The two-colored nature of the chessboard calls for a balanced control of white squares and black squares. Disturbances of this balance cause a state of *monochromy*, which is a serious weakness.

Monochromy presents itself as a "weakness on white squares" or a "weakness on black squares."

These usual terms suffer from the coincidence that in chess terminology "white and black" refer to the squares while "White and Black," spelled with capitals, indicate the players. It easily causes confusion when one has to talk about "white squares," "White's squares," "White's white squares," and so on.

Some writers therefore refer to the squares as "light and dark."

We prefer, in combined terms, *leuco* for *white*, and *melano* for *black*, consequently distinguishing between the two forms of monochromy as *leucopenia* or insufficient control of the white squares, and *melanpenia* or insufficient control of the black squares.

Monochromy is the drawback of the bad Bishop; it is either mechanical or dynamic in nature depending on the mechanical or dynamic immobilization of the critical pawns. For instance BQ3, PQ4, PK5 vs BQ2, PQ4, PK3 when Black suffers from *mechanical melanpenia,* or BQ3, PK3, PKB4 vs BQ2, PQ4, PK3 when Black is handicapped by *dynamic melanpenia.* Very often the monochromy is partly mechanical and partly dynamic as in case of BQ3, PQ4, PK5 vs BQ2, PQ4, PKB2. Mechanical monochromy is the more serious type.

The degree of monochromy depends on (1) the number of hampering pawns (2) the case of "bad Bishop vs Knight," when the monochromy is serious, or the milder case of "bad Bishop vs good Bishop" (3) the assistance rendered to the bad Bishop by one Knight or both Knights, because a Knight, for its roto-chromic function, is capable of substituting to some extent for the missing Bishop.

The following diagrams (*56-60*) show five degrees of monochromy of the leucopenic kind. White, owing to his bad Bishop, is the afflicted side.

The leucopenia of *Diagram 56* is mild, thanks to the presence of the Knights. White has a good chance to trade his Bishop. However, only BxB leads to full equality; BxN is less effective since Black then keeps his Bishop while there are good rams. Good rams usually make the Bishop slightly superior to a Knight.

In *Diagram 57* the white-bound assistance is reduced to only one Knight, which accentuates the leucopenia. However, White has a fair chance to reach full equality with BxN.

The leucopenia shown in *Diagram 58* is more distinct, inasmuch as definite relief depends on BxB, a trade which White has little chance to effectuate.

Reduced to an affair of "bad Bishop vs good Bishop," as shown in *Diagram 59,* monochromy is a serious affliction, and yet often bearable because the favored side has difficulty in making headway on squares heterochromic to the Bishops. Such progress usually depends on the presence of at least one pair of Rooks.

DIAGRAM 56

Mild leucopenia

White-bound assistance;
chance to trade bad Bishop

DIAGRAM 57

Accentuated leucopenia

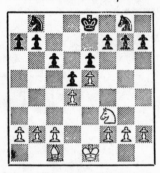

Some white-bound assistance;
chance for BxN

DIAGRAM 58

Distinct leucopenia

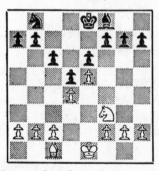

Some white-bound assistance;
little chance for relief by trade

DIAGRAM 59

Dangerous leucopenia

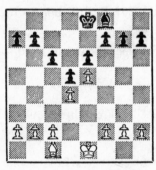

Serious but arrested

Reduced to a struggle of "bad Bishop vs Knight" (*Diagram 60*) monochromy usually takes a progressive and ultimately fatal course because the Knight, thanks to its rotochromic capacity, assures progress.

DIAGRAM 60

Alarming leucopenia

Serious and progressive

III–§4: Bad Bishop vs Knight

This case has great practical significance and deserves a more detailed discussion. Here is an example to the point.

AMOS BURN   ALEXANDER ALEKHINE

(From their game of the Karlsbad 1911 tournament)
(*See Diagram 61*)

Black suffers from severe melanpenia, but he is not entirely helpless as long as he can rely on the black-bound assistance rendered by his Knight.

At this point White offered a draw, but Black refused.
Both players had the impression that PQB3 must fall.

1		N–R2
2 K–B2		B–B3

Black now realizes that the intended 2..., N–N4, far from winning PQB3, only plays into White's hands because of 3 B–R4!, followed by 4 BxN.

3 K–K3	N–N4
4 K–Q2	....

4 B–R4 is now faulty because of 4 ..., NxQP.
At this point it was White who, of course, refused a draw.

4	K–B1
5 N–B2	K–K2
6 N–K3	P–B4

Another bad ram, but that does not matter any more. Black would like to close up the King side.

7 B–B3	....

Threatening 8 NxQBP.

7	K–Q2
8 P–N4!	....

DIAGRAM 61

Semi-final stage

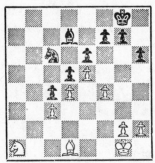

White's next objective is BxN

As usual in such cases it is vital to reduce the number of pawns so as to create assailable targets and provide maneuvering space for the pieces.

8	PxP

Exposing the base ... PK3 to assault. While this is inevitable, it can be done in a slightly better way by 8 ..., P–N3; 9 P–R4 (threatening 10 P–R5) 9 ..., PxP; 10 BxNP, P–R4. Then, White cannot easily operate with *zugzwang* as he lacks waiting moves with his R-pawn.

9 BxNP	....

Threatening 10 P–B5 (10 ... PxP; 11 NxKBP!).

9	P–N3

Necessary, but it creates another exposed target.

10 B–Q1	K–K2
11 N–N4!	P–R4

So it goes in such cases: the Knight drives an enemy pawn on a square of the wrong color, and may repeat the performance.
The text move completes the melanpenia of Black's position.

12 N–K3	K–B2
13 N–N2	K–N2
14 N–R4	B–K1
15 N–B3	K–B2
16 K–B2	B–Q2
17 K–N2	....

Preparing for the entry of the King via QR3. White does not threaten 18 B–R4, because of 18 ... NxQP, but he accomplishes it by means of *zugzwang*.

17	N–R2

There is no way of preventing K–R3 for long, e.g.

(1) 17 ..., K–N2; 18 B–R4, etc. (18 ... NxQP; 19 NxN, BxB; 20 NxPch);

(2) 17 ..., K–K2; 18 N–R4, B–K1; 19 B–B2 and wins the KNP;

(3) 17 ..., B–K1; 18 N–R4 (thematic; but 18 B–R4, N–B2; 19 BxBch, NxB; 20 K–R3 should also win) 18 ..., K–N2;

19 B–B2, K–R2(3); *20* N–B3, K–N2; *21* N–N5, B–Q2; *22* B–R4, etc.;

(4) *17* ..., B–B3; *18* N–R4, K–N2; *19* B–B2, B–K1; *20* P–R3, K–R2(3); *21* N–B3, K–N2; *22* N–N5, B–Q2; *23* B–R4, etc.

18 K–R3	N–B3
19 B–R4!	K–K2

If *19* ... N–N1, White wins either thematically with *20* B–B2, K–N2; *21* N–R4, B–K1; *22* K–N4, or with *20* BxB, NxB; *21* K–N4, in both cases thanks to penetration of his King on Q6.

20 N–R4	K–B2
21 BxN	BxB

The final stage is reached. Black's melano-bound resistance depends on his King which, however, is exposed to dislodgment by check or *zugzwang*.

White's ultimate objective is K–Q6.

DIAGRAM 62

Position after 21 ..., BxB

The final stage;
White's ultimate objective is K–Q6

22 K–N4	B–K1
23 N–B3	K–K2
24 N–N5	....

Here White starts to waver and lose time.

Since the win ultimately depends on K–Q6 when the base . . .
PK3 must fall, assistance to the King by means of N–K1–B2–N4
is indicated; both pieces must squeeze themselves through the
bottleneck on the Queen side in order to enter Black's position
with appropriate effect.

This, for instance, is a consistent line of play:

24 N–K1, B–B3; 25 N–B2 (25 K–B5, B–R5!); 25 . . . , K–Q2;
26 K–B5, K–B2; 27 N–N4, B–N2; 28 P–R3! (*zugzwang*) 28 . . . ,
B–B1; 29 N–B6, B–Q2; (29 . . . , K–Q2; 30 K–N6!); 30 N–K7,
B–K1; 31 N–N8, B–Q2; 32 N–B6, B–R5; 33 N–R7, B–K1;
34 N–B8, B–B2; 35 P–R4 and wins through *zugzwang*.

| 24 . . . . | B–B3 |
| 25 K–R3 | . . . . |

In the wrong direction.

25	B–Q2
26 K–N2	B–R5
27 K–B1	B–N6
28 N–B3	B–R5
29 N–R4	K–B2
30 N–N2	B–Q2
31 P–R4?	. . . .

A more serious error of basic significance.

White relinquishes the convenience of having this pawn available for one or two waiting moves for the purpose of *zugzwang*.
At this point there is no *zugzwang*, and no reason to seal off the
square KR4 either.

| 31 . . . . | B–K1 |
| 32 K–N2 | . . . . |

Back in the right direction.

32	B–R5
33 N–K3	K–K2
34 K–R3	B–B3

34 ..., B–N6, so as to prevent N–QB2, makes no difference since the Knight can reach the Queen side via other routes.

35 K–N4	K–Q2
36 K–R5	K–B2
37 N–B2	K–N2?

A grave mistake, losing quickly since the Knight is admitted to QB5.

After 37 ..., B–N2! the win offers a problem to which there hardly is a solution, e.g. 38 N–N4, B–B1; 39 K–N5 (39 N–R6ch, BxN!; 40 KxB, K–B3) 39 ..., B–N2; 40 K–B5, B–B1; 41 N–B6, B–Q2; 42 N–K7, B–K1; 43 N–N8, B–R5; 44 N–B6, B–B3; 45 N–R7, B–K1; 46 N–B8, B–B2; 47 K–N4 (White now misses the winning P–KR4); 47 ..., K–B3; 48 K–R5, K–B2; 49 K–N5, K–N2; 50 K–B5 (50 N–Q7??, B–K1!); 50 ..., K–B2. Too many immobilized pawns are in such cases a neutralizing factor because they hamper the Knight, too.

38 N–N4	B–Q2

If 38 ..., K–B2, White can proceed with 39 NxB, KxN; 40 K–R6, K–B2; 41 K–R7!, K–B3; 42 K–N8, etc. and win in the Queen ending. However, 39 N–R6ch wins much more conveniently.

39 N–R6	B–K1

The alternatives are even worse: 39 ..., K–B1; 40 K–N6; or 39 ..., K–B3; 40 N–N8ch, K–B2; 41 NxB, KxN; 42 K–N6; or 39 ..., K–R2; 40 N–B5, B–B1; 41 K–N5; or 39 ..., B–B1; 40 N–B5ch, K–B2; 41 K–N5.

40 N–B5ch	K–B3
41 NxP	and White won

III–§5: The rise of monochromy

Monochromy is a very common ailment; there are innumerable examples for its rise in practical play.

Let us discuss a drastic case.

EMANUEL LASKER   ERICH COHN

(From their game of the St. Petersburg 1909 tournament)

DIAGRAM 63

The Bishop in perfect health

But monochromy strikes

Black's position is slightly cramped but steady. The triad serves well, and so does the Bishop thanks to the absence of any hampering pawns. Naturally, White's head-duo with the Rooks behind it spells action, but there is no immediate action at hand except for the dangerous thrust P–B5–B6. And this Black can easily prevent.

The game continued:

> 1 ....   P–B4?

A bad move.

Lasker points out that 1 ..., P–B3 followed by a defensive attitude is indicated. This goes without saying.

> 2 P–K5   ....

Of course. Black now suffers from melanpenia as the bad ram hampers his Bishop.

Besides, there is the threat of 3 PxP.

> 2 ....   P–Q4??

A very bad move which, played by a master, must be rated as

a grave oversight. Black probably had the illusion that he could re-establish his duo with 3 . . . , P–B4 by force.

Lasker recommends 2 . . . , QR–K1; 3 R–K2 as slightly favoring White, adding that 3 P–KN4 is premature because of 3 . . . , B–B1.

3 N–R4!   Q–K2

It makes no difference where the Queen goes. The attempt of gaining a tempo with 3 . . . , Q–R6 is fruitless because of 4 Q–QB3 when 4 . . . , QxRP fails against 5 R–QR1.

4 Q–Q4!   . . . .

With the stopsquares Q4 and QB5 definitely under White's control, Black's melanpenia has reached fatal proportions. The Bishop is dead.

4 . . . .   KR–N1
5 N–B5   P–QR4

Threatening to seize control of the critical stops with 6 . . ., R–N4.

6 P–R3   . . . .

Parrying the threat, at the same time setting a fine trap.

6 . . . .   K–B2

It looks as if 6 . . . , R–N4; 7 P–QN4, PxP; 8 PxP, R–R7 would offer Black some counterplay thanks to control of the QR-file, e.g. 9 P–B3, R–N1; 10 R–QR1, R(1)–R1. However, 9 R–QR1! is much stronger; White then gets the open file himself, the tactical point being that after 9 . . . , RxBP??; 10 R–R8ch, K–B2; 11 Q–Q1!! he either wins the Rook or mates in two.

There is much of such tactical trim in Emanuel Lasker's play—probably more than is generally realized. Lasker himself was strangely reluctant to talk about the tactical details of his games.

7 R–QR1   R–N4
8 P–QN4   R(1)–QN1
9 P–B3   . . . .

White has consolidated his position and is ready for the final assault in one form or another. He might proceed with 10 P–QR4 followed by 11 PxP; or with 10 N–N3 gaining the QR-file after

10 ..., PxP; *11* RPxP, or winning the QR-pawn after *10* ...,
P–R5; *11* N–B5. Even an attack on the King side based on P–KN4
offers promise as Black is completely blockaded.

9 ....   RxN

In the absence of any hope, Black is entitled to shorten his
sufferings.

10 PxR   R–N4
11 R(R)–N1   QxP

Or *11* ..., RxP; *12* R–N7, R–B5; *13* Q–R7 and wins.

12 P–QR4!   Resigns

III–§6: Dynamic monochromy

Monochromy usually depends on rams but it is often enhanced
by dynamically immobilized pawns.

However, even monochromy of the purely dynamical type may
become an independent issue. Following is an example to the
point.

ALEXANDER ALEKHINE   F. D. YATES

(From their game of the Hastings 1925-6 tournament)

DIAGRAM 64

Black with a trace of monochromy

Harmless but not negligible

A position of two majorities of which Black's shows a trace of dynamic monochromy, inasmuch as the chain ... PQN2, PQB3, PQ4 confines the Bishop. However, since the base of this chain is part of a duo, Black should have no trouble in forming his head-duo and restoring full equality.

1 ....   N–B1?

But this is a waste of time.

Instead, *1* ... , P–B3!, as recommended by Alekhine, is most natural and satisfactory. Then, after *2* PxP, NxP, the salient of White's formation is eliminated while sufficient protection of ... PQ4 assures the proper use of Black's majority. And White has nothing better since *2* R–K1, PxP leads to the isolation of his K-pawn, while *2* BxNch, KxB; *3* PxP, PxP creates conditions more favorable to the Bishop than to the Knight.

2 P–QN4!   ....

So as to trade this pawn for the QB-pawn, thereby breaking up Black's formation on the Q-side. Success depends on the reduced mobility and inadequate protection of ... PQ4 (*2* ... , P–Q5?; *3* N–K4! or *2* ... , P–QN3; *3* P–N5, P–QB4?; *4* NxP).

2 ....   N–K3

Gaining a valuable tempo (of which Black however is unaware).

3 P–N3   ....

Of course not *3* P–B5 which loses a pawn to *3* ... , N–Q5.

3 ....   K–B1

Black should use the tempo he won for an extra protection of his Q-pawn playing *3* ... , N–B2!. Then, *4* P–N5 makes no sense any more because of *4* ... , P–QB4. Besides, Black can strive for ... P–QB4 anyhow starting with *4* ... , P–QN3. Once the duo ... PQB4 and PQ4 is established, and a penetration of White's Rook along the QN-file anticipated, the dispersion of Black's majority pawns is not likely to have any detrimental effect.

4 R–K1   ....

Apparently, White is not sure whether the advantage offered by the consistent 4 P–N5 has more than a theoretical significance. He first wants to see how Black would react to the possibility of 5 P–B5.

4 ....   P–KN3?

A passive reaction which has the drawback of creating slight monochromy on the King side, too.

With 4 ..., N–B2! Black can prevent 5 P–N5, and keep the balance in case of 5 P–B5, P–QN3; 6 P–N4, P–QB4 when the two head-duos match each other.

5 P–N5!   N–B4
6 PxP   PxP?

Conceding White the QN-file, which is unnecessary. Better 6 ..., BxP, when Black's Rook has future on the QB-file.

7 R–QN1   K–K2

Intending to neutralize the QN-file with ... K–Q1–B2.

8 R–N4!   ....

Preventing 8 ..., K–Q1 because of 9 N–R4!, Alekhine remarks. Indeed, Black then loses a pawn in case of 9 ..., NxN; 10 RxN or 9 ..., N–K3; 10 R–N7, while 9 ..., NxBch; 10 PxN, K–B2; 11 N–B5 leaves him in a hopeless state of melanpenia.

8 ....   P–KR4?

For no obvious reason Black abandons his only duo and increases the melanpenia of his King side. He is probably waiting for 9 N–R4?? which, as Alekhine points out, loses to 9 ..., P–R4; 10 R–Q4, N–K3.

The indicated move, serving as a preparation for ... K–Q1, is 8 ..., R–QB1.

9 N–K2   ....

Allowing ... K–Q1 since, after Black's last pawn move, the position became ripe for the exchange of the Rooks, according to Alekhine.

This "ripe" means that no further effort to achieve and accumulate small advantages is necessary, since Black's Bishop has become bad to a decisive degree.

9	K–Q1
10 R–N8ch	K–K2?

Of all the weak moves Black has made so far this one is the most serious as it allows the exchange of the Rooks.

Correct is 10 ..., B–B1 followed by the expulsion of the penetrated Rook, e.g. (1) 11 N–Q4, K–B2 (12 R–R8??, K–N2); (2) 11 R–R8 (a) 11 ..., R–K2?; 12 N–Q4, R–B2; 13 RxP!; (b) 11 ..., P–R3!; 12 R–N8 (12 R–R7??, B–N2!) 12 ..., K–B2.

11 RxRch	BxR
12 K–K3	....

So as to exchange a pawn with 13 P–B4 thus eliminating Black's chance for the duo ... PQB4, PQ4.

The monochromy of Black's position, although purely dynamic, has become hardly short of decisive.

12	NxBch

Black continues to co-operate; he now voluntarily parts with the last assistant to his bad Bishop.

The comparatively best although scarcely sufficient defense is, as pointed out by Alekhine, 12 ..., B–Q2, e.g.

(1) 13 P–B4?, NxB; 14 KxN, PxPch; 15 KxP, B–K3ch; 16 K–B5, BxP; 17 KxP, and White must fight for a draw;

(2) 13 P–QR3!, and White maintains his advantage (a) 13 ..., N–K3; 14 P–B4! (b) 13 ..., B–K3; 14 N–Q4! (c) 13 ..., NxB; 14 PxN! as in the game.

13 PxN!	P–QB4

This advance would serve well if Black could either maintain the duo or form a melano-bound chain with ... P–Q5 (14 ... P–Q5ch!; 15 K–K4??, B–B3 mate). But it is too late for that.

14 P–Q4!	P–B5

The conversion of the duo into a leuco-bound chain creates a bad ram and enhances the melanpenia of Black's position, but there is no choice.

After *14* ..., PxPch; *15* KxP White wins easily, e.g. *15* ..., K–K3; *16* P–KR3! (*16* ..., K–B4; *17* KxP threatening *18* N–Q4 mate).

The text move establishes a protected passed pawn which makes matters more difficult for White. However, Alekhine wins ingeniously.

DIAGRAM 65

Position after 14 ..., P–B5

Predominantly dynamic but fatal melanpenia

        15 P–B5!!   ....

Threatening *16* N–B4 (weaker *16* PxP, PxP; *17* N–B4 because of *17* ..., B–B2).

        15 ....   P–N4

The only reasonable defense.

If *15* ..., PxP; *16* N–B4, B–B3; *17* NxRP, White wins without any particular finesses.

        16 P–KR4!   P–B3
        17 RPxP!!   ....

Dangerous but well calculated.

Insufficient is *17* P–K6 because of *17* . . . , PxP; *18* PxP, K–Q3 when Black can temporize moving his King back and forth be-tween . . . QB3 and . . . Q3.

17	PxNP
18 N–N1!!	. . . .

One problem move after the other. The Knight threatens to land victoriously on KB4: *19* N–R3, P–N5; *20* N–B4.

18	B–Q2

Or *18* . . . , P–R5; *19* P–N4!, B–R5; *20* K–K2! and White wins easily, according to Alekhine.

This continuation is virtually the main line. It runs further as follows: *20* . . . , P–B6; *21* N–R3, P–B7; *22* K–Q2, B–N4; *23* NxP, B–K7; *24* P–B6ch, K–K1 (K–B1); *25* P–K6, BxP; *26* P–B7ch (N–R7ch), K–K2; *27* N–R7 and wins.

19 P–B6ch	. . . .

19 P–K6? is not only faulty because of *19* . . . , B–K1 followed by *20* . . . , K–B3, but also basically poor because of *19* . . . , BxP; these two tremendous pawns must net more than a piece.

19	K–K1

Or *19* . . . , K–B2; *20* N–B3, P–N5 (*20* . . . , K–N3; *21* NxP!); when White has the choice of two winning lines (a) *21* N–R4 followed by N–N2–B4 (b) *21* N–N5ch, K–N3; *22* P–B7, K–N2; *23* P–K6, BxP; *24* NxBch, KxP; *25* N–B4.

20 N–B3	P–N5
21 N–R4	B–K3
22 N–N6	B–B2
23 N–B4	. . . .

Now that the Knight has landed on this key square the win is easy even for ordinary mortals.

23	K–Q2
24 K–Q2	. . . .

The squeeze comes in.

24	P–R4
25 K–K3	B–N1

Or 25 ..., P–QR5; 26 P–R3, and Black must relinquish a pawn.

26 NxRP   and White won

III–§7: The Bishop's telepower

The conditions under which the Knight is stronger than the Bishop are easy to formulate, monochromy being the clue.

The other way round it is more difficult, for the possible advantages of the Bishop against the Knight are of a less concrete nature lending themselves to formulation only in general terms. Everything depends on the Bishop's potential long-distance activity or, as we prefer to call it, its *telepower*.

Telepower becomes a menace to the Knight when there are majorities or passed pawns on both sides or when good rams provide the Bishop with convenient targets.

Three examples follow.

MAX EUWE   MIKHAEL BOTVINNIK

(From their game of the Nottingham 1936 tournament)

DIAGRAM 66

The Bishop superior

Promoting agent: passers

White has a winning advantage, in spite of his double pawn, because in this fight between passers the telepower of the Bishop is a decisive factor.

The game itself was given a draw after *1* P–K6?, K–Q3.

Analysis revealed however the following win for White:

1 K–N3 ....

Threatening 2 K–R4.

1 .... K–N4

After *1* ..., K–Q2; 2 K–R4, White wins all pawns losing himself only the rather unimportant front-twin. Thus 2 ..., P–B5; *3* KxRP, P–B6; *4* KxP, P–B7; *5* B–N2, K–K3; *6* K–B4, P–B8 (Q)ch; *7* BxQ, KxP; *8* K–Q3 and wins.

2 P–K6 P–B5ch

2 ..., P–R5ch; 3 K–R2! leads, correspondingly, to the same.

3 K–B2! N–N3

There is no time for *3* ..., P–B6 because of 4 P–K7.

And *3* ..., P–N6ch loses to 4 K–N1!, N–N3; 5 P–R7, K–B3; 6 P–K7, K–Q2; 7 B–B6, P–R5; 8 K–N2. The situation KQN2 vs PQR5, PQN6, PQB5 as compared to KQN2 vs PQR7, PQN6, PQB7 in the text makes no basic difference.

4	P–R7	K–B3
5	P–K7	K–Q2
6	B–B6	P–R5
7	K–N1	....

White is going to win by *zugzwang*.

7 .... K–K1

The alternatives lead to the same: 7 ..., P–N6; 8 K–N2!; or 7 ..., P–R6; 8 K–R2, P–B6; 9 K–N3; or 7 ..., P–B6; 8 K–B2, P–R6; 9 K–N3.

8	P–K5	K–B2
9	P–K6ch	K–K1
10	B–N5	N–R1
11	B–R4	N–N3
12	B–B6	P–R6

Forced to move his pawns Black loses them one after the other.

13	K–R2	P–B6
14	K–N3	P–B7
15	KxBP	P–R7
16	K–N2	P–N6
17	K–R1!	and wins

Whereas 17 KxNP?, P–R8(Q) leads to a draw.

MAX EUWE   VASJA PIRC

(From a game of their 1949 match played in Yugoslavia)

DIAGRAM 67

The good Bishop superior

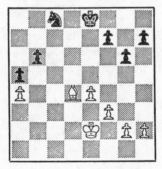

Majorities—good ram—assailable straggler

This pawn formation, which in itself is bad for Black since his majority is crippled by backwardness, offers the Bishop fine targets and invites White's King to penetration on either side. White has a great advantage. The game proceeded:

1 K–K3!   ....

Shrewdly giving the impression of intending 2 K–B4 with action on the King side.

1 ....   N–Q3

A seemingly shrewd reply. The QN-pawn is immune (2 BxP??, N–B5ch!) and Black threatens to mobilize his majority with great effect, e.g. 2 K–B4, P–QN4! (a) 3 P–K5, N–B4! (b) 3 B–B5, N–N2! (c) 3 B–K5, K–Q2!.

In reality this combination loses quickly, but there is no fully satisfactory alternative. For instance 1..., K–K2; 2 K–B4, P–B3; 3 P–N4 with these possibilities:

(1) 3 ..., P–N4ch (a) 4 K–B5??, N–Q3 mate (b) 4 K–K3, and White's advantage has increased, as the Bishop now has targets on the King side too;

(2) 3 ..., K–K3; 4 P–N5, PxPch; 5 KxP, K–B2 (a) 6 K–R6, K–N1; 7 P–R4, N–Q3! and Black, threatening 8 ..., N–B2 mate, has counterplay (b) 6 P–R4! and White, threatening 7 K–R6, KN1; 8 P–R5, maintains his great advantage.

2 K–Q3!　　　....

Now threatening 3 BxP while 2 ..., P–QN4 fails against 3 P–K5.

2 ....　　　N–B1

Necessary, but still disastrous because of the loss of time involved. Black now is helpless against the following penetration of the opposing King.

3 K–B4	K–Q2
4 K–N5	K–B2
5 K–R6	K–B3
6 B–K3	K–B2

Or 6 ..., P–B3; 7 P–N4, K–B2; 8 B–Q4 and wins.

7 B–N5!!　　　....

A fine maneuver designed to bring Black into *zugzwang*.

7 ....　　　K–B3

7 ..., N–Q3 fails against 8 B–B4.

8 P–K5!　　　K–B4

The alternatives are just as bad: *8 ..., K–Q2; 9 K–N7;* or *8 ..., K–B2; 9 B–B6, K–B3; 10 B–Q8, K–B4; 11 K–N7.*

9 K–N7   Resigns

EMANUEL LASKER   DAVID JANOWSKI

(From a game of their 1909 match)

DIAGRAM 68

Promotion of the Bishop

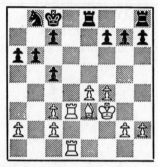

Rather backwardness than monochromy

White has the advantage of a sound majority. His minority, although crippled, is still good enough to prevent Black's crippled majority from producing a passer. With no pieces on the board White would win outright following the rule "Candidate first." As it is however, P–K5 has the drawback of causing monochromy, although only to a slight extent. Lasker resented that. His way of handling the situation is very instructive from the basic point of view.

1 P–B5!   ....

White acquiesces to the backwardness of his K-pawn giving priority to a proper co-operation between his Bishop and majority pawns. Since the Bishop is black-bound, the pawns should preferably advance white-bound.

While thus promoting the Bishop, the text move also serves the creation of levers; for after ... P–KB3, which Black can hardly avoid, there will be the excellent possibility of P–N4–N5, and also some chance for P–K5.

1 ....   P–KB3

Otherwise Black cannot prevent the duo-move P–K5 for long. For instance 1 ..., N–B3; 2 B–B4, R–K2

(1) 3 P–N4, R(R)–K1; 4 R–K3, N–K4ch, with a fully satisfactory game for Black, according to Tarrasch; however, since P–N4 should serve the lever PKN5 vs PKB3, there is little sense in playing it ahead of ... P–KB3;

(2) 3 R–Q5!, R(R)–K1; 4 R–K1, and White holds the initiative by provoking ... P–KB3 or getting in P–K5, e.g. (a) 4 .... P–B3; 5 P–N4! (b) 4 ..., N–K4ch; 5 BxN, RxB; 6 RxR, RxR; 7 K–B4, P–KB3; 8 P–B4! (8 P–N4, P–B5!) followed by 9 P–N4 (c) 4 ..., K–N2, or any other neutral move, then 5 P–K5.

2 P–N4	R–K2
3 B–B4	R(R)–K1
4 R–K3	N–B3
5 P–N5?	....

This move (not criticized by Tarrasch) is premature, because it distracts the Bishop from observing the vital stop K5.

Correct is 5 P–KR4! (5 ..., P–R3; 6 R–KN1!) with a fine game.

5 ....   N–R4?

Black misses his opportunity.
The alternatives are:

(1) 5 ..., N–K4ch; 6 BxN, RxB; 7 PxP, PxP, with a satisfactory game for Black, according to Tarrasch; however, this is true only after 8 R–KN1?, P–B5!, not after 8 P–B4!, R–N1 (else 9 R–KN1); 9 R–Q5 when White holds the initiative as he must get in P–K5 or seize control of the KN-file;

(2) 5 ... PxP!; 6 BxNP, N–K4ch; so far given by Tarrasch who rightly claims that Black has a good game (but wrongly concludes that this was a consequence of 1 P–B5); possible continuations are (a) 7 K–N3, R–B2; 8 B–B4, N–B5; 9 R(3)–K1 (9 R–K2?, RxBP!); 9 ..., N–R6; 10 B–B1, N–N4!; 11 B–Q2, N–Q3 (b) 7 K–B4, R–B2, and White must still play 8 K–N3, for the threat is 8 ..., P–R3; 9 B–R4, P–N4ch while 8 B–R4 loses a pawn to 8 ..., N–N3ch; 9 K–N3, NxB; 10 KxN, RxBP.

6 P–KR4!	....

Correcting the slip. White now has a distinct advantage.

6	N–B5
7 R–K2	R–B2

7 ..., N–K4ch; 8 BxN also favors White, but it offers a comparatively better defense.

8 R–KN1	K–Q2
9 P–R5!	....

Conclusive, as there is no adequate defense to the threat of 10 P–R6.

9	N–Q3

Or 9 ..., PxP; 10 RxP, also with a sure win for White.

10 P–R6!	....

The formidable chain lever. It breaks all resistance.

10	PxNP
11 RxP	P–N3

A desperate measure. Black sacrifices a pawn rather than conceding White connected passers. But White wins smoothly all the same: 12 PxP, PxP; 13 RxNP, R(1)–KB1; 14 R–N7!, RxR; 15 PxR, R–KN1; 16 R–N2, N–K1; 17 B–K5, K–K3; 18 K–B4, K–B2; 19 K–B5, and Black resigned.

III–§8: Good Bishop versus bad Bishop

The bad Bishop is rather helpless against a Knight, but not quite so against the good Bishop when there is the possibility of opposition, which may lead to an equalizing exchange. Basically however, the bad Bishop remains a handicap. The presence of heavy pieces is likely to accentuate the significance of this handicap, as the following example demonstrates.

GERHARD PFEIFFER   PETAR TRIFUNOVICH

West Germany   Yugoslavia

(From their game of the 1954 team match
between West Germany and Yugoslavia)

DIAGRAM 69

Good Bishop vs bad Bishop

Leucopenia and its consequences

Black suffers from leucopenia, and White takes advantage of the situation by remarkably instructive measures.

1 P–QN4!   ....

So as to proceed with PxP which (a) promotes PQ5 to a passer and PK4 to a candidate (b) reduces the unassailable triad to the assailable chain...PQB4, PQ5 (c) provides scope for White's Rooks along the QN-file and QB-file (d) serves well inasmuch

as monochromy generally counts most when there are neither
too many pawns on the board (eight or seven) nor too few (four
or less).

> 1 ....   Q–Q2

Threatening 1 ..., Q–N4, which would turn the tables because
of Black's getting in his head-duo by force.

> 2 P–QR4   KR–B1

And now threatening 2 ..., P–B5 (when giving up the exchange would be White's best chance: 3 QxQP, B–B3).

> 3 PxP   PxP

Whereby Black's leucopenia has become purely dynamic.

> 4 Q–B4!   ....

The occupation of this stopsquare renders Black's connected
passers useless and is consequently decisive.

Note that here the Queen successfully does a job for which it
is basically least suitable.

> 4 ....   QR–N1
> 5 QR–N1   ....

Not 5 QxRP because of 5 ..., P–B5. It would be silly to concede Black his head-duo for as little as a pawn.

> 5 ....   RxR
> 6 RxR   Q–B2
> 7 P–B4   R–N1
> 8 RxRch   QxR
> 9 P–K5   ....

The head-duo.

White's spearhead of pawns, although comprising only one
passer, is capable of forming successive duos and therefore superior to Black's connected passers.

The immediate threat is 10 P–Q6 followed by 11 QxBP.

> 9 ....   Q–N8ch
> 10 K–B2   Q–Q8

Nor is *10 . . .* , Q–QN3 any better because of *11* B–B1 threatening *12* B–R3 and *13* P–Q6.

11 Q–QB1!	QxQ

Or *11 . . .* , QxP; *12* P–Q6 followed by *13* QxP, also with a sure win for White.

12 BxQ	P–B5

Now or never. Indeed this advance cures Black from leucopenia, but too late. For in this end-game the superior activity of White's King is decisive.

13 P–Q6	B–Q1

13 . . . , B–B1 loses to *14* B–R3 threatening *15* P–Q7.

14 P–B5!	K–B1
15 B–R3	K–K1
16 P–K6	. . . .

Threatening *17* P–Q7 mate.

16	PxP
17 PxP	B–N3
18 K–B3	P–QR4

Vaguely hoping for some counterplay with *19* P–Q6 as *20* B–N4 is prevented.

19 B–B1	. . . .

Threatening *20* B–N5 (which is stronger than *20* P–Q7ch).

19	P–R3
20 B–B4	B–B4

20 . . . P–Q6 or *20 . . .* , P–B6 also loses to *21* K–K4.

21 K–K4	P–Q6
22 P–Q7ch	K–Q1

Or *22 . . .* , K–K2; *23* B–B7.

23 K–Q5	Resigns

The main threat is *24* K–B6.

III–§9: The pair of Bishops

The pair of Bishops is reputedly stronger than a Bishop and a Knight, and still stronger than two Knights. In point evaluations of positions, special ratings have been suggested allowing, for instance, two points for each minor piece but five for the pair of Bishops. Tarrasch claimed that a Rook and two Bishops combined would have a fighting power at least equal to two Rooks and a Knight.

We rather abstain from a special rating of the Bishops, because too much depends on the circumstances. Basically, two Bishops have no extra value, but they may gain some if their telepower is favored by the pawn formation or, possibly, by the position of the Kings.

In the opening, a Bishop can often be exchanged for a Knight with no harm, and sometimes even advantageously.

In the Canal variation of the Giuoco Piano, White obtains some initiative in the center with BxN. Thus *1* P–K4, P–K4; *2* N–KB3, N–QB3; *3* B–B4, B–B4; *4* N–B3, N–B3; *5* P–Q3, P–Q3; *6* B–KN5, P–KR3; *7* BxN, QxB; *8* N–Q5, Q–Q1; *9* P–B3.

In the Steinitz defense of the Ruy Lopez, White's BxN is a strong move: *1* P–K4, P–K4; *2* N–KB3, N–QB3; *3* B–N5, P–Q3; *4* P–Q4, B–Q2; *5* N–B3, N–B3; *6* BxN (Best. But *6* 0–0, B–K2; *7* R–K1, PxP; *8* NxP, 0–0; *9* BxN is also good; it offers White a slight edge.) *6* ..., BxB; *7* Q–Q3, PxP; *8* NxP, and White has a fine game, his main trump being 0–0–0.

The Nimzo-Indian defense (*1* P–Q4, N–KB3; *2* P–QB4, P–K3; *3* N–QB3, B–N5) is perfectly sound although Black commits himself to ... KBxN.

Dutch Reversed (*1* P–KB4, P–Q4) is an opening system where White, intent to control the diagonal QR1–KR8, gladly exchanges his King Bishop for Black's Queen Knight if he gets the chance: *2* N–KB3, P–QB4; *3* P–K3, N–QB3?!; *4* B–N5!. In this way the white-bound Bishop indirectly helps to control the black-bound diagonal.

In the Stonewall formation, QBxN or ... QBxN is definitely a partial success, e.g. *1* P–KB4, P–Q4; *2* P–K3, N–KB3; *3* N–KB3, B–N5; *4* P–KR3, BxN; *5* QxB, QN–Q2; *6* P–Q4, N–K5; *7* B–Q3, P–KB4, with a good game for Black.

More difficult to evaluate, and open to personal opinions, is the significance of the pair of Bishops in the exchange variation of the Ruy Lopez: *1* P–K4, P–K4; *2* N–KB3, N–QB3; *3* B–N5, P–QR3; *4* BxN, QPxN. This position is characterized by both Black's damaged pawn formation and his pair of Bishops. It has been mentioned before (*Diagram 45*) that while Black is supposed to have a good game, Emanuel Lasker used to prefer White. He had a particular technique in guarding against the Bishops and using his majority after the usual *5* P–Q4, PxP; *6* QxP, QxQ; *7* NxQ. The famous game he won from Capablanca in the 1914 St. Petersburg tournament went on: *7* ..., B–Q3; *8* N–B3, N–K2; *9* 0–0, 0–0; *10* P–B4, R–K1; *11* N–N3, P–B3; *12* P–B5. This daring advance (see also *Diagram 68*) has been sharply criticized by Capablanca. However, Lasker was also somebody, after all, and he must have known what he was doing. His view on this whole variation is most remarkable.

The following example gives an idea of the circumstances which favor the pair of Bishops.

SAMUEL RESHEVSKY   FREDERICK OLAFSSON

(From their game of the Dallas 1957 tournament)
(*See Diagram 70*)

This position is far from ideal for the Bishops because there are neither passed pawns nor local majorities, while the defender holds a Bishop and a Knight, which is basically better to have than two Knights.

However, White has a distinct plus in assets because: (1) there are pawns on both wings (2) his King is in a dominating position (3) Black's Bishop is bad with respect to ... PQR4.

DIAGRAM 70

The pair of Bishops superior

White wins very closely

White still faces a problem, inasmuch as it is very difficult to make headway.

1 P–R3!!   ....

A temporary sacrifice, which enables White to attack the pawns on the K–side or operate with *zugzwang*.

Ineffective are (a) *1* B–K8 because of *1* ..., N–Q3 (b) *1* K–K5 because of *1* ..., B–Q5ch (c) *1* B–Q3 because of *1* ..., N–K6ch; *2* K–K5, N–N5ch.

1 ....   NxP

After *1* ..., N–Q3; *2* B–Q3, K–Q2; *3* P–N4, PxP; *4* PxP, Black faces *zugzwang*, e.g. *4* ..., K–B2; *5* P–B5!, PxP; *6* B–KB4!. However, *4* ..., B–Q1; *5* B–K3, B–B2 may hold.

2 B–K8		N–B8
3 B–K1		N–K6ch
4 K–K5		N–B5ch
5 K–B6		B–Q5ch
6 KxBP		N–Q3ch
7 K–B8		NxB
8 KxN		....

Superior chances for a favorable BxB or BxN is one of the basic advantages offered by the combined telepower of the pair of Bishops.

In this case, White has initiated such an exchange indirectly. He now wins thanks to the superior activity of his King.

	8		B–K6

After 8 ..., K–N3 or 8 ..., B–N3, White wins quite simply with 9 K–B7.

9	BxPch	K–B3
10	K–B7	BxP
11	KxP	P–R5
12	K–R5	Resigns

The point is that Black, after losing his last pawn, is unable to sacrifice his Bishop for the KR-pawn (which would lead to a draw). For instance 12 ..., B–N6; 13 B–Q8, B–K8; 14 BxP, B–N5; 15 K–N4, K–N2; 16 B–N3, B–K2; 17 B–B4, K–R3; 18 B–N5, B–N5; 19 P–R4, and so on.

Positions with two Bishops on either side are subject to the question of whether there is a hampering ram on the board, and if so, which of the bad Bishops is better posted. For instance KKN1, BQN2, BQ3, PQR3, PQN4, PK5, PKB2, PKN2, PKR2 vs KKN1, BQN3, BQ4, PQR3, PQN4, PK3, PKB2, PKN2, PKR2 when Black has the edge because of the active position of ... BQ4 as against the inactive position of BQN2.

III–§10: Bishops of opposite color

Bishops of opposite color are an element that easily causes stagnation because of mutual monochromy, one side being in absolute control of the squares of white color, a state we call *leucarchy*, the other having the same advantage on the squares of black color, which we call *melarchy*. For instance BQ3, PQB4, PK4, PKB5 vs BQ5, PQB4, PK4, PKB3, a situation where White's leucarchy is matched by Black's melarchy.

As against leucopenia and melanpenia, which are descriptive of one-way weakness, leucarchy and melarchy describe one-way strength. This one-way strength often compensates for a pawn or two. For instance KKB4, BQ3, PQB4, PK4, PKB5 vs KKB3, BQ5, PQB4 is a draw, since White is unable to form a duo.

With additional pieces on the board, particularly heavy pieces, Bishops of opposite color often have the effect of a stimulant rather than a sedative. The question of whether the Bishop is used in front of the pawns or behind them assumes great importance; an attack against the King might easily become irresistible thanks to unopposed one-way strength; and when it comes to using an extra pawn in an otherwise sterile position, there is good chance that a sacrifice of the exchange, RxB that is, will serve as a decisive amplifier.

Following are two examples.

SAMUEL RESHEVSKY   SAVIELLY TARTACOVER

(From their game of the Kemeri 1937 tournament)

DIAGRAM 71

Extra pawn plus extra chance

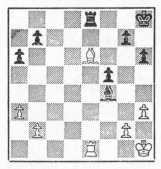

Black has a great advantage

This is a situation where the extra pawn in itself means little. However, Black has an extra chance; he can either eliminate the

Bishops of opposite color or win another pawn, in both cases
with a substantial increase of his advantage.

> 1 .... P–KN4?

But this is weak.

Better, although still of little promise, is the thematic continuation 1 ..., P–KN3; 2 R–K2, K–N2; 3 B–B4, B–K4. This line is
designed to produce a passer on the K-side, for the purpose of
which Black's majority pawns must advance leuco-bound as far
as possible.

Best is 1 ..., B–B8!!, e.g. 2 R–K2, P–QN4, or 2 RxB, RxB,
with a win for Black, according to the tournament book. White
may have some drawing chances in the Rook end-game after
3 R–B7.

> 2 P–KN4! PxP
> 3 PxP ....

The K-side is now frozen because of mutual monochromy and
the demotion of Black's extra pawn from a candidate to a helpless straggler.

> 3 .... K–N2
> 4 R–K2 K–B3
> 5 B–B4 RxR
> 6 BxR B–B8

Black still wins another pawn, but to no avail since he emerges
with a completely paralyzed formation.

> 7 B–B3 P–N3
> 8 P–R4 BxP
> 9 B–K2! P–QR4

A deadlock typical for leucarchy vs melarchy is reached.
Black's two extra pawns are useless owing to irremediable backwardness. A draw is inevitable.

In the game itself Black played 9 ..., P–N4, with no better
result.

ALEXANDER ALEKHINE   RUDOLPH SPIELMANN

(From their game of the Karlsbad 1923 tournament)

DIAGRAM 72

Extra pawn and active Bishop

Black should win

White is a pawn down, and he also suffers from dispersion as well as from the inactivity of his Bishop. This Bishop is hampered by PQ4 and PKB4. Because of these pawns, there is simply no square on the board where White's Bishop would perform as well as Black's Bishop does. Even K5 is inferior to ... Q4, for it lacks diagonal connection with the hinterland.

Black should win.

1	Q–K3	R(Q)–QB1
2	Q–K5	P–KR3
3	R(N)–N2	R–B6
4	Q–K2	Q–R6
5	R–Q1	QxR!

A neat liquidation, which offers Black substantial progress.

6	QxQ	R–B7
7	R–Q2	....

Obviously forced.

7	RxQ
8 RxR	R–B5

With the main threat of 9 ..., R–R5.

9 B–N4	....

Since 9 R–N4?? fails against 9 ..., R–B7!, White must give up a pawn. He rightly saves his QR-pawn, which is far more important.

9	P–QR4

Black can make further progress with 9 ..., RxP (10 B–Q6?, BxRP!) but he rather follows the sound principle of preserving the pawns that hamper White's Bishop.

The move he makes, however, is somewhat impatient causing technical inconvenience. True, his white-bound Bishop calls for the black-bound advance of his majority, and the backwardness of ... PQN3 is bearable since RxQNP is out of question for the time being because of ... R–B7. Yet, Black has a safer way of doing it; he should first bring his King to the Q-side, as suggested in the tournament book.

10 B–Q6	K–B2
11 P–R3	R–B3
12 B–N8	K–K1
13 B–R7	R–B2!
14 B–N8	....

The Bishop must leave its prey as 14 BxP loses to 14 ..., R–N2 followed by ... K–Q2–B3, the hampering PQ4 precluding B–Q4.

14	R–B1
15 B–K5	....

After 15 B–R7?, R–R1! the Bishop is lost.

On K5 the Bishop is well placed for attack—but White has no attack since his Rook is still pinned to the second rank. Besides, as has been mentioned before, the Bishop is perilously cut off from its hinterland.

15	P–N3
16 P–N4	R–B6

It is important to refrain from 16 ..., PxP so that White's KR-pawn remains a target.

17 PxP	NPxP
18 RxP	....

The Rook is finally free to leave the second rank, although at the expense of conceding Black a passer.

In the tournament book the text move is criticized but no improvement suggested. We do not think there is one. After 18 B–Q6, B–N6 Black must soon get a passer, anyhow.

18	RxP
19 B–Q6	R–QB6
20 B–B5	....

The counterattack 20 R–R6 is better, at least from the practical point of view, e.g.

(1) 20 ..., P–R4; 21 RxP, P–R5; 22 R–R1!, R–B7ch; 23 K–N1, R–N7ch; 24 K–B1, R–KR7 or R–N6; 25 R–R3, and the defense holds;

(2) 20 ..., R–B7ch; 21 K–N3, R–QR7; 22 K–R4, B–B6; 23 R–R7, and White has some counterplay;

(3) 20 ..., R–B3; 21 RxR (21 R–R8ch??, K–Q2!) 21 ..., BxR, with most likely a win for Black.

20	P–R4!

Threatening 21 ..., P–KR5; e.g. 21 R–N1, P–KR5; 22 R–QR1, P–R5! and ... K–Q2–B3–N4 (23 RxP??, R–B8!).

21 P–R4	....

Necessary, but it spoils the possible escape of the King via KR4.

21	....	P–R5
22	R–R6	R–B7ch
23	K–N1?	....

Losing quickly as the R-pawn becomes untenable. Instead, 23 K–N3 offers tough resistance.

23	....	R–N7ch
24	K–B1	R–N5!

This switch to the K-side is decisive.

25	RxP	RxRP!

In avoiding 25 ..., RxPch Black assures the smooth advance of his passer since White's Bishop remains cut off from the King side.

26	B–Q6	R–R8ch
27	K–B2	P–R5
28	R–R7	R–R7ch
29	K–B1	....

Or 29 K–K3, P–R6; 30 R–R7, R–QN7! with the same result.

29	....	P–R6
30	R–K7ch	K–Q1
31	R–KR7	R–R7

White resigns

Chapter IV

PAWNS AND KNIGHTS

The best squares for the Knight are, basically, those in the central zone of the board. Nimzovich called a Knight thus placed *centralized*. We use his term only with regard to the squares Q5 and K5 (...Q5 and...K5). These squares are of particular importance, especially in the opening and the middle-game. A Knight posted on Q5 or K5, on enemy territory but not far from home, that is, usually constitutes a fine nucleus for further action.

Apart from centralization, a Knight is likely to serve well on any square in the front line from which it cannot be easily dislodged. Consequently, pawn structures of reduced mobility showing isolation, backwardness, doubling or rams are favorable to the Knights.

IV–§1: Good squares for the Knight

The merits and shortcomings of a Knight as compared to a Bishop have been discussed before, mainly in III-§4.

There now follows a series of diagrams showing Knights in more or less favorable positions close to the enemy ranks, the general supposition being that other elements are equal.

The situation of *Diagram 73* is very common; it requires evaluation from the tactical point of view as a symmetrical pawn formation always does, provided there is no monochromy. If corresponding pieces are available and correspondingly used, time becomes the dominating factor. In this case the centralization of the Knight may be justified by Black's inability to (a) proceed correspondingly with ... N–K5 (b) dislodge the Knight quickly with ... P–KB3 (c) exchange the Knight and form quickly a lever with ... P–KB3.

DIAGRAM 73

Centralized Knight; symmetry

Only tactical edge, if any

DIAGRAM 74

The Knight well placed

Thanks to half-open King file

New situations arise from *Diagram 73* after:

(1) *1* ..., P–KB4, which obviously strengthens the position of the Knight but, creating a Stonewall formation, is not necessarily harmful;

(2) *1* P–KB4, which creates a Stonewall formation on White's part and may be particularly justified in the course of a King-side attack;

(3) *1* P–KB4, P–KB4, which creates another symmetrical formation (Double Stonewall) with all its consequences.

In *Diagram 74* the Knight is well placed since ... P–B3 would tangibly weaken ... PK3 exposing it to frontal pressure.

New situations arise from *Diagram 74* after:

(1) *1* ..., P–B4, which has the serious drawback of making ... PK3 backward;

(2) *1* P–KB4, which cancels out P–KB3 thereby slightly weakening K4, but might still serve well if the further advance and exchange of this pawn is assured;

(3) *1* P–KB4, P–B4, which basically transposes to *Diagram 88*, provided Black can post a Knight on ... K5.

The situation of *Diagram 75* illustrates the possibility mentioned under *Diagram 74*, point 2. Since an open file usually enhances the activity of the pieces, while activity usually emphasizes the significance of weaknesses, the straggler ... PK3 has become a serious liability, and the Knight stopping the straggler is in a really dominating position.

<table>
<tr><td>DIAGRAM 75</td><td>DIAGRAM 76</td></tr>
<tr><td>*Straggler with neighboring open file*</td><td>*Hanging pawns stopped*</td></tr>
</table>

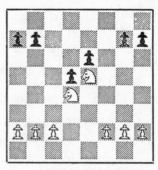

Great advantage for White   *A particularly great advantage*

The situation of *Diagram 76* almost doubles the positional advantage White has in *Diagram 75*. Either Knight is excellently placed. If a distinction must be made, however, the centralized Knight (NK5), being fully independent, deserves a higher rating. The other Knight (NQ4) is in a somewhat dependent state, for if NK5 moves, ... P–K4 might be played.

The position of *Diagram 77* is a counterpart of *Diagram 74*. Of course, either Knight may land on Q5, but it usually is the Queen Knight that does.

The situation often occurs with PK4 instead of PK3. White then has increased chances on the King side, but is also more exposed to possible counterplay resulting from the advance and subsequent exchange of Black's KB-pawn.

The next two cases (*Diagrams 78, 79*) usually occur as details of the same position. The stopping Knight (... NQ4) is in itself much better placed than the centralized one (NK5), but the latter renders better service in attack. To keep the attack going, however, minor pieces are important for the purpose of possible sacrifices. Hence the opposite concern of White and Black in these two diagrams.

DIAGRAM 77

The Queen Knight centralized

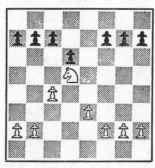

Fine position

DIAGRAM 78

Backed by the isolated Q-pawn

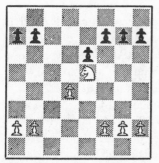

Menacing in the middle-game; the more minor pieces; the better

DIAGRAM 79

Stopping the isolated Q-pawn

Excellent; the fewer minor pieces, the better

The forking power of a Knight is generally appreciated in its major tactical functions, but little known for its great strategic value when it comes to keeping two pawns of a chain under pressure as the Knights in *Diagram 80* do. Pressure of this type has a certain tendency to explode in a sacrificial combination.

DIAGRAM 80

Chainforking

Effective positions

DIAGRAM 81

Chainforking from the base

Particularly effective

All the Knights in *Diagram 81* perform particularly well as their chainforking includes a base, with Black's Knights doing their job from behind. A Knight thus posted takes advantage of the fact that a base by its nature has no pawn protection.

The Knights of *Diagram 82* have in common that each one is attached to a ram, protected and unassailable by pawns. A Knight thus posted will in most cases serve well.

Diagram 83 shows a particular case of the *Diagram 82* type. A Knight thus placed is perfectly active and hard to dislodge since the opposing center pawn has bypassed the critical square (QB4 or KB4, and ... QB4 or ... KB4 respectively).

The most common situation of this sort is PQR2, PQN2, PQB4,

PQ5, PK4 vs NQB4, PQR4, PQN2, PQB2, PQ3, PK4. Action to dislodge this Knight requires the pattern *1* P–QN3; *2* P–QR3; *3* P–QN4, usually with some moves in between. This is a slow process, but the immediate *1* P–QR3? fails against *1* ..., P–QR5! when the position of the Knight becomes permanent because of the backwardness of PQN2.

A similar action to dislodge a Knight from KB4 (...KB4) is usually not feasible, as it impairs the safety of the King.

DIAGRAM 82

Attached to a ram

Usually well posted

DIAGRAM 83

Attached to PQ3 vs PQ5 or PK5 vs PK3

QB4 vs KB4 classic Knight squares

The Knight in *Diagram 84* is attached to a ram as in *Diagrams 82* and *83*, but its position is ideal since both opposing pawns have bypassed the square that the Knight occupies.

Such a square is called a *hole*.

Holes are weaknesses, inasmuch as they offer the enemy pieces ideal strongholds.

Most suitable for the occupation of a hole is a Knight, particularly if the weak square is located in the central zone. If that involves the centralization of the Knight as it does in *Diagram 84*, so much the better.

DIAGRAM 84

Hole and stronghold

Ideal for a Knight

DIAGRAM 85

Rendering duo service

Better behind the pawn than in front of it

In supporting a pawn, a Knight serves best when acting from behind in the function of an imaginary duo-pawn. As NK4 does in *Diagram 85* substituting for PK5. The next stage is reached after *1 P–B6* and *2 N–N5*, when the Knight replaces an imaginary PKN6, and again the next after *3 P–B7* and *4 N–K6*, when the Knight acts for PK7. Acting in front of the pawn (see ... NQB7 in *Diagram 85*) the Knight has more trouble in rendering proper duo service, as it is more exposed to attack and, of course, unable to control the promotion square.

Acting from behind is also indicated when the Knight must serve on behalf of levers. See NQ3 in *Diagram 86*. The position of this Knight is ideal, since the pawn formation requires P–QN4 and/or P–KB4 (to be prepared or not by P–QR3 and/or P–KN3 respectively).

Stopping a passer is a task for which in most cases a Knight is the proper piece, particularly if the passer is located in the central zone. Black's Knight in *Diagram 87* not only stops the passer but renders active service, too, in hitting at PQ4 and PKB4 and doing lever duty as well in view of a possible ... P–N4. No other piece on that square could perform as well. The fine service of this Knight compensates at least partly for White's having a protected passer. Also, Black's isolated and outside passer keeps NQN3 away from the center and from targets.

DIAGRAM 86

On lever duty

Covering the key squares

DIAGRAM 87

Stopping a passer

Black's Knight is better posted

The Knight in *Diagram 88,* thanks to its double pawn protection and immunity against pawn attack, shields PQB3 against frontal assault, so that the backwardness of this pawn has little significance.

DIAGRAM 88

Shielding a straggler

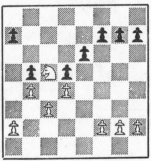

Valuable service

DIAGRAM 89

Stopping a twin

Ideal for a Knight

Shielding is another task for which a Knight is more suitable than any other piece, mainly because a Knight is particularly capable of reaching the critical square and returning from it with ease.

Action against a shielding piece requires levers against the protecting pawns, in this case thus ... P–QR4 and/or ... P–K4. The capture of such a piece creates a protected passer and is rarely of promise.

The shielding of a Rook pawn is necessarily imperfect as the shielding piece lacks double pawn protection.

A situation of the type of *Diagram 89*, with some additional features, has been discussed before (see III–§5).

IV–§2: The centralized Knight

Following are two examples demonstrating the centralization of a Knight.

MAX EUWE   SALO FLOHR

(From the tenth game of their Karlsbad 1932 match)

DIAGRAM 90

Centralized Knight and lever

Sponsors of annihilation

Black suffers from several ailments such as the broken and predominantly vertical pawn wall around his King, the lamentable position of his King Rook, and the inactivity of his Bishops good and bad alike. He would need ten moves or so to put his house in order, but there is no time for that. White has at his disposal a lever that enables him to use his well-developed forces, led by the centralized Knight, for an annihilating attack.

1	P–KN4!	PxP
2	QxP	P–KR4
3	Q–B3	....

So as to proceed with the new lever 4 P–B5 or, after 3 ..., P–B4, penetrate along the KN-file.

These threats are overwhelming.

3	....	P–R3
4	P–B5	B–N4ch
5	K–N1	K–K2
6	PxP	PxP
7	R–N1	B–R3

Or (a) 7 ..., R–N2; 8 RxB! (b) 7 ..., R–KN1; 8 P–KR4! (c) 7 ..., KB–B3; 8 N–N6ch, K–B2; 9 R(Q)–KB1, Q–Q1; 10 N–K5ch.

8	R(Q)–KB1	Q–N5
9	P–QR3!	Resigns

For after 9 ..., Q–R4; 10 Q–B7ch!, White mates.

ISAAC FARBER   H. WALLACH

(From a 1955 tournament played by mail in the US)
(*See Diagram 91*)

White obviously has the edge, thanks to control of the open file. However, it is difficult for him to make headway since the opposing minor pieces are separated by four rams while there is neither an easy lever to form nor a promising sacrifice in sight.

DIAGRAM 91

A dream comes true

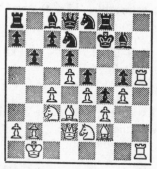

White brings a Knight to Q5

The game continued:

          1 B–B2!   ....

White discovers the only possibility of strengthening his position without resorting to cumbersome pawn action; he is going to bring his bad Bishop via QR4 in front of the pawn wall.

          1 ....   B–QR3

An attempt to provoke 2 P–N3, which would shut the door to White's bad Bishop.

          2 B–QR4!   ....

So as to meet 2 ..., BxP with 3 BxN, QxB; 4 RxP. This indirect exchange of pawns would decisively broaden White's attacking front.

          2 ....   N–B4

Or 2 ..., B–B3; 3 B–B6, R–QN1; 4 N–N5 when Black also must make the concession of parting with his good Bishop (4 ..., BxN).

          3 B–B6   B–N2

The alternatives are just as bad (a) 3 ..., N–N2; 4 P–N4! (b) 3 ..., R–QN1; 4 P–N4!, N–Q2; 5 BxN, QxB; 6 P–N5 and 7 RxP.

4 BxN!	BxB
5 PxB	NPxB

Nor is 5 ..., QPxB any better.

6 N–Q5!   ....

With this centralization, a dream has come true and White wins at will: 6 ..., R–KN1; 7 N(2)–B3, P–R3; 8 Q–R2, B–B3; 9 R–R7ch, R–N2; 10 Q–R5ch, K–B1; 11 R–R8ch, R–KN1; 12 RxRch, KxR; 13 QxNch!, QxQ; 14 NxBch, and White won.

IV–§3: The shielding Knight

The following example deals with the element of shielding.

AKIBA RUBINSTEIN   DUS-CHOTIMISKY

(From their game of the Karlsbad 1911 tournament)

DIAGRAM 92

Operation shielding

Measures and counter-measures

This position offers about even chances. The ensuing struggle is particularly instructive inasmuch as all the Knights become engaged in shielding at one time or another.

1 N–R5! ....

White shields his backward QR-pawn in order to proceed with P–QR4, thus hitting at one of the supporting pawns of Black's shielding Knight.

The text move constitutes a special case inasmuch as the shielding works satisfactorily although it concerns a Rook pawn.

1 .... RxN

Best. The alternatives are promising for White: (a) *1* ..., NxN; 2 PxN, B–Q1; 3 P–QR4! (b) *1* ..., Q–B2; 2 NxN, QPxN; 3 P–QR4, RxP; 4 BxP!.

2 BxN ....

Best, too. The indirect exchange of a Rook resulting from 2 PxR, N–R6 would only stress the negative significance of White's double pawn.

2 .... R–R3
3 B–N3 ....

White has made substantial progress, it seems; he threatens 4 P–QR4 while Black's straggler is no longer shielded.

However, there is a Knight left.

3 .... N–K5
4 R(B)–B1 B–B3
5 B–K1 ....

So this Bishop will not be loose after 6 P–QR4.

5 .... Q–R2
6 Q–Q3 N–Q3!
7 B–B3 ....

A preparation for R–R1, which White needs as he is aiming at P–QR4.

7 .... BxB
8 QxB N–B5!

The other Knight has taken over the shielding. Further developments now depend on the question of whether and with what effect White may get in P–QR4 and/or P–K4.

9 R–Q1   R–R6

The backward QR-pawn, far from being assailable, cannot be trusted; it might effectively advance to QR4 any moment. Hence this move. Of course the Rook there serves only as a road-block, but it serves satisfactorily.

10 R–Q4   ....

White is preparing for the other lever: P–K4.

10 ....   R–K3
11 R(1)–Q1   Q–K2

Allowing the following lever, which Black can afford though.

12 P–K4!   ....

A little combination.

12 ....   RxKP
13 RxR   PxR

There is the little point of 13 ..., QxR?? losing to 14 R–K1.

14 Q–B1!   ....

White's main point. By threatening to win a piece, he recovers the pawn.

14 ....   R–R1
15 BxN   PxB
16 QxP   ....

And so the part of the game which illustrates shielding has ended, with the chances still in the balance. The players eventually agreed to a draw.

IV–§4: The versatile Knight

The following example illustrates the versatility of the Knight.

MIGUEL NAJDORF   ISAAC I. KASHDAN
La Plata   New York

(From their game of the 1947 cable match between the Jockey Club in La Plata, and the Manhattan Chess Club in New York)

DIAGRAM 93

White's Knight provokes weaknesses

... and helps to utilize them

White is a pawn down but he obviously has attacking chances. Making excellent use of the versatility of his Knight he wins.

> 1 N–N5!   ....

Threatening both 2 Q–R5, and 2 NxBP, KxN; 3 Q–B4ch.
But the real purpose of this move is to bring the Knight with due effect to KB5.

> 1 ....   Q–Q2
> 2 Q–R5   P–KR3
> 3 N–B3   ....

Now that White has provoked ... P–KR3, he threatens to recover the pawn very favorably with 4 N–R4.

3 ....   P–QN3

The immediate 3 ..., P–B5 fails against 4 R(B)–B1, White winning the Bishop. Nor is 3 ..., K–R2 playable because of 4 N–K5.

A more reasonable alternative is 3 ... P–R4, although after
4 R(B)–B1, B–N5; 5 BxB, PxB; 6 RxNP White still has the edge.

4 R(B)–B1	B–R4
5 N–R4	P–B5
6 N–B5!	....

One of the fine places from which the Knight would exercise
forking pressure against a chain (compare *Diagram 81*).

White threatens (a) thematically 7 Q–N4 (b) 7 N–K7ch,
K–R2; 8 QxP. His attack is decisive.

6 ....   R–K1

After 6 ..., P–N3; 7 NxPch, K–N2; 8 Q–R4 White wins more
quickly, e.g.

(1) 8 ... PxP; 9 PxP, B–Q7; 10 N–N4, R–R1; 11 Q–B6ch, K–N1
    (11 ..., K–R2; 12 Q–B4); 12 R–B1;

(2) 8 ..., R–R1; 9 P–Q5!, P–B3; 10 PxP, NxP; 11 R–Q1, Q–N2;
    12 R–Q6, R(QR)–KB1; 13 QxP (13 ..., RxN; 14 RxN!).

7 Q–N4	P–B3
8 QxP	N–R3
9 Q–N4	....

Threatening 10 NxPch as well as 10 RxP.

The situation is characteristic of a combined action of Queen
and Knight.

9	K–R2
10 RxP	....

With a pawn to the good and his attack still gathering strength,
White won easily: 10 ..., R(R)–B1; 11 R–Q6, Q–KB2; 12 NxNP!,
R(K)–Q1; 13 N–R5, P–B4; 14 Q–R4, RxR; 15 BxR, B–N5;
16 N–B6ch, K–N2; 17 B–K5, B–B1; 18 P–R3, Q–N3; 19 P–R5,
P–B5; 20 N–K4ch, K–R2; 21 QxP, and Black resigned.

IV–§5: Knights stronger than Bishops

Finally an example showing under which circumstances two Knights are of better use than two Bishops.

WOLFGANG UNZICKER   FRITZ SAEMISCH

(From a tournament played in 1949 at Oldenburg, Germany)

RUY LOPEZ

1	P–K4	P–K4
2	N–KB3	N–QB3
3	B–N5	P–QR3
4	B–R4	P–Q3
5	0–0	N–B3
6	R–K1	. . . . .

A move for which Emanuel Lasker had a preference. The usual continuation, serving to retain the King Bishop, is 6 P–B3.

6	. . . .	P–QN4
7	B–N3	N–QR4

The exchange of White's Bishop is generally considered a partial success, even though it is achieved with a slight loss of time.

More modest and perfectly safe is 7 . . . , B–K2.

8	P–Q4	NxB

8 . . . PxP?? loses immediately because of 9 P–K5!.

9	RPxN	B–N2
10	B–N5!	. . . .

Lasker's continuation, to which in general little attention has been paid. White threatens 11 PxP winning a pawn.

10 PxP, NxP, leads to a fully satisfactory game for Black.

10	. . . .	P–R3

10 . . . , PxP; 11 NxP gives White a good game.

11	B–R4!	. . . .

An improvement on Lasker-Rubinstein, Maehrisch-Ostrau 1923, where *11* BxN, QxB; *12* N–B3, P–B3; *13* P–Q5, P–B4; *14* Q–Q3, Q–Q1; *15* NxNP followed; White's attack, although dangerous, led only to perpetual check.

The text move, based on a sharp point, was introduced by C. Poulsen of Denmark.

11 ....   Q–K2?

Avoiding the consistent *11* ..., P–N4; *12* B–N3, NxP; *13* PxP, P–Q4 as White then obtains a powerful attack with *14* P–K6! (C. Poulsen's point).

Yet Black must accept the challenge or admit that his entire setup starting with *7* ..., N–QR4 is poor.

With the text move Black holds the center, planning to take cover behind his firm pawn wall until his development is completed with ... P–N3; ... B–N2, and ... 0–0.

However, this is a rosy dream; Black's pawn formation is too poor in duos to keep White's Knights successfully at bay. These Knights now develop a pernicious activity.

DIAGRAM 94

Position after 11 ...., Q–K2?

*White's Knights starting
pernicious activity*

12 N–B3 ....

Threatening *13* N–Q5. Black's reply is forced.

12 .... P–B3
13 Q–Q3 ....

Again a threat: *14* P–Q5, P–B4; *15* BxN! (a) *15* ..., QxB; *16* NxNP! with a winning attack (b) *15* ..., PxB; *16* N–KR4! with a winning positional advantage.

13 .... P–N5

A stopgap, as is *13* ..., P–N4; *14* B–N3, N–Q2. Both continuations parry the immediate threat, but the one weakens ... QB5, the other ... KB4 thus creating excellent possibilities for White's Queen Knight (N–Q1–K3).

There is no steady line of defense.

14 N–Q1! Q–K3

The consistent *14* ..., P–N3 is bad, e.g. *15* N–K3, B–N2; *16* PxP, PxP; *17* N–B4, R–Q1; *18* Q–K3, P–N4; *19* B–N3, N–Q2; *20* Q–R7, B–QB1; *21* Q–B7 and White wins.

Black therefore changes his plan intending ... B–K2. But his position is beyond repair.

15 BxN! ....

So as to gain still more time.

15 .... QxB
16 N–K3 ....

The point; White threatens to win the KP with *17* PxP, PxP; *18* N–N4.

16 .... Q–K3

16 ..., R–Q1 fails against *17* Q–B4 threatening *18* QxNP (*17* ..., P–Q4; *18* PxP, PxP; *19* Q–B7!).

Nor is 16 ..., PxP any good as it opens the game—of which White can take advantage in several ways, e.g. with 17 P–K5! (17 ..., PxP; 18 N–N4).

17 PxP!	PxP
18 QR–Q1	....

Threatening 19 NxP, while 18 ..., B–K2 fails against 19 N–B5 (19 ..., 0–0; 20 Q–Q7!). Black's reply is forced.

18	P–B3

What a position Black now has! Seven pawns and no chance for any duo! Five pieces and only two of them developed (or, better, just moved)!

He has two Bishops, yes. But under the circumstances the Bishops are lamentably inferior to the Knights.

19 N–R4	....

Also KN6 has become an ideal spot for a Knight.

19	P–QB4
20 N(K)–B5	....

We would prefer 20 N–N6 followed by 21 P–KB4, but this is a matter of taste.

20	R–KN1
21 Q–N3	P–N4
22 Q–N4!	PxN

An oversight.

Instead, 22 ..., Q–B2; 23 N–B3, P–KR4; 24 Q–N3 (threatening 25 NxKP) 24 ..., Q–B2 is necessary, but then too Black's position is hopeless.

23 N–N7ch	Resigns

Chapter V

PAWNS AND ROOKS

The Rooks may have plenty of mobility behind the wall of their own pawns, but they are active only when attacking the enemy position.

The preparation for active Rook play entails what is called the opening of lines, which largely depends on pawn play, especially on the proper use of levers.

V–§1: The status of a file

The status of a file depends on the presence or absence of pawns.

A file is classified as *closed* as long as it is locked by a white pawn and a black pawn, *open* when unlocked for both sides so that no pawn remains, and *half-open* when unlocked unilaterally so that only one pawn remains.

The unlocking creates an outlet for the Rooks so they can attack the enemy position; it makes the file what we call *navigable*.

The act of unlocking, if it consists in the exchange of a pawn as it normally does, creates two outlets, one for White and one for Black; it offers navigability to both sides, either on the same open file, or on two different half-open files.

The doubling or loss (sacrifice) of a pawn creates only a single outlet which limits the navigability to one side. Files of these types are also called half-open, but we prefer to list them separately because each of them has independent qualities of its own.

Finally there is what we call the *Rook lift*, the use of a Rook in front of a locking pawn, e.g. *1* P–QR4; *2* R–R3; *3* R–R3, when this Rook controls the frontspan of PKR2 and is active no matter whether the file is unlocked on the other side or not. However, the lift is rarely practicable in the early stages of the game because it exposes the Rook to attack by minor pieces.

Accordingly, there are these six types of files:

The closed file: This is the original state of every file. The closed file is useless except that its interspan may be controlled by a lifted Rook.

The open file: This is a file unobstructed by pawns. It normally results from a symmetrical exchange of pawns (*Diagram 26*).

The half-open file and its counterfile: This is a set of files of which, due to an unsymmetrical exchange of pawns, one is unlocked for White, the other unlocked for Black (*Diagram 27*). Such files are adjacent if the pawn is recaptured by a piece, e.g. *1* P–K4, P–Q4; *2* PxP, QxP, or separated by a file if the recapture is carried out by a pawn, e.g. *1* P–Q4, P–QB4; *2* P–K3, PxP; *3* PxP. Indirect exchange may cause a greater distance between the files and create local majorities, e.g. *1* P–QN4, P–K4; *2* B–N2, BxP; *3* BxP.

The hybrid file: This is our term for a file unlocked by means of doubling, e.g. *1* P–Q4, P–K3; *2* P–QB4, B–N5ch; *3* N–QB3, BxNch; *4* PxB, when the QN-file is hybrid on White's side. Unlike the half-open file, the hybrid file involves no elimination of pawns and is not neutralized by a counterfile of the same status.

The void file: This is what we call a file unlocked through the accidental or intentional loss of a pawn, e.g. *1* P–K4, P–K4; *2* B–B4, B–B4; *3* P–QN4, BxP, when White has the void QN-file. The void file entails a material disadvantage, thus presenting questions which, because of their predominantly tactical or technical nature, lie beyond the scope of this book.

The lift file: This is the file which the Rook has occupied by means of a lift, e.g. KKN1 vs RKN3, PKN2.

V–§2: Span control

The control of a file is an asset.

Controlling a singly unlocked file means holding its navigable part, which is the frontspan of the interfering locker. For instance PQB4 vs PQ3 when the Q-file is open for White, the QB-file open for Black. White controls the squares Q1–Q5, while Q7 and Q8 count against him; he has a *span-plus* of 5:2. On the QB-file, however, White has a *span-minus* of 3:4. The general *span-proportion* in this case is 5:2 vs 4:3—a slight advantage for White.

There is always a plus and a minus with respect to a single file, namely 6:1, 5:2 or 4:3. However, equality in span-control is possible in that the span-count for a half-open file and its counterfile may be the same. For instance *1* P–K4, P–QB3; *2* P–Q4, P–Q4; *3* PxP, PxP, when the span-proportion on the two half-open files is 6:1 vs 6:1.

Slight differences in span-control, with their slightly disturbing effect on the balance in controlled space, constitute the basic problem in opening play.

The length of the frontspan is not the only factor on which the value of its control depends; just as important is the vulnerability of the interfering locker. The weakness of a locker may amply compensate for a span-minus, e.g. PQR2, PQN2, PQB2 vs PQR2, PQN2, PQ5, which favors White, his negative span-count of 3:4 vs 6:1 notwithstanding. An isolated pawn is usually a poor locker.

The best locker, making control of its frontspan useless for the opponent, is a firmly protected passer. For instance PQB5, PQ6 vs PQN4, PQB3 when White's positive span-count of 4:3 vs 2:5 has only indirect significance in that the longer frontspan offers better chances to stop the opposing passer.

Span-control by means of the lift normally emanates from a point on the third rank, e.g. RKR3, PKR2, where the Rook is comparatively less exposed than farther along the file, e.g. RKR5, PKR4.

V–§3: Types of pawn formations

The opening usually leads to the forming of a lever or to an exchange of pawns, so that after a few moves an outlet for the Rooks is mutually created or assured. From then on measures and plans are required in compliance with the specific traits of the pawn formation, particularly as far as navigability is concerned.

Since there are only a few characteristics pertaining to navigability, namely outlets for the Rooks, and prospective outlets due to levers and possible levers, it is possible to distinguish between positions of several basic types, each one leading to its own type of middle-game.

During the brief initial stage of the game, the pawn formation normally assumes sufficient character to be classified under one of the following headings.

(1) *Open formations:* those with at least one open file (*Diagram 95*).

DIAGRAM 95

Open formation

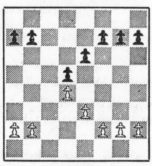

Open file

(2) *Half-open formations:* those with a half-open file and counterfile. There are two types of positions belonging to this group:

(2a) *Ram formations*, where the opposing pawn walls are connected by at least one ram (*Diagram 96*);

(2b) *Jump formations*, where the opposing pawn walls are separated by the open fifth rank while the two head-pawns face each other at the distance of a Knight's jump (*Diagram 97*).

DIAGRAM 96

Ram formation

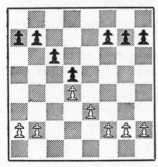

Half-open files; ram

DIAGRAM 97

Jump formation

Half-open files; open fifth rank; head-pawns at a Knight's jump distance

(3) *Free formations:* those with all pawns on the board, none of them advanced across the middle-line (*Diagram 98*).

(4) *Closed formations:* those with all pawns on the board, at least one of them advanced across the middle-line (*Diagram 99*).

(5) *Half-closed formations:* those with half-open files and at least one pawn advanced across the middle-line (*Diagram 100*).

(6) *Hybrid formations:* those with all pawns on the board and a hybrid file (*Diagram 101*). We shall discuss the hybrid file but not hybrid formations independently.

DIAGRAM 98

Free formation

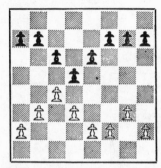

All pawns on the board, none
advanced across middle-line

DIAGRAM 99

Closed formation

All pawns on the board,
middle-line crossed

DIAGRAM 100

Half-closed formation

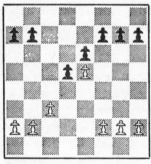

Half-open files; middle-line
crossed

DIAGRAM 101

Hybrid formation

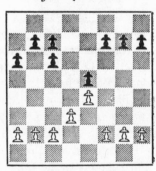

All pawns on the board;
hybrid file

(7) *Gambit formations:* those where one side has more pawns than the other (*Diagram 102*). These formations we only mention as a possibility.

DIAGRAM 102

Gambit formation

Pawns unequal in numbers

V–§4: The open file

The position of *Diagram 103* shows an elementary case where everything depends on control of the open file. Black, whose move it normally must be, has perfect equality after *1* ..., R–B1, or *1* ..., Q–Q2 followed by either ... KR–B1 or ... QR–B1.

But if White has the move, he shares the open file in something like a 55:45 proportion, thus holding a slight edge. His next step is an attempt at tripling his pieces on the open file starting with *1* R–B3 or *1* R–B5. Remember: the Rook moves (a) to a protected square (b) far enough so that its rearspan can accommodate the other two pieces.

After *1* R–B3, Q–Q2; *2* Q–B2, R(R)–B1; *3* R–B1, RxR; *4* QxR White is in full control of the file. He then must try to penetrate Black's position and make progress horizontally, but this is a problem in view of *4* ..., R–Q1!; *5* Q–B7, P–KR3!. Black may be able to hold his own.

The change from *Diagram 103* to *Diagram 104,* although slight, is of great significance. Both sides have a stronghold on the fifth square of the open file, the occupation of which offers a great advantage. Hence the great importance of the move. White gets his advantage with *1* R–B5, Black with *1* ..., R–B5. The Rook thus anchored assures either trebling followed by the full exploitation of the open file, or, if it is captured, an outside protected passer as against a mere candidate on the Q-file (*1* R–B5, RxR; *2* QPxR!).

DIAGRAM 103	DIAGRAM 104
Open file; symmetry; no good levers	*Open file with mutual strongholds*

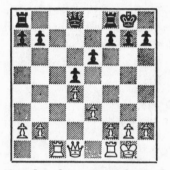 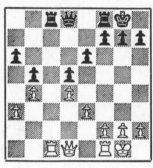

Equality, but only with Black to move   *The move decisive*

This example also shows what great importance the first move may have in a symmetrical position. Since it normally should be White's move, one must assume that Black has maintained the symmetry too long. His last move might have been ... R–B1? while it should have been the lever move ... P–QR4!. Navigational equality often depends on the unlocking of another file.

V–§5: The horizontal switch

The open file, being cleared of pawns, offers no permanent targets. The advantage of controlling an open file consists mainly in the chance of penetrating the enemy position and switching to horizontal activity.

Horizontal activity of the Rooks is often the decisive factor in the course of a mating attack, e.g. in a case like RKR8, RKR7 vs KKN2, PKB3, PKN3. Strategically however the switch is most important for the general purpose of exploiting the original rank of the pawns, i.e. the seventh.

Control of the seventh rank usually offers the advantage that there are pawns to attack which cannot protect each other, while the opposing King is pinned to the eighth rank or to a corner. In such cases (*Diagram 105*) the issue depends on the width of the navigable zone of the rank as well as on the vulnerability of the pawns that lock the zone on both sides.

DIAGRAM 105

Horizontal activity

Navigable zone Q7–K7 vs lockers PQB2 and PKB2

In this position Black threatens to equalize, but White to move wins as follows:

1 P–N6!   ....

With this attack on one of the lockers White broadens the navigable zone to three squares making the rank suitable for exploitation.

Any neutral move permits *1* ..., P–KN3!, after which White cannot effectively break through any more, while otherwise ... K–B1–K1 expels his Rook. For instance (1) *1* P–R4, P–KN3!; *2* P–B5, NPxP (a) *3* K–R4, K–N2! (b) *3* P–N6, PxP; *4* K–B4, R–B1; *5* RxP, R–B2; (2) *1* K–N4, P–KN3!; *2* P–B5, KPxPch; *3* K–B4, K–B1; *4* P–K6, PxP; *5* K–K5, R–K1; *6* K–B6, P–K4!.

1	PxP

There is nothing better. After *1* ..., P–KB3 White wins easily with 2 P–B5!, PxBP; 3 P–K6. In case of *1* ..., P–KB4; 2 K–R4, K–B1; 3 K–N5, K–N1 White should not capture the K-pawn as long as his Rook has no moves on the sixth rank; the proper way of doing it is a general advance of pawns aiming at a broadening of the navigable zone by means of P–N6.

2 K–N4	....

2 R–K7 is ineffective because 2 ..., K–B1; the Rook then must return to Q7, for after 3 RxKP??, K–B2! it is trapped.

2	P–QN4

No matter how Black proceeds, he quickly runs out of playable moves.

3 K–N5	K–R2
4 R–K7	....

Less accurate is *4* P–N4 because of *4* ... P–B4, which offers Black some counterplay. (In situations of this kind, the defender must try somehow to activate his Rook, even at the expense of a pawn or two.)

4	R–Q1

As good as any move.

5 RxKP	R–Q7
6 R–QB6	and wins easily

V–§6: Half-open plus open

While the open file often has a neutralizing effect by favoring the exchange of the Rooks, the half-open file tends rather to delay action by preventing the Rooks from becoming fully active.

Excellent for the Rooks, however, is an open file with an additional half-open file in its neighborhood. The indicated chronological order of the procedure is "half-open file plus lever plus open file," because the half-open file implies an unsymmetrical pawn formation with adequate chances for the necessary lever.

Following is an example of considerable demonstrative power and actuality.

DIAGRAM 106

Half-open ram formation

White has the better lever

This formation, arising from the Queen's gambit or the Nimzo-Indian defense, is frequently met in today's tournaments. We strip the position of minor pieces in order to emphasize what is essential for the Rooks.

Both sides have a half-open file, and there is a 5:2 vs 5:2 equality in span control.

There is also equality inasmuch as the head-duo offers little promise, P–K4 leading to the isolation of PQ4, and ... P–QB4 doing the same to ... PQ4. And if P–K4 is prepared with P–B3 (or ... P–QB4 with ... P–QN3) the result is a hanging duo—not too bright a proposition either.

No; the position calls for levers rather than duos.

The indicated levers are PQN5 vs PQB3 for White, and ... PKB5 vs PK3 for Black. They must serve to create poorly protected pawns and stopsquares on the half-open files or in their neighborhood.

To get in P–QN5 against the resistance of ... P–QR3, White needs P–QR4. By the same token, *1* ..., P–KB4; *2* P–KN3 requires *2* ... P–KN4, but this advance weakens the position of Black's King. The situation therefore favors White.

White with the move obtains a strong initiative with *1* P–QN4. Note that the pawn formation, which for its unsymmetrical nature favors the attacker, remains unsymmetrical no matter what further exchange results from P–QN5.

Black with the move plays *1* ..., P–QR4, which under these circumstances is a good defense as it hampers White's pawn action (*2* P–QR3, P–R5!; or *2* P–QN3, Q–R6!).

The lever action with P–QN4–N5, commonly called *minority attack,* opens the QN-file or the QB-file, thus leading from the half-open formation of *Diagram 106* to one of the open formations of *Diagrams 107-110.*

DIAGRAM 107	DIAGRAM 108
PQN5 vs PQN2 eliminated	*PQN5 vs PQB3 eliminated*

Distinct advantage for White

Also a distinct advantage for White

Diagram 107, as compared to *Diagram 106,* shows that White has made substantial headway because (a) his half-open file has gained in significance in view of the increased vulnerability of ...PQB3, which now is a poorly protected straggler (b) he firmly controls the stopsquare QB5 (c) he is favored by the open QN-file which Black, being occupied with the protection of the straggler, has difficulty in contesting (d) he has a chance to penetrate on QN7 or, if Black's QR-pawn ever moves, on QN6 (e) he can keep Black's QR-pawn under fire while his own QR-pawn is unassailable.

Also *Diagram 108,* as compared to *Diagram 106,* shows great progress on the part of White who now threatens both to win a pawn with *1* Q–N3, and to treble with *1* R–B5 (which *1* ..., P–QN3 does not prevent because of *2* R–N3 and *3* R–B3).

Black's position is very bad; the pawn formation alone spells more trouble for him because (a) his Q-pawn is ailing and exposed to possible lever action with P–K4, or P–B3 and P–K4 (b) there is pressure against...PQN2 while...P–QN3 provokes powerful lever action with P–QR4–R5.

DIAGRAM 109

*P–QN5 frustrated
by ... P–QB4*

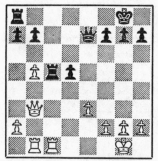

White has a slight edge if any

DIAGRAM 110

QRP vs QRP eliminated

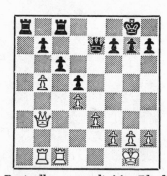

Basically some relief for Black

Diagram 109 illustrates how P–QN5, if it does not lead to the exchange of this pawn, is detrimental to White's position; there is less advantage here than in *Diagram 106*, probably none at all. True, Black's Q-pawn is isolated, but the aimlessly advanced PQN5 also constitutes a weakness—mainly because it is no longer available for control of QB4 or QB5, so that Black can use these squares as strongholds on the open file. The pros and cons of this pawn formation are debatable; a possible advantage of White would normally depend on the minor pieces.

As a rule, P–QN5 should be played only when the exchange of this pawn is assured.

In a position as shown in *Diagram 106* Black's task is at any rate difficult (so that he probably is better off in meeting *1* P–Q4, P–Q4; *2* P–QB4 with *2* ..., P–QB3 rather than with *2* ..., P–K3).

But once such a position is reached, Black should strive for the exchange of the QR-pawns by interpolating ... P–QR3 or ... P–QR4.

The elimination of the QR-pawns offers Black:

(1) some relief in comparison with *Diagram 107* (where his own QR-pawn tends to weakness);

(2) not much relief in comparison with *Diagram 108* in view of his then isolated QN-pawn;

(3) substantial relief, possibly to the point of a tangible advantage, in comparison with *Diagram 109*, such in view of White's then isolated and vulnerable QN-pawn;

(4) basically some relief thanks to possible exchanges along the open QR-file.

V–§7: Louis Paulsen's ram formation

In the tournaments since 1945, another half-open ram formation has risen to great importance; we speak of it as the *Ram system* of the Sicilian defense.

This formation differs basically from the formation of *Diagram 106* by the absence of strongly indicated levers. Its special characteristic is the backwardness of Black's Q-pawn. Also remarkable is that the span proportion slightly favors Black with 5:2 vs 6:1, but this is characteristic for the Sicilian as a whole.

The ram system is one of the three main systems of the Sicilian; the two others are characterized by ... P–K3 and ... P–KN3 respectively.

All three systems have been worked out and bequeathed to the chess world by Louis Paulsen; they should bear his name or have some descriptive names. However, only the fianchetto system has such a name; it is called the *Dragon system,* its name depicting the qualities of Black's fianchettoed Bishop. The system with the duo-move ... P–K3, which we accordingly call the Duo system, is known as the Scheveningen variation. And the Ram system is called the Boleslavsky variation.

DIAGRAM 111

Sicilian ram system

Louis Paulsen's heritage

The ram-move ... P–K4 had been played now and then before Paulsen's time, but it took Paulsen to work it out to a perfect system. This happened in the eighties. Sixty more years elapsed, however, before Louis Paulsen found a worthy interpreter in Isaac Boleslavsky. Louis Paulsen's merit in the matter has also been recently pointed out by Imre König of Los Angeles.

The Duo system was Paulsen's main hobby during his entire life. Time and again he experimented with ... P–K3, trying out with self-sacrificing zest all kinds of supplementary ideas. Indeed this system is named after him—provided Black continues with ... QN–Q2. Usual today however is ... QN–QB3, a move adopted by Euwe around 1920 with so much success that the duo system and with it the Sicilian as a whole gained enormously in popularity.

We therefore distinguish between the Paulsen branch (... QN–Q2) and the Euwe branch (... QN–QB3) of the Duo system.

The Euwe branch suffered a blow in the Maroczy-Euwe game of the Scheveningen 1923 tournament. Strangely enough it has since then been called the Scheveningen variation, although the name virtually refers to White's system of attack.

Paulsen's name is never mentioned in connection with the Dragon system, yet it seems that he invented it himself. At any rate, Steinitz made the remark in the New York 1889 tournament book that "the new move ... P–NK3" was introduced by Louis Paulsen at the Frankfurt tournament (evidently a reference to the tournament of 1887).

Paulsen's invention of the Dragon is the more likely since he generally had a strong predilection for the fianchetto of the King Bishop, which was very strange in his time. He also most likely invented and certainly introduced the King's Indian (1 P–Q4, N–KB3; 2 P–QB4, P–KN3) some forty years before this defense began to gain popularity. Equally he contributed to that variant of the King's Indian which today is called the Yugoslav or Pirc defense (1 P–K4, P–Q3). For there is a documentary remark in the Nuremberg 1883 tournament book, reading: "The actual inventor of this defense is Wilfried Paulsen but [his brother] Louis Paulsen submitted it to a closer investigation."

Enormous, indeed, is Louis Paulsen's contribution to present-day chess.

We may mention in passing that Louis Paulsen (1833-1890) of Germany resided in the United States as a businessman for four years. In the New York 1857 tournament he finished second, after Paul Morphy.

Now back to *Diagram 111*.

There are many variations of the Sicilian ram system, due mainly to Black's playing ... QN–QB3 or ... QN–Q2, and ... B–K3 or ... B–QN2.

We have chosen a variation of average importance so as to have a suitable background for the following general explanation of the situation.

The position of *Diagram 111* is normally reached as follows: *1* P–K4, P–QB4; *2* N–KB3, P–Q3; *3* P–Q4, PxP; *4* NxP, N–KB3; *5* N–QB3, P–QR3; *6* B–K2, P–K4; *7* N–N3, B–K2; *8* 0–0, 0–0; *9* B–K3, B–K3.

For a long time, Black's backward Q-pawn was considered as the outstanding mark of the position and evaluated as a serious weakness. But when Boleslavsky and others started to follow Louis Paulsen's example, it soon became evident that the straggler is unassailable and even somewhat dangerous because of its tendency to advance. This brings us to the question of the levers.

There are three first-hand levers offered by the pawn formation, one for White: P–KB4, and two for Black: ... P–Q4 and ... P–B4.

Of these, ... P–B4 is practically out of question because of KPxBP, which leaves Black with hanging pawns in the center and a weakened King side, while on the other hand White's pieces gain considerably in scope, thanks to the disappearance of PK4.

That makes the lever situation virtually even: P–KB4 vs P–Q4. However, these levers have different qualities, so that the situation raises difficult problems.

In general, P–KB4 is assured but of little promise, while ... P–Q4 is of promise but not assured. White cannot expect much from the exchange of his KB-pawn, mainly since he has no pawns available for the effective support of an action along the half-open KB-file. Black, on the other hand, is well off if he exchanges his Q-pawn at the proper time, because he then has a dangerous majority on the King side, while the open Q-file, thanks to his center pawn and span-plus on the QB-file, may also count as an asset for him.

Indeed, ... P–Q4 is the key move of this entire system. However, ... P–Q4 may easily fail if played prematurely, for instance *1* P–K4, P–QB4; *2* N–KB3, P–Q3; *3* P–Q4, PxP; *4* NxP, N–KB3;

5 N–QB3, P–QR3; *6* B–Q3, P–K4; *7* KN–K2, P–Q4??; *8* PxP, NxP; *9* B–QB4!, N–KB3; *10* BxPch with a winning advantage for White (O'D. Alexander–Z. Milev, International team tournament, Amsterdam 1954).

Of course, White is highly interested in preventing . . . P–Q4 directly or indirectly and keeping the square Q5 open so he can centralize his Queen Knight and correct his span-minus with P–QB3 or P–QB4. However, he can rarely achieve all this: QN–Q5 usually leads to a change of the pawn formation in that PK4 lands on Q5 sealing off the critical stopsquare and creating majorities. In this new situation, White still has a good game if he acts on the Q–side but remains passive on the K-side with P–KB3, as has been repeatedly demonstrated by Bisguier. Instead, the often played P–KB4 is dangerous for White, mainly since . . . KPxBP clears the K-file and the square . . . K4 for Black's pieces (which has far less significance as long as the Q-file is half-open).

Consequently, these are the most reasonable continuations in *Diagram 111* (and similar positions):

(1) *10* P–B4. Most usual. White threatens to strengthen his grip on the vital square Q5 by means of *11* P–B5. Black has this choice:

> (1a) *10* . . . , PxP. A radical measure—somewhat strange since it isolates the straggler, but playable since it also isolates PK4 thus making . . . K4 a fine square for Black's pieces.

> (1b) *10* . . . , Q–B2; *11* P–B5, B–B5. The usual measure; the ensuing situation is very tense inasmuch as White should strive for his head-duo with P–KN4–N5 but remains in constant danger that the counterthrust . . . P–Q4 would blow up his position.

(2) *10* P–B3. As preferred by Bisguier. White obtains the slightly better majority two ways:
> (2a) *10* . . . , P–Q4; *11* PxP, NxP; *12* NxN, BxN; *13* P–QB4;

(2b) *10* ..., Q–B2; *11* N–Q5, BxN; *12* PxB (Bisguier–Barcza, Zagreb 1955).

(3) *10* N–Q5. This leads more directly to 2b (*10* ..., NxP??; *11* B–N6!).

One must conclude that Paulsen's ram formation is very difficult to assail. There is no convenient system of attack comparable to the minority attack in the formation of *Diagram 106*. Lacking any strong lever White is unable to bring his Rooks into action quickly and must rely on slow maneuvering.

Remarkable in this connection is the great popularity which the following line has today: *1* P–K4, P–QB4; *2* N–KB3, P–Q3; *3* P–Q4, PxP; *4* NxP, N–KB3; *5* N–QB3, P–QR3; *6* B–KN5, which practically prevents *6* .... P–K4 because of *7* BxN, QxB; *8* N–Q5, Q–Q1; *9* N–B5, with a strong game for White.

We mention this case as a curiosity. Not long ago the Sicilian ram system was considered poor, while today White usually avoids it.

V–§8: Jump formations

Jump formations constitute a large and very important group of half-open formations (defined heretofore as having in common the open fifth rank and head-pawns facing each other at the distance of a Knight's jump).

In a jump formation, the span proportion is always 5:2 vs 4:3 offering the side with the span-plus (not necessarily White) a slight advantage in space. To maintain this edge and probably increase it, the attacker usually is better off if he (a) holds his pieces in a state of readiness (b) avoids exchanges as far as possible (c) counteracts the forming of levers rather than striving for it (d) works with occasional threats (e) generally bides his time for major action.

As far as the use of the Rooks is concerned, jump formations offer some choice. On the part of the attacker, not even the occupation of the half-open file is always indicated; he might do better by forming his head-duo and placing a Rook behind either duo-pawn. Nor is it advisable to double the Rooks without a special reason, because heavy pieces generally reach a higher state of preparedness if placed next to each other rather than behind each other. Rather characteristic for jump formations is a Rook lift to the third rank, adopted by the attacker for the sake of action on the K-side.

The full opening of a line might easily lead to the exchange of the Rooks thereby helping the defender.

The levers offered to the defender, hitting at the opposing head-pawn, have a tendency to free his game, and we therefore call them *liberation levers*. For instance, after 1 P–K4, P–K4; 2 N–KB3, P–Q3; 3 P–Q4, PxP; 4 NxP Black's liberating lever moves are ... P–Q4 and ... P–KB4.

The value of a liberation lever depends on the proper use of the thus opened file or files. Formed prematurely, a liberation lever is apt to serve only the attacker. To avoid such an adverse effect, the defender must have his Rooks at hand before taking the critical step. He would normally be better off with one Rook on his half-open file and the other behind the lever-pawn he intends to advance.

The need for a liberation lever diminishes in accordance with the exchange of pieces, because a reduction in material for the available space helps just as much as an increase in space for the available material.

The defender's task is especially difficult in those cases where the liberation lever must also serve to liberate his Queen Bishop; delicate problems then arise from the urgency of the lever on behalf of the Bishop, and its possible prematurity with regard to the Rooks. The solution sometimes requires three stages according to the pattern of (1) RQR1, BQB1, PQR2, PQN2, PQB3 (2) RQR1, BQN2, PQR2, PQN3, PQB3 (3) RQB1, BQN2, PQR2, PQN3, PQB4. Thus the move P–QB4, supposed to form the liberating lever PQB4 vs PQ4, is postponed until the Bishop and the Rook got ready to cope with the opening of lines, which sometimes requires additional preparations. The Bishop must stay inactively in its nest on QN2 (usually ... QN2) for some time, and we therefore call this characteristic procedure the *nest method.*

The position of the defender's Queen Bishop, either in front of the pawn wall or behind it, is also one of the characteristics by which jump formations differ from each other. Further distinction depends on the half-open files for White and Black, the possibilities being practically restricted to the QB-file, the Q-file, and the K-file, with two of these files virtually involved in every single case. Rarely involved is the KB-file, because a jump formation as e.g. QR2, QN2, QB2, Q3, K4, KN2, KR2 vs QR2, QN2, QB2, Q3, KB2, KN2, KR2, which in the middle-game would clearly favor White, can hardly arise from any logical setup.

The most important types of the jump formation are:

(1) the Spanish formation (*Diagram 112*)
(2) the French formation (*Diagram 113*)
(3) the French formation expanded (*Diagram 114*)
(4) the Caro-Kann formation (*Diagram 115*)
(5) the Orthodox formation (*Diagram 116*)
(6) the Slav formation (*Diagram 117*)

Each of these formations ordinarily arises from the opening indicated, but it might also be reached in some other way.

DIAGRAM 112

The Spanish formation

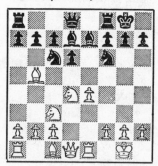

Minor pieces important; no levers required

This formation normally arises from the Spanish (Ruy Lopez) opening as follows: *1* P–K4, P–K4; *2* N–KB3, N–QB3; *3* B–N5, N–B3; *4* 0–0, P–Q3; *5* P–Q4, B–Q2; *6* N–B3, B–K2; *7* R–K1, PxP; *8* NxP, 0–0.

Both sides have developed their light forces, and White has a slight edge, thanks to superiority in controlled space. For the time being however, White's chances lie in the line of mainte-nance rather than progress, for he lacks a lever of promise. He should first of all avoid any unnecessary exchange of minor pieces. Black, on the other hand, needs some exchanges, but no lever for the time being. However, any time-wasting play on White's part may enable Black to use one of his levers aggres-sively. White has this choice:

(1) *9* KN–K2 (An obsolete system.) *9* ..., P–QR3; *10* B–Q3 (The most objectionable move of this system; the Bishop hampers the Queen and is hampered itself by PK4.) *10* ..., N–KN5!; *11* N–N3 (Or *11* P–B4?, P–Q4!) *11* ..., B–B3; *12* P–KR3, BxN; *13* PxB, KN–K4; *14* P–KB4, Q–R5!; *15* N–B1, NxB; *16* PxN, P–B4!, with a fine game for Black (Janowski–Em. Lasker, match 1909, eighth game).

(2) *9* B–B1 (A more reasonable system, and yet dubious as it also entails a loss of time.) *9* ..., R–K1; *10* P–B3, NxN; *11* QxN, B–K3; *12* Q–B2, P–B3, and Black has a fully satis-factory game (Euwe–Capablanca, London 1922).

(3) *9* BxN!. The usual and best continuation, making White's modest advantage more permanent in nature because P–K5 becomes a constant threat in view of Black's double pawn. For instance *1* P–K4, P–K4; *2* N–KB3, N–QB3; *3* B–N5, P–QR3; *4* B–R4, N–B3; *5* 0–0, P–Q3; *6* BxNch, PxB; *7* P–Q4, PxP; *8* NxP, P–B4; *9* N–KB3, B–K2; *10* N–B3, 0–0; *11* R–K1, B–N2; *12* B–N5, P–R3; *13* B–R4, R–K1; *14* P–K5! (The characteristic lever which, if destroying the triad one way or the other, creates assailable targets.) *14* ..., PxP; *15* RxP, QxQch; *16* RxQ, B–Q3; *17* RxRch, NxR; *18* N–Q2, and White definitely has the edge (Smyslov–Botvinnik, match 1954, eleventh game).

DIAGRAM 113

The French formation

Liberation lever indicated

This pawn formation is characteristic for some variations of the French defense. The shortest way to reach it is the Rubinstein variation: *1* P–K4, P–K3; *2* P–Q4, P–Q4; *3* N–Q2, PxP; *4* NxP (*Diagram 113*).

The French formation requires a liberation lever to be formed (a) normally with the unfree QB-pawn, which in turn sometimes requires the nest method (b) exceptionally with the half-free K-pawn.

Following a few plausible lines starting from *Diagram 113*:

(1) *4* ..., N–KB3 (Dubious because of *5* NxNch.) *5* B–KN5 (Transposing to the Burn variation.) *5* ..., B–K2; *6* NxNch (*6* BxN, BxB; *7* N–KB3 is more enterprising.) *6* ..., BxN; *7* BxB, QxB; *8* N–B3, 0–0; *9* P–B3, N–Q2; *10* B–K2, P–K4 with full equality (Capablanca-Alekhine, New York 1927). This is an example of the exceptional lever with the K-pawn.

(2) *4* ..., N–Q2; *5* N–KB3, KN–B3; *6* B–Q3, B–K2; *7* 0–0, NxN; *8* BxN, N–B3; *9* B–Q3, 0–0

(2a) *10* P–B3 (Dull play; White takes no measures against the liberation lever.) *10* ..., P–QN3; *11* Q–K2, B–N2;

12 N–K5, Q–Q4; *13* P–B3, P–B4! (Liberation accomplished.) *14* B–K3, PxP; *15* BxP, B–B4; *16* BxB, QxBch; *17* K–R1, QR–Q1 with a good game for Black (Wolf–Rubinstein, Karlsbad, 1907).

(2b) *10* Q–K2! (Forcing Black to form the lever at once, when it is somewhat premature, or apply the nest method, which in this case is particularly laborious since Black cannot rely on ... Q–QB2.)

(i) *10* P–QN3; *11* R–Q1, B–N2; *12* P–B4, P–B3; *13* N–K5, and Black is in trouble, mainly in view of *13* ..., Q–B2; *14* B–B4;

(ii) *10* ..., P–B4 (Best under the circumstances.) *11* PxP, BxP; *12* R–Q1, and White has the edge; holding an advance in development he may also count the local majorities as an asset.

DIAGRAM 114

The French formation expanded

Liberation lever urgent

The French formation is also common in the Queen's gambit although in the expanded shape of PQB4, PQ4 vs PQB3, PK3 rather than PQB2, PQ4 vs PQB2, PK3.

The French expanded is usually reached as follows: *1* P–Q4,

P–Q4; 2 P–QB4, P–QB3; 3 N–KB3, N–B3; 4 N–B3, P–K3; 5 P–K3, QN–Q2; 6 B–Q3, B–Q3; 7 P–K4, PxKP; 8 NxP. And the usual continuation is 8 ..., NxN; 9 BxN (*Diagram 114*).

In this position Black urgently needs a liberation lever. Let us keep this in mind when looking at the following possibilities:

(1) 9 ..., N–B3? (Inconsistent. The Knight should keep the lever points ... QB4 and ... K4 under observation.) 10 B–B2
   (1a) 10 ..., B–N5ch? (As usual, playing for exchanges before the Queen Bishop is liberated causes delay in development.) 11 B–Q2, BxBch; 12 QxB, 0–0? (12 ..., Q–K2, possibly followed by ... 0–0–0, is comparatively better.) 13 N–K5, Q–B2; 14 0–0–0, P–B4; 15 Q–K3, P–QN3; 16 PxP, PxP; 17 P–KN4!, R–N1; 18 KR–N1, Q–N3; 19 P–N3, R–N2; 20 P–N5, N–K1; 21 BxPch!, KxB; 22 Q–R3ch, K–N1; 23 R–N4, and Black resigned (Szabo–Bisguier, Buenos Aires 1955).
   (1b) 10 ..., 0–0; 11 0–0 (Threatening 12 B–N5 followed by Q–Q3.) 11 ..., P–KR3.
      (i) 12 Q–K2, P–QN3!; 13 P–QN3, B–N2; 14 B–N2, Q–K2; 15 QR–Q1, QR–Q1; 16 B–N1, P–B4!, and the nest method has worked, Black has a satisfactory game;
      (ii) 12 Q–Q3!, P–QN3; 13 P–QN3, B–N2; 14 B–N2, and the nest method has failed, the threat of 15 P–Q5 is decisive.

(2) 9 ..., 0–0; 10 0–0
   (2a) 10 ..., N–B3?. A poor move; it might lead to 1b.
   (2b) 10 ..., Q–B2. A good move; it might lead to 2c.
   (2c) 10 ..., P–QB4!; 11 B–B2, Q–B2; 12 Q–Q3, P–B4!. This is Black's best line of play (Gruenfeld–Bogolyubov, Berlin 1926). White's attack is halted; the backwardness of the K-pawn is neutralized by the pressure against the Q-pawn; and Black is adequately prepared for a duel between opposing majorities. The chances are about even.

(3) *9 ..., P–QB4.* This might serve satisfactorily. However, since Black is not forced to start action before having castled (see 2c) he can better first castle.

(4) *9 ..., P–K4.* The lever with the candidate, before castling at that, is too risky. After *10 O–O!* Black is in trouble, mainly since the natural *10 ..., O–O* loses a pawn: *11 PxP, NxP; 12 NxN, BxN; 13 BxPch!.*

DIAGRAM 115

The Caro-Kann formation

No liberation problems; no tension

This position arises from the Caro-Kann defense as follows: *1 P–K4, P–QB3; 2 P–Q4, P–Q4; 3 N–QB3, PxP; 4 NxP, B–B4; 5 N–N3, B–N3; 6 N–B3, N–Q2.* Black, with his Queen Bishop in front of the pawns, has no problems; he can complete his mobilization smoothly without a lever or relieving exchange. His span-minus has very little significance if any.

White is unable to use his good King Bishop appropriately because Q3, its best square according to the pawn formation, is under enemy control. The exchange of the Bishops is convenient for Black, e.g. *7 P–KR4, P–KR3; 8 P–R5, B–R2; 9 B–Q3, BxB; 10 QxB, P–K3; 11 B–Q2, KN–B3; 12 O–O–O, Q–B2; 13 K–N1, O–O–O.* This system, including many minor deviations, is the old main line. It offers White no tangible advantage and is rarely adopted in present-day tournaments.

Another factor of importance is the insignificance of White's pair of Bishops resulting from NxQB or ... QBxN. After 7 N–R4 Black gets a satisfactory game not only with 7 ..., P–K4, which is the generally recommended move, but also with 7 ..., P–K3. By the same token *1* P–K4, P–QB3; *2* N–QB3, P–Q4; *3* N–B3, which is fairly usual today, can be safely met with *3* ..., B–N5; *4* P–KR3, BxN; then, *5* QxB, P–K3; *6* P–Q4, PxP transposes to the Caro-Kann jump formation.

DIAGRAM 116

The Orthodox formation

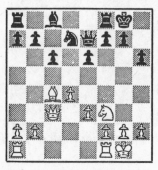

Liberation lever necessary

The Orthodox formation is characterized by (a) White's half-open QB-file versus Black's half-open Q-file (b) Black's confined Queen Bishop.

Consequently, Black needs a liberation lever urgently. His first choice is the lever on the closed file: ... P–K4; his second choice the lever with the candidate: ... P–QB4.

Positions of this type normally originate from the Orthodox defense of the Queen's Gambit. The position of *Diagram 116* is taken from the following game, which offers a good background to discuss the Orthodox formation.

KARL GILG   ERICH ELISKASES

(Championship of Germany 1939)

ORTHODOX QUEEN'S GAMBIT

| 1 P-Q4 | P-Q4 |
| 2 P-QB4 | .... |

The Queen's gambit—which leads to a jump formation if this pawn is captured sooner or later, as happens in many variations.

| 2 .... | P-K3 |

The Classic defense—which entails possible transposition to a jump formation of the orthodox type.

The orthodox jump formation requires that ... QPxBP be followed up quickly by either ... P-QB4 or ... P-K4. If the lever move is postponed, White may profit from his superiority in the center.

2 ... PxP, the Queen's Gambit Accepted, offers these possibilities:

(1) 3 P-K3, P-K4, with a satisfactory game for Black. White is supposed to do better if he prevents this immediate lever with the K-pawn.

(2) 3 N-KB3, P-QR3; 4 P-K3
   (2a) 4 ... N-KB3; 5 BxP, P-K3; 6 0-0, P-B4!; 7 Q-K2, P-QN4; 8 B-N3, B-N2, with a satisfactory game for Black. Note the *expanded fianchetto* of Black's Q-Bishop. This pattern of play is characteristic for many variations of the Queen's gambit.
   (2b) 4 ..., B-N5; 5 BxP, P-K3. This is a remarkable transposition to a jump formation of the Slav type (compare *Diagram 117*). It leads to complicated play after 6 Q-N3. Black is supposed to have a satisfactory game.

| 3 N-QB3 | N-KB3 |
| 4 B-N5 | B-K2 |

This is the so-called Orthodox defense.

5	N–B3	P–KR3

Or 5 ..., 0–0; 6 P–K3, QN–Q2; 7 R–B1, P–B3; 8 B–Q3, PxP; 9 BxP, when the liberation lever with the K-pawn works satisfactorily: 9 ..., N–Q4; 10 BxB, QxB; 11 0–0, NxN; 12 RxN, P–K4!. This is actually the main line of the Orthodox defense, but it is rarely played today.

6	B–R4	0–0
7	P–K3	N–K5

The so-called (Emanuel) Lasker variation. However, this continuation is adoptable in many variations of the Queen's Gambit, so that a name such as *Lasker twist* is more to the point.

The Lasker twist increases Black's freedom of movement through the exchange of a minor piece or two.

8	BxB	QxB
9	Q–B2	....

Instead, 9 PxP, NxN; 10 PxN, PxP; 11 Q–N3, which Tarrasch thought had refuting power, is usually recommended, but it offers White only a slight advantage, if any.

9	....	P–QB3
10	B–K2	....

10 NxN, PxN is satisfactory for Black (11 N–Q2, P–KB4; or 11 QxP, Q–N5ch and 12 ..., QxNP).

10	....	N–Q2
11	0–0	NxN
12	QxN	....

The conservative view that in a case like this the recapture with the pawn strengthens the center is not very reliable because there are drawbacks to consider, too.

After 12 PxN, PxP!; 13 BxP, P–QB4 White's center formation has a touch of clumsiness, inasmuch as any capture initiated by PQ4 entails isolation of PQB3.

12	....	PxP

The development of Black's Bishop is called for, and it requires this preliminary exchange in view of (a) *12* ..., P–K4?; *13* NxP! (b) *12* ..., P–QB4?; *13* PxQP! which isolates ... PQ4 (c) *12* ..., P–QN3?; *13* PxP!, BPxP, when the unexchangeable ... PQ4 definitely confines Black's Bishop.

13 BxP   ....

This is the Orthodox jump formation of *Diagram 116*.

13 QxP allows *13* ..., P–K4!, which is more convenient for Black.

13 ....   P–QN3

The immediate *13* ..., P–QB4 looks premature, for Black opens the QB-file before being ready to contest it. Yet, after *14* Q–R3, R–K1! the defense holds (*15* B–N5, PxP!).

However, Black decides rather on the nest method, which is more elaborate, but also of a more active nature.

As a rule, it is good policy to postpone the lever when in doubt.

14 P–K4   ....

White is preparing for P–Q5, to be played in answer to ... P–QB4 or independently. Counting on his span-plus he is striving for a lever himself.

14	B–N2
15 KR–K1	KR–B1!

Preventing *16* P–Q5, and doing so the right way.

In keeping the other Rook on ... QR1 Black is prepared to meet a possible P–QN4 with ... P–QR4!.

16 QR–Q1	P–QR3
17 B–Q3?	....

An inconsistency amounting to neglect of the key square Q5.

Correct is *17* B–N3. Then, White has the edge since *17* ..., P–QB4 is unfeasible because of *18* P–Q5, threatening *19* P–Q6. Black's best would be *17* ..., Q–B3.

17 ....   P–QB4!

Played at the right moment, the liberation lever has a fully satisfactory effect.

18 P–Q5   ....

This advance is now harmless, for White lacks the threat of 19 P–Q6.

18 ....   N–B1!

The only good reply, but a very good one. Black wants to control the stop-square of the Q-pawn with a Rook.

19 N–K5   ....

With 19 P–Q6, QxP; 20 BxP White can liquidate the tension reaching a drawish position.

19 ....   Q–B2

Omitting the immediate 19 ..., R–Q1 because of the obscure consequences of 20 N–B6.

20 B–B4   ....

The liquidation with 20 P–Q6 is still possible, but White strives for more. He threatens 21 P–Q6.

20 ....   R–Q1!
21 PxP?   ....

A serious aberration.

It is strictly necessary to play 21 P–QR4 so as to maintain the pawn on Q5 and prevent Black's majority from advancing.

21 ....   PxP!

Protecting the square ... Q4 against invasion. Besides, Black threatens 22 ..., RxR; 23 RxR, BxP.

22 B–Q3   ....

22 RxR, RxR; 23 P–QR4 fails against 23 ..., R–Q5!.

| 22 .... | QR–B1 |
| 23 B–B2 | .... |

23 P–QR4, R–Q5; 24 N–B4, P–QN4 also favors Black.

| 23 .... | P–QN4 |

Black now has a superior game thanks to his advanced majority on the Queen side. He won.

DIAGRAM 117

The Slav formation

No liberation problems but tension

This position arises from the Slav defense as follows: *1* P–Q4, P–Q4; *2* P–QB4, P–QB3; *3* N–KB3, N–B3; *4* N–B3, PxP; *5* P–QR4, B–B4; *6* P–K3, P–K3; *7* BxP, KB–N5.

Typical for the Slav formation are the half-open files (QB-file vs Q-file, as in the Orthodox) and the position of Black's Queen Bishop (in front of the pawns, as in the Caro-Kann). *Diagram 117* shows the most common position of this type.

The Slav formation has a more vivid character than the Caro-Kann because P–K4 may restrict the activity of Black's Queen Bishop, although this is not necessarily to White's advantage.

As far as activity of the Rooks is concerned, the Slav formation has the same delaying tendency as the Caro-Kann because White lacks a suitable lever while Black does not need one.

V–§9: Blitz formations

There is a type of position where one side, usually White, has a broad, menacing pawn center which the other has chances to blast. We call such pawn centers *Blitz formations,* indicating the sharp and sometimes explosive character they lend to the game.

The basic means of the blasting are (a) the half-open Q-file or K-file (b) a lever or two against the opponent's pawn center (c) usually a fianchettoed Bishop.

Following are three well-known formations of this type.

DIAGRAM 118

Alekhine's Blitz formation

Rather favoring White

This formation arises from Alekhine's defense as follows: 1 P–K4, N–KB3; 2 P–K5, N–Q4; 3 P–QB4, N–N3; 4 P–Q4, P–Q3; 5 P–B4, PxP; 6 BPxP, N–B3; 7 B–K3, B–B4; 8 N–QB3, P–K3.

White is exposed to pressure along the Q-file as well as to the concentric levers ... P–KB3 and ... P–QB4. The situation is very tense. But since White himself has a dangerous lever at his disposal, namely P–Q5, and since Black's setup lacks the support of a fianchettoed Bishop, the balance in chances rather favors White.

DIAGRAM 119

Gruenfeld's Blitz formation

Approximate equality

This position results from Gruenfeld's defense as follows:
1 P–Q4, N–KB3; *2* P–QB4, P–KN3; *3* N–QB3, P–Q4; *4* PxP,
NxP; *5* P–K4, NxN; *6* PxN, B–N2.

Black has powerful means of focusing pressure against PQ4,
i.e. vertically, diagonally, and by the lever move ... P–QB4
(which, by the way, is usually played as early as possible: *6* ...,
P–QB4 instead of *6* ..., B–N2; but that has no particular bearing on the general situation). After the lever usually comes the
reinforcing ... N–QB3, and again thereafter stands Black's long-
range plan of establishing a majority on the Queen side (...
PQB4xPQ4) and using it in connection with play along the then
open QB-file.

White has a fine center duo, but his chances for attack are
vague owing to the absence of a guiding lever. Action on the
K-side is by and large indicated, but there is only an outside
chance for P–KB5 or P–KR5. Whatever chances White has
would appear in the middle-game rather than in the end-game.
All in all, White's position is satisfactory, but most players distrust it. The less committing lines of the Gruenfeld defense are
much more usual.

DIAGRAM 120

Euwe's Blitz formation (Blitz Benoni)

Rather favoring Black

This important formation has a story connected with the King's Indian defense as follows:

1	P–Q4	N–KB3
2	P–QB4	P–KN3
3	N–QB3	B–N2
4	P–K4	P–Q3
5	P–B4	....

The Four-pawns-attack, which since the time of Louis Paulsen has been considered a menace to the King's Indian.

5	....	0–0
6	N–B3	P–B4!

Starting with this move Euwe succeeded in discrediting the Four-pawns-attack some thirty years ago.

Up to then the accepted but inadequate continuation was 6 ..., QN–Q2; 7 B–K2, P–K4, e.g. 8 QPxP, PxP; 9 PxP, N–N5;

10 B–N5!, Q–K1; *11* N–Q5!, KNxKP; *12* B–K7 (Englisch–
Tarrasch, Hamburg 1885).

7 P–Q5   ....

The main line.

Attempts have lately been made to improve White's setup
with 7 PxP, but the results reached after 7 ... Q–R4!; *8* B–Q3,
QxBP are not convincing.

7 ....   P–K3!

A strong lever.

8 B–Q3   ....

Again the main line.

8 B–K2, PxP; *9* KPxP, R–K1; *10* 0–0, which has recently been
tried with some success, offers White hardly any advantage by
force.

8 ....   PxP
9 BPxP   ....

Or *9* KPxP, R–K1ch, with a comfortable game for Black.

9 ....   Q–N3!

This is the position of *Diagram 120* (Saemisch–Euwe, Wies-
baden, 1925).

Black has a good game.

The position belongs to the great family of Benoni formations.

V–§10: Sicilian formations

As explained before (*V-§7*) we distinguish between the Ram,
Duo, and Dragon systems of the Sicilian. They all have the char-
acteristics of Q-file vs QB-file and a 5:2 vs 6:1 span-plus for
Black.

The Ram system has been discussed with *Diagram 111*.

Let us now take a look at the Duo system and the Dragon
system which together constitute a special branch of the Jump
formations.

DIAGRAM 121

Sicilian duo system

Duos in jump distance

This position is typical for the Duo system. Its basic trait is the duo ... PQ3 and PK3. The counter-duo PK4 and PKB4 then leads to a kind of double Jump formation.

The counter-duo offers White an advantage in space on the K-side which compensates for Black's span-plus on the Q-side.

The given lever moves are P–K5 and P–KB5 for White, and ... P–Q4, ... P–K4 for Black. Originally none of them has the significance of a threat; they are possibilities to be kept in reserve for use at the proper moment. Proper moments are e.g. (a) for P–K5 when the dislodgment of ... NKB3 and/or removal of PK4 is desirable (b) for P–KB5 where there is a chance to use the KB-file, or to gain access to Q5, or to form the head-duo PKB5, PKN5 (c) for ... P–Q4 when the basically dangerous reply of P–K5 has been recognized as harmless (d) for ... P–K4 when this transposition to the Ram system offers reasonable scope.

As far as the use of the Rooks is concerned, Black's line of play is more clearly indicated than White's.

Black must occupy the QB-file and support his pressure there by bringing his Queen Knight to ... QB5 and playing ... P–QN4 so as to dislodge NQB3 or, if this is met with P–QR3, for a lever with ... P–QN5. In the course of these operations, both sides must carefully watch the possibility of ... RQB1xNQB3; this sacrifice of the exchange, if it leads to the fall of PK4 and the doubling of White's QB-pawn, offers Black a distinct advantage.

White, on the other hand, has little chance of making any headway along the Q-file. His span-plus on that file is insufficient for a stronghold comparable to Black's ... QB5. Nor has he at his disposal any such supporting action as Black has. Indeed, were it only for the half-open files, Black would have the edge.

However, White has considerable chances for attack on the K-side. Apart from P–K5 and/or P–KB5 there is the possibility of P–KN4–N5 to be followed up with either P–KB5, or a Rook lift to KR3.

DIAGRAM 122

Sicilian Dragon system

Focus Q5 (... Q4)

This is a position typical for the Dragon system.

With his King Bishop fianchettoed, Black cannot afford to move his K-pawn because of the resulting weakness of ... PQ3. Consequently, the square Q5 (... Q4) is of great importance for both sides; White may use it for the centralization of his Queen Knight, while Black may free his game with ... P–Q4. However, White has a better grip on the critical square since it is located on his half-open file; his advantage in this regard compensates for Black's span-plus.

The importance of the critical square lends a centralized

character to the proceedings. As compared to the Duo system, the initial chances of White on the K-side are reduced, and so are Black's on the Q-side.

The possible N–Q5 enables White to improve his span proportion on the QB-file with P–QB3 or P–QB4. Black is better off if he prevents P–QB4 and heads for ... N–QB5. The centralized Knight he usually must exchange quickly.

The possible transfer of PK4 to Q5 increases White's chances on the K-side, for in trading the Q-file for the K-file he improves his span-control from 5:2 to 6:1 and brings the front nearer to Black's King, too. In particular, White then can comfortably strive for the lever move P–KB5, which no longer involves the disadvantage of making PK4 backward.

White usually has a slight pull.

V–§11: Maroczy bind and Boleslavsky wall

These are two special and very important formations of the jump type, one characterized by PQB4, PK4 vs PQ3, PK2, the other by PQB4, PK4 vs PQB3, PQ3.

DIAGRAM 123

The Maroczy bind

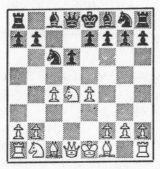

Span control improved by P–QB4

The so-called Maroczy bind is arrived at in the Sicilian if White is permitted to interpolate 5 P–QB4 before playing

N–QB3. For instance *1* P–K4, P–QB4; *2* N–KB3, P–Q3; *3* P–Q4, PxP; *4* NxP, N–QB3; *5* P–QB4 (*Diagram 123*).

The Maroczy bind offers White a span-plus of 5:2 vs 4:3 as against the span-minus of 5:2 vs 6:1 which he normally has. This advantage in space has long been considered as very important, leading to the conclusion that *4* ..., N–KB3 is necessary; for White's best then is *5* N–QB3, but that precludes the Maroczy bind.

However, the Maroczy bind has also a drawback, as the Russian analyst Symagin has recently pointed out. The move *5* P–QB4 delays the development of White's pieces, of which Black can take advantage by getting in ... P–KB4—the lever for which there is otherwise very little chance.

Symagin's system requires ... P–KN3 and ... N–KR3. Moreover, ... P–KB4 should be played prior to ... P–Q3, according to recent experiences. Black's best way of doing it is considered to be this:

1 P–K4	P–QB4
2 N–KB3	N–QB3

If Black wants to challenge the Maroczy bind, he should play this move instead of the otherwise more usual *2* ..., P–Q3 (which may lead to *Diagram 123*, where White has the edge).

3 P–Q4	PxP
4 NxP	P–KN3
5 P–QB4	B–N2
6 B–K3	N–R3

Necessary for the Symagin system.

Another line of play, designed to take advantage of the slight melanpenia of the Maroczy bind, runs as follows: *6* ..., N–B3; *7* N–QB3, N–KN5; *8* QxN, NxN; *9* Q–Q1 with two possibilities (a) *9* ..., P–K4, as in Smyslov—Botvinnik, Alekhine Memorial tournament, Moscow 1956 (b) *9* ..., N–K3, as in Gligorich—Larsen, Dallas 1957. Neither of these games is convincing. Black's general idea is questionable.

7 N–QB3	0–0

7 ..., N–KN5 leads to the other system (see the preceding note).

8	B–K2	P–B4!
9	PxP	BxN!
10	BxB	NxP
11	B–B5	P–Q3
12	B–R3	KN–Q5

Black has broken the bind and obtained a fully satisfactory game (Fuhrman–Spassky, USSR Championship 1957).

The idea of challenging the Maroczy bind goes virtually back to Richard Réti (1889-1929) who, playing White, successfully tried a line which is nothing else but the Dragon-Maroczy in reverse, e.g. *1* N–KB3, P–Q4; *2* P–B4, PxP; *3* N–R3, P–QB4; *4* NxP, P–B3; *5* P–KN3, P–K4. However, the significance of this particular system became eclipsed because of the custom of labeling as Réti system whatever opening may arise from *1* N–KB3.

DIAGRAM 124

The Boleslavsky wall

King's Indian jump formation

The Boleslavsky wall as shown in *Diagram 124* is reached as follows: *1* P–Q4, N–KB3; *2* P–QB4, P–KN3; *3* N–QB3, B–N2;

4 P–K4, P–Q3; *5* N–B3, 0–0; *6* B–K2, QN–Q2; *7* 0–0, P–K4; *8* R–K1, PxP; *9* NxP, R–K1; *10* B–B1, P–B3.

There are several other lines of the King's Indian leading to the same characteristic pawn formation in the central zone. The formation itself (but hardly the exact position) may also arise from the Ruy Lopez.

We call this formation the *Boleslavsky wall* because it was the Russian grandmaster *Isaac Boleslavsky* who introduced this line of defense, with its key move of . . . KPxQP, and became famous for his virtuosity in handling it.

The Boleslavsky wall is extremely rich in possibilities and has great importance in present-day tournament play. Its outstanding feature is the Q-pawn—seemingly weak as it lacks protection by a pawn, but virtually healthy as it forms part of a duo. White has a slight advantage in span control (5:2 vs 4:3) and consequently a very slight edge. For the time being, however, his King Bishop is less active than Black's King Bishop, while his Knights lack such stopsquares in the frontline as are offered to Black's Knights by . . . QB4 and . . . K4.

The basic levers of this formation are P–QB5 and P–K5 vs . . . P–Q4 and . . . P–KB4.

The levers on the closed files, namely P–QB5 and . . . P–KB4, have an aggressive tendency: either of them normally creating a majority on the K-side for White, and a majority on the Q-side for Black. However, there is more attacking power in a 4:3 majority than in a 3:2 one. Accordingly, P–QB5 is apt to favor White offering him 4:3 on the K-side, while . . . P–KB4 has the opposite effect as it offers Black 4:3 on the Q-side.

The levers with the candidates, namely P–K5 vs . . . P–Q4 (of which only the latter is sometimes desirable), are likely to have a pacifying effect.

All the basic levers are very hard to initiate; the game usually keeps its half-open character for a long time.

Tactical reasons might at times enable White to play P–KB5 with impunity—a second-rate lever which has the obvious drawback of causing backwardness or isolation of PK4. Superior chances for attack might justify this action.

Black is offered an additional lever action in P–QR4–R5–R6. This action is time-consuming but basically sound, provided Black can prevent the establishment of White's QN-pawn on QN4. Advantageous for Black is a possible ... PQR6xP; promising for Black are the situations PQR2, PQN3 vs NQN5, PQR6 and, to a lesser degree, PQN3 vs NQN5, both on the condition that the Knight can be safely maintained. But if Black loses control of the vital stopsquare ... QN5 thus allowing P–QN4, he faces the necessity of a general retreat which might easily become a rout.

V–§12: Free formations

Free formations (all pawns on the board, none across the middle-line) are ripe for planning Rook play when a ram and/or lever has established contact between the pawns. Lacking such contact the position is not yet ripe for Rook play.

DIAGRAM 125

An unripe formation

No indication for Rook play

This position occurred in the New York 1927 tournament (Vidmar–Nimzovich).

It is noteworthy what Alekhine says about the next two moves in the tournament book.

1 QR–Q1   ....

A tolerable move, for the Q-file will most likely be opened sooner or later, Alekhine explains. He prefers however *1* N–KN5 followed by *2* B–B3, e.g. ..., P–KR3; *2* B–B3!.

1 ....   KBxN

This move has Alekhine's full approval. Otherwise Black could move only a Rook, he points out, whereas the position offers no clue as to where the Rooks belong.

There is more wisdom and instruction in such a remark than in a series of brilliant variations.

DIAGRAM 126

Stonewall (Dutch type)

Ripe formation of permanent character

Most important among the free and ripe formations is the Stonewall; it occurs frequently and is not subject to quick changes.

There are many Stonewalls depending mainly on differences in the development of the pieces. Most usual is the Dutch Stonewall characterized by the fianchetto of White's K-Bishop. All Stonewalls have in common the pawn formation in the central zone, possibly with colors reversed.

The Stonewall offers neither side an immediate chance for changing the pawn formation with impunity.

Black's transposing to a half-open formation with ... QPxBP

is rarely sound; even winning a pawn this way is dangerous. For ... PQ4 and ... PKB4 are the pillars of the wall; as soon as one of them gives way, the other one becomes exposed to lever attack by P–K4, the wall as a whole crumbles, and weaknesses behind such as ... PK3 in the state of full backwardness are the result. However, ... QPxBP may serve well if immediately followed by the liberation lever ... P–K4; Black sometimes gets this chance in the middle-game.

White's BPxQP, which is rarely strong, offers three possibilities for a change in formation depending on Black's recapture. These are:

(a) ... NxQP, or any recapture with a piece; this leads to the same type of half-open formation as ... QPxBP; it is poor, but practically never forced.

(b) ... BPxQP; this creates an open formation; it is satisfactory, provided Black can immediately proceed with ... QN–QB3; otherwise the open QB-file is likely to favor White.

(c) ... KPxQP; this is the normal way of recapturing; creating a half-open formation in which the pillars of ... PQ4–PKB4 are maintained it is convenient for Black thanks to the removal of the hampering ... PK3; the formation on the Q-side is then the same as in *Diagram 106*, but White has little chance for a successful minority attack since Black, mainly thanks to his readiness for an effective ... N–K5, has strong chances on the K–side.

White can also change the formation by P–B5, making it a closed one, and speculating on the lever attack with P–QN4–N5. However, this too is a measure which usually works adversely since White, in lifting the pressure on ... PQ4, gets exposed to the very dangerous counterlever ... P–K4. Besides, ... P–QN3 might also thwart his plan.

Whereas breaking up the lever PQB4 vs PQ4 one way or the other is thus likely to be a concession rather than a step forward, both sides are better off by assuming a more or less waiting attitude for the time being, White biding his chance for some lever action, Black building an attack on the King side.

White should keep an eye on these three additional lever chances he has (a) the chain-lever PQN5, PQB4 vs PQB3, PQ4–

which ought to be very effective but is particularly hard to get in (b) the fork-lever PK4 vs PQ4, PKB4—which may or may not work well since it requires the somewhat clumsy preparation by P–B3 (c) the lever PKN4 vs PKB4—which is especially indicated and likely to be very effective in a case of 0–0–0 vs 0–0.

Black must abstain from any early lever action. He has no reason to make any pawn moves except . . . P–KN4. This duo-move he needs sooner or later in connection with . . . N–K5, . . . QN–Q2, . . . Q–K1–R4, followed by . . . K–R1 and . . . R–KN1. This is the new-style procedure developed mainly by Botvinnik. Old-style, and often a source of trouble, are the key moves of (originally) . . . B–Q3 and (later) . . . R–KB3.

Detailed indications for action, particularly lever action, vary with the type of the Stonewall depending on:

(1) the position of the pieces, which involves such differences as BQ3 or BKN2;

(2) the extension of the pawn formation to the Counter-Stone-wall: PQB4, PQ4, PK3, PKB4 vs PQB3, PQ4, PK3, PKB4;

(3) the doubling of White's and/or Black's K-pawn, normally caused by the exchange of a Knight, which entails a hybrid Q-file and may, for its frequent occurrence, be considered as characterizing the second stage of the Stonewall;

(4) the delayed completion of the Stonewall, possibly preceded by the doubling of the K-pawn and/or a significant exchange of Bishops.

Following are some examples given mainly for the purpose of demonstrating lever action in a variety of Stonewalls.

CAPABLANCA—AMATEUR (Havana 1912): *1* P–Q4, P–Q4; *2* P–K3, P–K3; *3* B–Q3, P–QB3; *4* N–KB3, B–Q3; *5* QN–Q2, P–KB4; *6* P–B4, Q–B3; *7* P–QN3, N–KR3; *8* B–N2, 0–0; *9* Q–B2, N–Q2 (An inferior Stonewall, Black's Queen, K-Bishop and K-Knight being poorly placed.) *10* P–KR3!, P–KN3; *11* 0–0–0 (Getting ready for P–KN4, as is usually indicated in a case of 0–0–0 vs 0–0.) *11 ...*, P–K4 (This lever move, if adopted while the lever PQB4 vs PQ4 is still in force, constitutes a monstrosity. In this case, however, Black has the excuse of lacking a reasonable defense against the looming threat of P–KN4. White now wins very elegantly.) *12* QPxP, NxP; *13* PxP, PxP; *14* N–B4!!, PxN; *15* BxPch, KN–B2; *16* RxB!, QxR; *17* NxN, B–K3; *18* R–Q1, Q–K2; *19* R–Q7!!, BxR; *20* NxB, KR–B1; *21* Q–B3, RxB; *22* PxR, and Black resigned.

TAIMANOV, USSR, vs KARAKLAICH, Yugoslavia (Team match between the two countries, 1957): *1* P–QB4, N–KB3; *2* N–QB3, P–K3; *3* N–B3, P–Q4; *4* P–Q4, P–B3; *5* P–K3, QN–Q2; *6* Q–B2, B–Q3; *7* B–Q2, 0–0; *8* 0–0–0, N–N5 (... P–B4!); *9* B–K1, P–KB4 (A time-wasting delayed Stonewall, particularly dangerous since the 0–0–0 vs 0–0 feature strongly indicates P–KN4.) *10* P–KR3, N–R3; *11* B–K2 (Threatening *12* P–KN4.) *11 ...*, N–B3; *12* N–K5, N–B2; *13* P–B4 (Counter-Stonewall) *13 ...*, N–K5; *14* QNxN, QPxN? (The regular way of entering the second stage of the Stonewall, which in this case however is the major evil. Instead, Black must anticipate the lever attack of P–KN4 by means of *14 ...*, BPxN.) *15* P–KN4! (Devastating.) *15 ...*, B–Q2; *16* P–B5, BxN; *17* QPxB, Q–K2; *18* R–N1, P–QN3; *19* QB–B3, P–N3; *20* B–B4, QxP; *21* Q–K2, P–QN4; *22* PxP!, QxB; *23* Q–R5!, N–R1; *24* PxNP, PxP; *25* RxPch, NxR; *26* QxNch, K–R1; *27* Q–R5ch, and Black resigned.

ELISKASES–CANAL (Maehrisch-Ostrau 1933): *1* P–Q4, P–Q4; *2* N–KB3, N–KB3; *3* P–B4, P–B3; *4* P–K3, QN–Q2; *5* B–Q3, P–K3; *6* 0–0, N–K5; *7* QN–Q2, P–KB4; *8* N–K5, QNxN; *9* PxN, Q–B2; *10* N–B3, B–K2; *11* P–QN3, 0–0; *12* B–N2, N–N4 (... B–Q2!); *13* NxN, BxN; *14* P–B5, Q–B2; *15* P–B4, B–K2; *16* B–Q4 (This is a Counter-Stonewall in its second stage. Black is rather cramped owing to the three rams and White's control of the stop Q4. The formation calls for lever attack with P–KN4 or, possibly, P–QN4–N5. In cases of 0–0 vs 0–0, the playability of P–KN4 usually depends on White's hybrid Q-file together with the possible duo PKB4, PKN4. By the same token, Black also may strike with ... P–KN4, provided he is ready for attack.) *16* ..., P–KN4?? (Plain suicide, under the circumstances, for it adds tremendously to the effect of White's following lever move.) *17* P–KN4! (A murderous cross-lever.) *17* ..., NPxP (... B–Q2 is a little better.) *18* K–R1!, PxP; *19* RxP, Q–R4; *20* QxPch, QxQ; *21* RxQch, and Black resigned.

PRZEPIORKA, Warsaw, vs GOTTESDIENER, Lodz (Inter-city match 1924): *1* P–Q4, P–KB4; *2* P–KN3, P–K3; *3* B–N2, N–KB3; *4* KN–R3, (Harmless, unless Black adopts the Stonewall.) *4* ..., P–Q4 (... P–Q3!); *5* 0–0, B–Q3 (... B–K2!); *6* P–QB4, P–B3 (An inferior Dutch Stonewall. Black cannot rely on ... N–K5, and his precious K-Bishop is exposed to exchange.) *7* Q–Q3, 0–0; *8* N–B3, K–R1 (... N–K5, although of little value, is still Black's best.) *9* B–B4, BxB; *10* NxB (Also *10* PxB is reasonable, for it emphasizes Black's melanpenia.) *10* ..., Q–K2; *11* P–B3 (indeed, P–K4 ought to be strong under these circumstances.) *11* ..., QN–Q2 (Black cannot afford playing for a lever himself; after *11* ..., PxP; *12* QxQBP, P–K4; *13* PxP, QxP; *14* P–K4 he also is in trouble.) *12* PxP! (*12* P–K4, P–K4!) *12* ..., KPxP; *13* P–K4! (*13* QxP, Q–K6ch) *13* ..., BPxP; *14* PxP, N–N3 (Or *14* ..., PxP; *15* NxP, a: *15* ..., NxN; *16* BxN, N–B3; *17* BxRP! b: *15* ..., N–N3; *16* N–N5!) *15* QR–K1!, PxP; *16* BxP! (*16* NxP, B–B4!) *16* ..., NxB; *17* RxN, Q–Q3; *18* R–K5, N–Q2; *19* R–KR5, N–B3; *20* N–K4!, and Black resigned.

HERMAN STEINER–BOTVINNIK (Groningen 1946): *1* P–Q4, P–K3; *2* P–QB4, P–KB4; *3* P–KN3, N–KB3; *4* B–N2, B–N5ch; *5* B–Q2, B–K2!; *6* N–QB3, 0–0; *7* Q–B2, P–Q4; *8* N–B3 (Not *8* N–R3 because of *8* ..., PxP threatening *9* ..., QxP.) *8* ..., P–B3 (... PxP; *9* P–K4!) *9* 0–0, Q–K1; *10* B–B4, Q–R4 (This is a

regular Dutch Stonewall.); *11* QR–K1 (With P–K4 in mind—
a much too optimistic idea.) *11* ..., QN–Q2; *12* N–Q2 (Pernicious consistency.) *12* ..., P–KN4!; *13* B–B7 (The poor Bishop
has no reasonable square.) *13* ..., N–K1; *14* B–K5, NxB;
15 PxN, P–B5! (A lever, yes; however, the main purpose of this
advance is a siege. Since *16* P–B4 is prevented, while *16* P–B3
fails against *16* ..., B–B4ch, and *16* P–K4 does so against *16* ...,
P–B6 or *16* ..., P–Q5, White's army suffers severely from lack
of space.) *16* NPxP (*16* N–B3, P–N5!) *16* ..., NPxP; *17* N–B3
(Indeed, PK5 is now safe. However, White must lose as he
cannot appropriately share the open KN-file.) *17* ..., K–R1;
18 K–R1, N–N2; *19* Q–B1, B–Q2; *20* P–QR3, R–B2; *21* P–N4,
R–KN1; *22* R–N1, N–B4; *23* N–Q1, R(2)–N2; *24* QxP, R–N5;
25 Q–Q2, N–R5; *26* N–K3, NxN; *27* PxN (*27* BxN, QxPch!)
27 ..., R–R5; *28* N–B1, B–N4, and White resigned.

RÉTI–BOGOLYUBOV (New York 1924): *1* N–KB3, P–Q4;
2 P–QB4, P–K3; *3* P–KN3, N–KB3; *4* B–N2, B–Q3; *5* 0–0, 0–0;
6 P–N3, R–K1; *7* B–N2, QN–Q2; *8* P–Q4, P–B3; *9* QN–Q2, N–K5;
10 NxN, PxN; *11* N–K5, P–KB4 (A delayed Stonewall starting with
its second stage. Black is in trouble because of RK1? and BQ3?
which should be RKB1! and BK2!; then, with Black to move, the
game would be even.) *12* P–B3! (White's most important lever in
the second stage of the Stonewall; as usual, it serves as a preparation for P–K4. A characteristic team of levers.) *12* ..., PxP;
13 BxP!, Q–B2; *14* NxN, BxN; *15* P–K4!, P–K4 (Only this counterlever might justify the position of ...KRK1 and ...BQ3. But it
fails, tactically.) *16* P–B5!, KB–B1; *17* Q–B2!, KPxP; *18* PxP,
QR–Q1; *19* B–R5!, R–K4; *20* BxP, RxKBP; *21* RxR, BxR; *22* QxB,
RxB; *23* R–KB1, R–Q1; *24* B–B7ch, K–R1; *25* B–K8!!, and Black
resigned.

FLOHR–BOTVINNIK (Match 1933): *1* P–Q4, P–K3; *2* P–QB4,
P–KB4; *3* P–KN3, N–KB3; *4* B–N2, B–K2; *5* N–KB3, 0–0;
6 0–0, P–Q4; *7* P–N3, P–B3; *8* N–B3 (After *8* QB–R3 Black
must act against melanpenia. See Botvinnik–Bronstein, game

seven of their 1951 match: *8* ..., P–QN3!; *9* BxB, QxB; *10* N–K5, B–N2; *11* N–Q2, QN–Q2; *12* NxN, NxN!; *13* P–K3, QR–B1; *14* R–B1, P–B4 with equality.) *8* ..., QN–Q2?! (... Q–K1! or ... N–K5!); *9* B–N2 (N–KN5!?); *9* ..., Q–K1; *10* Q–Q3, K–R1 (A trap, typical for the Stonewall.) *11* PxP? (Falling into it. White counts on *11* ..., BPxB; *12* QN–N5! with a strong initiative.) *11* ..., KPxP!; *12* N–Q2 (White now sees that he would lose the Queen after *12* QxP??, N–K5!, e.g. *13* Q–K6, QN–B3; *14* Q–K5, N–N5; *15* Q–B7, B–Q1. Which proves that dissolving the lever was a useless concession.) *12* ..., N–K5; *13* P–B3, NxQN; *14* BxN, P–B5! (Lever action in the neighborhood of the half-open file! Black opens the KB-file too, obtaining a lasting initiative. Correspondingly, White needs P–QN5 in order to exploit the half-open QB-file, but he has no chance to. *15* KR–K1, Q–R4; *16* N–B1, B–Q3; *17* P–K3, PxNP; *18* NxP (*18* PxP?!, RxP!?) *18* ..., Q–R5; *19* N–B1, N–B3; *20* R–K2, B–Q2; *21* B–K1, Q–N4; *22* B–N3, BxB; *23* NxB (*23* PxB, N–R4!) *23* ..., P–KR4!; *24* R–KB2 (There is no adequate defense.) *24* ..., P–R5; *25* P–B4, Q–N5; *26* B–B3,PxN!; *27* BxQ, PxRch; *28* K–N2, NxB; *29* P–KR3, N–B3; *30* KxP, N–K5ch, and White resigned.

MISS MENCHIK–BECKER (Karlsbad 1929): *1* P–Q4, P–Q4; *2* N–KB3, N–KB3; *3* P–B4, P–B3; *4* N–B3, P–K3; *5* P–K3, N–K5; *6* B–Q3, P–KB4; *7* N–K5, Q–R5; *8* 0–0, N–Q2; *9* P–B4 (The Counter-Stonewall, which stabilizes the center but creates the additional lever possibility ... P–KN4; the latter compensates for White's lever chances on the Q-side. Remarkable is *9* Q–B2, B–Q3; *10* P–B4, which transposes to Pillsbury–Marshall, Monte Carlo 1903, where Black obtained a dangerous attack with the gambit lever *10* ..., P–KN4!?; *11* N–B3, Q–R4; *12* BxN, BPxB; *13* NxNP, N–B3; *14* Q–K2, Q–N3; the game continued: *15* P–B5, B–B2; *16* K–R1, P–KR3; *17* N–R3, R–KN1; *18* B–Q2?, P–N3!; *19* P–QN4, PxP; *20* NPxP, B–R3! and Black won.) *9* ..., B–K2; *10* B–Q2, QNxN; *11* QPxN! (*11* BPxN, B–N4! is convenient for Black, e.g. Teichmann–Réti, Teplitz–Schoenau 1922:

12 R–B3?, NxB; *13* QxN, QxP!) *11* ..., B–B4; *12* BxN (Parting
with the good Bishop is in itself a concession. But White has the
subsequent BxB in mind.) *12* ..., BPxB (*12* ..., QPxB is safer,
e.g. *13* P–QN4, B–K2!) *13* Q–N3! (Threatening *14* ..., PxP and
15 NxQP!) *13* ..., Q–Q1!; *14* N–R4, B–K2; *15* B–N4!, with a good
game for White. However, Black held his own until he blundered.

DIAGRAM 127

The Briton wall: QB4, Q3, K4, KB4

Independent of Black's setup

This formation might have been introduced by Staunton. At
any rate it is of British origin, and we therefore call it the
Briton wall.

Unlike the Stonewall, the Briton wall is originally a system
of attack but as such of little promise. White has basically three
chances for making headway (1) P–Q4, possibly leading to an
effective variant of the Maroczy bind (2) attack on the K-side
with P–KB5 (3) attack on the Q-side with P–QN4.

Consequently, these counter-measures are indicated on the
part of Black (1) a firm control of the stop ... Q5 normally requiring ... P–QB4 (2) firm control of ... Q4, mainly for the
purpose of the possible lever thrust ... P–Q4, which prevents
White from acting freely on either wing (3) the lever thrust
... P–QN4, which is virtually Black's main trump.

Diagram 127 shows a good setup on Black's part.

In general, it is difficult to discuss the Briton wall in detail for the practical reason that there are on the one hand too many potential variations depending on Black's attitude, and on the other hand no recognized variations since the system is too rarely adopted.

Worth mentioning however is the *Minor Briton wall* as the formation PQB4, PQ3, PK4 might be called.

The following example, where Black consistently strives for ... P–QN4, is characteristic for both branches of the Briton wall:

1 P–QB4, N–KB3; *2* N–QB3, P–KN3; *3* P–KN3, B–N2; *4* B–N2, 0–0; *5* P–K4, P–B4; *6* KN–K2, N–B3; *7* 0–0, P–Q3; *8* P–QR3, B–Q2; *9* P–R3, N–K1; *10* P–Q3, N–B2; *11* R–N1, R–N1; *12* B–K3, P–QN4!, with a good game for Black (Botvinnik —Smyslov, first game of their 1957 match).

V–§13: Closed formations—Benoni preview

These formations are represented mainly by the Benoni family.

The name *Benoni* is derived from the opening with that name: *1* P–Q4, P–QB4: *2* P–Q5. However, we use this name in the wider sense to describe any position with the ram PQ5 vs PQ3, which necessarily includes some formations other than the closed ones.

In distinguishing between Benoni formations we go by the pawn situation on the QB-file and K-file thus getting these three groups of them: (1) *Full Benoni formations*, characterized by PQ5 vs PQB4, PQ3, PK4 (2) *Open Benoni formations*, with no pawns on the QB-file and/or K-file (3) *Part Benoni formations*, namely those which are neither Full nor Open.

There is so much variety among Benoni formations, so suitable are they for the study of pawn play, and so important in present-day chess, that we have deemed it proper to treat them at length in our Games Department. Consequently, we mention them only briefly at this point.

We shall discuss only the formations specified as Full and Part. As for Open Benoni formations, these are virtually the offspring of other formations, and we shall treat them only in passing.

Benoni formations as a whole bring out a sharp distinction

between good and bad Bishops and pose formidable problems with regard to lever actions. They are difficult to handle for both sides.

V–§14: Half-closed formations—Franco survey

Leading among half-closed formations (a pawn across the middle-line, half-open files) are those marked by the ram PK5 vs PK3 and the file situation of Q-file vs QB-file. We call them *Franco formations* as they frequently arise from the French defense.

There would be no basic difference between Benoni positions and Franco positions were it not for the entirely different effect of the corresponding lever moves ... P–KB4 in the Benoni, and ... P–QB4 in the Franco; both are highly desirable, but the former requires careful preparation as it may easily impair the safety of the defending King, while the latter involves no such danger and is strongly indicated at the earliest possible moment.

Franco formations, unlike Benoni formations, would therefore rarely stay closed for long. Besides, they have the tendency of posing only minor questions of pawn play.

The next two diagrams demonstrate the difference between ... P–KB4 in the Benoni, and ... P–QB4 in the Franco.

Positions of the *128* type result from a premature ... P–KB4 in the Benoni. White has excellent chances for attack as his pieces are no longer hampered by PK4 while Black's King lacks the protection of ... PKB2.

In cases of the *Diagram 129* type Black's position is perfectly sound. His King is safe, although ... 0–0 will require tactical alertness. However, Black can just as well rely on ... 0–0–0. He faces no lever attack on either side but has a constant lever threat of his own: ... P–B3.

True, White has the situation in hand; only he must take proper precautions against Black's lever to the point of getting permanent control of the stop K5 whenever ... PxKP is played. To be sure of that, he must keep PK5 under firm protection by pieces ("over-protection," as Nimzovich called it).

DIAGRAM 128

Half-closed Benoni formation

*Very good for White
but hard to get*

DIAGRAM 129

Half-closed Franco formation

Easy to get but only equal

Following is a brief survey of Franco formations as they arise from what we call the *Ram system of the French defense:*

1 P-K4	P-K3
2 P-Q4	P-Q4
3 P-K5	....

The French ram system (as distinguished from the Sicilian ram system; see *Diagram 111*).

Also *3* N-QB3 and *3* N-Q2 usually lead to Franco formations.

3	P-QB4!
4 P-QB3	....

4 PxP, the Nimzovich variation, leads after *4* ..., N-QB3! (*4* ..., BxP; *5* Q-N4!); *5* N-KB3, BxP to the position of *Diagram 129*.

The criterion of this half-closed variation is the evacuation of the stop Q4. Variants of the same idea, also frequently adopted by Nimzovich, are (1) 4 N–KB3, PxP; 5 QxP or 5 B–Q3 (2) 4 Q–N4, PxP; 5 N–KB3.

4	N–QB3
5 N–KB3	....

The Paulsen variation.

5 P–KB4, the MacDonnell variation, is an obsolete system of attack. Since White has no real chance for P–KB5, he only loses a tempo, weakens his K-side, and definitely confines his Q-Bishop.

5	Q–N3
6 B–K2	....

6 P–QR3, as preferred by Paulsen, is designed to shake off the forking pressure of Black's Queen by means of P–QN4, e.g. 6 ..., B–Q2; 7 P–QN4, PxQP; 8 PxP, P–QR4; 9 P–N5, N–R2; 10 N–B3, R–B1; 11 B–N2, with a fine game for White (Bisguier –Whitaker, U.S. Open Championship 1954).

However, 6 P–QR3 has the drawback of justifying 6 ..., P–B5!. This advance is bad in cases of the type PQR2, PQN2, PQB3, PQ4 vs PQB4, PQ4 when White can react with the powerful duo-lever P–QN3. Not so when the formation has changed to PQR3, PQN2, PQB3, PQ4 vs PQB4, PQ4; then ... P–B5 is all right, because after P–QN3 and ... PxP the shielded backwardness of PQN2 emerges as full backwardness of PQB3, the effect being about the same as if Black had carried out a successful minority attack. Nor has White any other good lever at his disposal so that the position is likely to remain closed for some time, which for a Franco formation is exceptional. The situation may change when Black, after due preparation possibly by ... 0–0–0, starts a lever action with ... P–B3.

However, ... P–B5 is usually omitted; only in recent years have there been signs of discrimination between ... P–B5? and ... P–B5!. The following old game may therefore be quoted as a historical document:

Louis Paulsen–Theodor von Scheve (Frankfort 1887): 1 P–K4, P–K3; 2 P–Q4, P–Q4; 3 P–K5, P–QB4; 4 P–QB3, N–QB3;

5 N–B3, B–Q2; *6* B–K2, Q–B2; *7* 0–0, KN–K2; *8* R–K1, N–N3; *9* B–Q3, R–B1; *10* P–QR3, P–B5!. Black got a good game and won.

$$6 \dots \qquad \text{PxP}$$

So as to immobilize PQ4 and make it a target.

$$7 \text{ PxP} \qquad \dots$$

Whereby the formation has changed from closed to open.

The position is difficult, but the chances are about even. The open file is neutral.

After *7* ..., KN–K2, White must take one of these three measures against the threat of *8* ..., N–B4 (1) *8* N–B3, N–B4; *9* N–QR4 (2) *8* P–QN3, N–B4; *9* B–N2, B–N5ch; *10* K–B1 (3) *8* N–R3, N–B4; *9* N–B2, B–N5ch; *10* K–B1.

No major pawn action is indicated for the near future.

Following are a few examples illustrating half-closed Franco formations mainly with regard to the consequences of the initial lever PQ4 vs PQB4.

NIMZOVICH–MISS MENCHIK (Karlsbad 1929): *1* P–K4, P–K3; *2* P–Q4, P–Q4; *3* P–K5, P–QB4; *4* Q–N4, PxP; *5* N–KB3, N–QB3; *6* B–Q3, Q–R4ch; *7* QN–Q2, KN–K2? (... Q–B2!) *8* 0–0, N–N3; *9* R–K1 (White had the time for a convenient protection of PK5.) *9* ..., B–K2; *10* P–KR4 (*10* N–N3?, QNxP!) *10* ..., B–B1; *11* P–R5, KN–K2; *12* N–N3, Q–B2; *13* QNxP, NxN; *14* NxN, B–Q2; *15* B–KN5, P–KN3; *16* QR–B1, and White has a winning advantage.

CANEPA–ALEKHINE (Montevideo 1938): *1* P–K4, P–K3; *2* P–Q4, P–Q4; *3* P–K5, P–QB4; *4* Q–N4, N–QB3; *5* N–KB3, KN–K2!; *6* P–B3, N–B4 (Black has the edge.) *7* B–Q3? (PxP!) *7* ...,

PxP!; *8* 0–0, B–Q2; *9* R–K1, PxP; *10* NxP, P–KN3; *11* B–KN5, B–K2; *12* Q–KB4, QN–Q5; *13* B–B6, NxNch; *14* PxN, R–KN1; *15* K–R1, B–B3; *16* BxN, NPxB; *17* BxB, QxB; *18* N–K2, P–Q5!; *19* NxP, Q–N5!; *20* R–KN1, RxRch; *21* RxR, 0–0–0; *22* R–Q1, QxP; *23* R–Q2, RxN!; *24* RxR, QxBP, and White resigned.

ALEKHINE–EUWE (Nottingham 1936): *1* P–K4, P–K3; *2* P–Q4, P–Q4; *3* P–K5, P–QB4; *4* N–KB3, N–QB3; *5* B–Q3, PxP; *6* 0–0, P–B3; *7* B–QN5 (It is vital to get back the pawn and strengthen the control of K5, too. White has nothing better, according to Alekhine.) *7* ..., B–Q2; *8* BxN, PxB; *9* QxP, PxP (Most consistent but slightly double-edged as White remains in control of the stop K5. More modest but steady and still promising is *9* ..., P–KB4.) *10* QxKP, N–B3; *11* B–B4, B–B4; *12* N–B3, 0–0, and the difficult position offers about equal chances. The rest of the game is marred by inaccuracies. White won.

KERES–EUWE (Zandvoort 1935): *1* P–K4, P–K3; *2* P–Q4, P–Q4; *3* P–K5, P–QB4; *4* N–KB3, PxP; *5* QxP, N–QB3; *6* Q–KB4, P–B4 (This advance often serves better than ... P–B3, particularly in the early stage of the game, when Black's main concern is development. It then should be played before the K-Knight has moved, such in view of PxP e.p.? vs KNxP!) *7* B–Q3, KN–K2; *8* 0–0, N–N3; *9* Q–N3, B–K2; *10* R–K1, 0–0; *11* P–QR3, N–N1 (Intending ... N–R3–B4–K5—which White prevents, though.) *12* QN–Q2, P–QR4; *13* N–N3, N–R3; *14* P–QR4, N–N5; *15* KN–Q4, B–Q2; *16* B–QN5, N–B3; (The game is about even.) *17* P–QB4? (A lever that works adversely. Correct is *17* P–QB3.) *17* ..., NxN; *18* NxN, B–B4!; *19* Q–Q3 (*19* N–N3, B–N5!) *19* ..., BxB; *20* NxB, Q–R5!; *21* Q–B1, QR–Q1!; *22* B–K3 (A desperate remedy against Black's impending seizure of the Q-file.) *22* ..., P–Q5; *23* B–Q2, P–Q6; *24* P–QN3, P–B5; *25* R–K4, R–B4; *26* QR–K1, R–R4; *27* P–R3, R–N4!; *28* N–Q6, QxP; *29* BxBP, NxB; *30* RxN, Q–N6!; *31* R(4)–K4, R–R4, and White resigned.

TARRASCH–EM. LASKER (St. Petersburg, 1914): *1* P–K4, P–K3; *2* P–Q4, P–Q4; *3* P–K5, P–QB4; *4* PxP, N–QB3!; *5* N–KB3, BxP (The position of *Diagram 129.*) *6* B–Q3, P–B4 (An indication that Lasker had no confidence in the pretentious *6* ..., P–B3.) *7* P–B3, P–QR3; *8* QN–Q2, KN–K2; *9* N–N3, B–R2; *10* 0–0, 0–0 (*10* ..., N–N3; *11* R–K1, B–N1; *12* QN–Q4, QNxP?; *13* NxN, NxN; *14* BxBP!, PxB; *15* P–KB4 favors White, as Tarrasch points out.) *11* R–K1, N–N3; *12* QN–Q4, B–N1; *13* NxN, PxN, and the game is even.

SPIELMANN–KERES (Noordwijk, 1938): *1* P–K4, P–K3; *2* P–Q4, P–Q4; *3* N–QB3, N–KB3; *4* P–K5 (The Steinitz system—an improved but still somewhat dubious version of the Mac Donnell variation.) *4* ..., KN–Q2; *5* P–B4 (Leading to a half-closed formation which may be called the "Steinitz Minor" as against the closed "Steinitz Major": *5* QN–K2, P–QB4; *6* P–QB3, N–QB3; *7* P–KB4. In the latter case Black often runs into a mating attack because of a premature ... 0–0. He should either play *7* ..., P–QN4 striving for an additional lever on the Q-side, or proceed with *7* ..., Q–N3 and, after *8* P–QR3, lock the Q-side with *8* ..., P–B5. Remote from questions of pawn play is the Gledhill attack: *5* Q–N4, when White intends to abandon PK5.) *5* ..., P–QB4; *6* PxP, N–QB3; *7* P–QR3, BxP; *8* Q–N4, P–KN3! (Much safer than the up to then usual *8* ..., 0–0.) *9* N–B3, P–QR3; *10* B–Q3, P–QN4; *11* P–N4, B–R2; *12* P–KR4, P–KR4; *13* Q–N3, Q–K2 (The game is in the balance. There is little chance for quick action owing to lack of convenient levers.) *14* P–B5?? (This violent lever action has a catastrophic flaw. White dwells on *14* ..., NPxP?; *15* BxBP, PxB??; *16* NxQP, Q–Q1; *17* P–K6.) *14* ..., B–N1!! (The refutation. Black now threatens both *15* ..., N(2)xP and *15* ..., NPxP.) *15* PxNP (Or *15* B–KB4, NPxP; *16* BxBP, N(2)xP; *17* NxN, NxN; *18* BxN, PxB and wins.) *15* ..., N(2)xP; *16* PxPch, QxBP; *17* N–N5, Q–B3; *18* R–B1, N–N5!; *19* Q–B3, QxNch; *20* K–Q1, Q–N2!; *21* Q–K2, R–B1; *22* RxRch, KxR; *23* NxPch, BxN; *24* QxB, N–B7ch; *25* K–K1, NxBch, and White resigned.

V–§15: Dragon cue and St. George attack

The situation KKN1, BKN2, PKB2, PKN3, PKR2, which appears in several openings, among them the Dragon system of the Sicilian, constitutes a characteristic which we call *Dragon cue*.

The Dragon cue is independent from the Bishop on KN2, but it would rarely occur without.

When the Dragon cue appears in the setting of KK1, RKR1, PKB2, PKN2, PKR2 vs KKN1, PKB2, PKN3, PKR2, lever action by means of P–KR4–R5 deserves consideration, for it may lead to a powerful attack based on the open KR-file. We call this the *St. George attack*, indicating the sharp antagonism between the two characteristics.

DIAGRAM 130

Dragon cue and St. George attack

Characteristic lever PKR5 vs PKN3

Diagram 130 shows the St. George attack in its initial stage under excellent conditions. White has a very fine game as he can use the Q-file for additional pressure.

The situation in the center is of great importance for the St. George attack. Two open verticals in the central zone usually cancel out the attack since they require the full attention of the Rooks. As for a single open vertical, the K-file would rather favor the defender offering full activity to the pieces of his K-side, while the Q-file rather does the opposite.

The Q-file is also likely to favor the attacker if it is half-open on his side, as for instance in the following popular line of the Dragon system: *1* P–K4, P–QB4; *2* N–KB3, P–Q3; *3* P–Q4, PxP; *4* NxP, N–KB3; *5* N–QB3, P–KN3; *6* B–K3, B–N2; *7* P–B3, 0–0; *8* Q–Q2, N–B3; *9* 0–0–0. We do not claim a definite advantage for White (although that might be correct). All we want to say is that in this case the St. George attack is justified.

The Dragon cue and the half-open Q-file normally oppose each other; only in positions of the Gruenfeld type (*1* P–Q4, N–KB3; *2* P–QB4, P–KN3; *3* N–QB3, P–Q4; *4* PxP) are they on the same side, and then usually to the effect of precluding the St. George attack through activity in the center.

A strong indication for the St. George attack is the closed center formation PQ5, PK4 vs PQ3, PK4 as exemplified by the Saemisch variation of the King's Indian: *1* P–Q4, N–KB3; *2* P–QB4, P–KN3; *3* N–QB3, B–N2; *4* P–K4, P–Q3; *5* P–B3 (Saemisch!) *5* ..., 0–0; *6* B–K3, P–K4; *7* P–Q5, when this plan for White is indicated: Q–Q2 followed by 0–0–0, P–KN4, P–KR4, KN–K2–N3, and P–R5. Black can counteract with ... P–KB4, but that exposes him to other dangerous levers, e.g. *7* ..., N–K1; *8* Q–Q2, P–KB4 (1) *9* 0–0–0, P–B5; *10* B–B2 with the possibilities of P–KN3 and P–QB5 (2) *9* PxP, PxP; *10* 0–0–0 with the possibilities of P–KN4 and P–B4.

This Saemisch variation is frequently adopted in present-day tournament chess.

V–§16: The queue method

The task of opening a vertical with due effect sometimes requires a specific procedure which we call the *queue method.*

Diagram 131 explains what we mean with a queue: a lever pawn with as many heavy pieces behind it as are available. There is a queue on either side: PQB5, RQB3, QQB2, RQB1 vs PKN5, RKN3, QKN2, RKN1.

It is the purpose of the queue to open the critical file after its definite control is assured. The exchange of the pawn is postponed until the defender has no chance to contest the control of the file by means of opposition.

Obviously, the queue depends first of all on a plus in rear-span space on the crucial vertical, which in *Diagram 131* is 4:1 vs 4:1. It is also obvious that a queue lever on the fifth rank (PQB5 vs PQ3 and . . . PKN5 vs PKB3 in the diagram) offers fine conditions. These conditions are still better if the lever pawn is part of a head-duo (see PQB5, PQ5 vs PKN5, PKB5) becoming better again if the lever pawn has pawn protection (see PQN4, PQB5 vs PKN5, PKR4).

DIAGRAM 131

The queue method

Heavy pieces behind the lever pawn

A queue directed against the King is particularly dangerous, provided that there are enough pieces available for attack; if not, the defending King becomes an obstacle rather than a target.

The position of *Diagram 131* is a border case: Black's queue has the more dangerous direction, but since the chances for attack are limited because of the absence of minor pieces, the KN-file appears to be better defended than the QB-file.

Indeed, Black to move wins by force with *1* . . . , NPxP.

White to move, however, holds his own with *1* PxNP. Then, Black has two basic possibilities:

(1) the recapture with the piece and subsequent use of his queue file—which in this case has the advantage of dis-

tracting White's forces from the QB-file; thus *1* ..., RxP; 2 R–R3, Q–N4; *3* R–KN1, leading to a state of stagnancy;

(2) the recapture with the pawn so as to maintain the head-duo, which becomes half-free, and subsequent switch to the neighboring vertical that has become half-open; thus *1* ..., RPxP—which in this case involves the danger that after 2 P–N3 White might use the QB-file before Black can switch to the KR-file.

<table>
<tr><td>DIAGRAM 132</td><td>DIAGRAM 133</td></tr>
<tr><td>*Queue PQB5, RQB3*</td><td>*Queue PQB3, RQB2, RQB1*</td></tr>
</table>

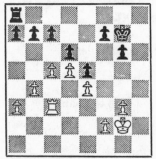
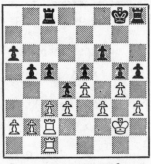

Protection the issue, not space   *Span-minus insignificant*

The power of the queue is usually explained with a plus in rear-span space. However, there is more to it as indicated by *Diagrams 132* and *133*.

In the position of *Diagram 132* Black's limited span space is still sufficient for "all" his heavy pieces, but he cannot use this space for lack of the necessary extra protection: *1* ..., R–QB1; 2 PxP!. Or *1* ..., K–B1, but the King comes too late: 2 PxP, PxP; *3* R–B7, R–N1; *4* P–B4 (Threatening *5* R–Q7. After 4 R–Q7, K–K1 White must play *5* R–B7 as *5* RxQP?? loses to *5* ..., K–K2!.) *4* ..., K–K1 (Or *4* ..., PxP; *5* PxP, K–K1; *6* K–B3 and wins, the immediate threat being *7* P–K5.) *5* K–B3, and White wins by proceeding as in *Diagram 105*. Nor is *1* ..., PxP any better: 2 RxP, R–QB1; *3* P–Q6, P–QB3; *4* RxP, R–Q1; *5* R–K7 and wins.

Diagram 133 demonstrates that the effect of a queue does not necessarily depend on a rear-span plus. Here it is Black who has the plus, but since his pieces are scattered, he lacks an adequate defense to the threat of *1* PxQP. For instance: (1) *1* ..., R–Q1; *2* PxQP (a) *2* ..., BPxP; *3* R–B6 (b) *2* ..., RxP; *3* RxP, RxQP??; *4* R–B8ch! (2) *1* ..., QPxP; *2* RxP, R–Q1; *3* RxP (3) *1* ..., P–B5; *2* PxQP, KPxP; *3* QPxP, P–Q6; *4* R–Q2, RxP (... NPxP; *5* RxQP!) *5* R(1)–Q1! with a winning advantage. (*5* RxR, PxR; *6* P–N3 also wins a pawn, but is less convincing because of *6* ..., BPxP; *7* RPxP, PxP; *8* RPxP, K–N2; *9* RxP, R–QN1.)

In the same diagram Black has a queue on the KR-file which, however, is incomplete and ineffective since the ... RKR1 alone is unable to overcome the resistance of KKN2.

Following are two examples from practical play.

MAX BLUEMICH   ALBIN BECKER

(From their game of the Breslau 1925 tournament)

DIAGRAM 134

Ideal queue with assisting pieces

Black has a winning attack

Black's queue is particularly strong as it aims at the King, while the presence of all minor pieces provides ample possibilities for attack.

The game continued:

1	PxP
2 BPxP	....

Or 2 NxP, BxN; *3* BPxB, RxPch; *4* NxR, QxNch; *5* K–N1, NxKP! and wins.

2	N–N3

The immediate 2 ..., RxP is not convincing.

3 B–K1	....

After *3* B–KB3, which is desirable in order to stop the passeı, Black can convincingly sacrifice the exchange getting two con-nected passers for it: 3 ..., N–R5; *4* R–B2, NxB; *5* QxN, RxP!; *6* NxR, QxN; 7 QxQ, RxQ; 8 R–B3, R–R1.

3	P–B6!

So the Knight can take PKR3 under fire. The total opening of the queue-file is at stake.

4 BxP	....

Or *4* N(2)xP, N–B5 (a) 5 NxPch, K–Q3 and wins, the main threat being 6 ..., RxPch (b) 5 NxP, NxRP!; *6* N(1)xN, RxNch and wins.

4	N–B5
5 B–N3	....

The best there is.

5	NxRP!

Also the best, and decisive.

6 NxN	RxN
7 BxP	B–Q3!
8 BxB	KxB
9 Q–K2	....

An oversight. Instead, 9 R(1)–R2 is necessary. However, Black then wins by bringing his remaining Knight on ... KB5.

Thus *9* ..., N–Q2; *10* R(R)–KB2, N–K4 (threatening *11* ...,
NxB) *11* B–K2, N–N3!, etc.

The rest is easy: *9* ..., NxNP!; *10* BxN, BxB; *11* QxB, RxNch;
12 K–N1, R–R8ch; *13* K–B2, Q–B2ch; *14* K–K2, RxR; *15* P–K5ch,
K–B4, and White resigned.

ALEXANDER KOTOV, USSR   HERMAN STEINER, USA

(From their game of the 1955 team match)

DIAGRAM 135

Preliminaries to the queue

Essential change of the pawn formation

White has a slight edge. The game continued:

1 NxB   R(N)xN?

Bad, as is *1* ..., QxN? for the same reason.
Correct is *1* ..., R(K)xN! with these possibilities:

(1) *2* BxN, PxB; *3* P–B4 (so as to prevent *3* ..., P–K4) *3* ...,
N–K5, and Black has reasonable counterplay;
(2) *2* N–B4, Q–Q3 (a) *3* NxN, PxN, and Black gets in the vital
...P–K4 (b) *3* BxN, PxB; *4* N–Q3, N–Q2; *5* P–B4, P–QN3,
with adequate counterplay.

2 N–B4!   R(B)–Q1?

It is right to lift the pin, but the Rook should be placed behind an exchangeable or at least mobile pawn. Correct is 2 ..., R–N1, e.g. 3 NxN, PxN; 4 B–N6, R(K)–QB1; 5 P–B4, P–N3. Black must rely on the lever thrust ... P–QB4.

3 NxN	PxN
4 B–N6!	R–K2
5 P–B4	....

White now has a definite advantage. It looks as if Black had played Stonewall and somehow allowed the elimination of his vital ... PKB4.

| 5 .... | N–K1 |

Black may or may not be lost; at any rate he must try to get in ... P–B4. Therefore, 5 ..., N–Q2 is indicated.

6 R–B3	N–Q3
7 P–KN4	R–KB1
8 K–R1	K–R1
9 R–KN1	....

White has the possibility of establishing a lever with P–KN5. Based on this lever he is building a queue on the KN-file.

9	Q–Q1
10 R(3)–N3	R–Q2
11 P–N5!	....

The queue is established, and White threatens to complete it with 12 Q–N2.

| 11 .... | N–B4 |
| 12 BxN | .... |

Forced, but powerful. White must not worry about the backwardness of PK3 because his advantage on the queue-file is overwhelming.

| 12 .... | PxB |
| 13 PxP | .... |

Most accurate as White now wins by force thanks to absolute control of the open file.

13	PxP
14 Q–N2	....

White now threatens *15* R–N6!, R–R2; *16* R–N7!! and mate.
Note that *16* RxRP only draws because of *16* ..., R–N1!. Also,
that Black's Rook must be driven to ... KR2 before White can
victoriously penetrate on KN7.

DIAGRAM 136

Position after 14 Q–N2

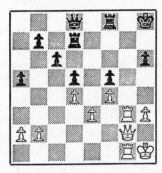

Triumph of the queue method

14 ....   R(2)–KB2

One move is as good as the other.

14 ..., Q–K1 (so as to escape the worst after *15* R–N6, Q–K5)
fails against *15* K–R2!, e.g. *15* ..., Q–B2; *16* R–N6, Q–R2;
17 Q–N3 and *18* Q–R4.

15 R–N6   Q–K2

There is no defense to the threatened mate (*15* ..., K–R2;
16 R–Pch; or *15* ..., R–R2; *16* R–N7!!).

16 R–N8ch   Resigns

V–§17: The hybrid file

Let us finally take a look at the file which is unlocked unilaterally through the mere transfer of a pawn by means of doubling, e.g. PKB2, PKN2, PKN3 vs PKB2, PKN2, PKR2. Such a file runs against a pawn front which is numerically intact and difficult to assail. Therefore, the control of a hybrid file has basically less value than the control of a half-open file.

Increased vulnerability of the counterpawn obviously enhances the value of the hybrid file. For instance PKB2, PKN2, PKN3 vs PKB2, PKN4, PKR3 when ... PKR3 is backward; or PKB2, PKN2, PKN4 vs PK4, PKB3, PKR3 when the half-open files (K-file vs KN-file) neutralize each other while the hybrid KR-file has great value because of the backwardness and isolation of ... PKR3.

An important factor is the active and passive exchangeability of the twin pawns depending on their ability to initiate levers or to become targets of levers. For instance PK3, PK5, PKB4 vs PQ4, PK3, PKB2 when PK3 is apt to form a lever (P–K4) while PK5 provides a lever for Black (... P–B3). The exchange of a twin pawn creates half-open files, thus basically changing the character of the position. The possibility of initiating such an exchange is an asset; for instance PKB4, PKN2, PKN3 vs PKB4, PKN3, PKN5 when the KR-file is hybrid on both sides while Black has the basic advantage of being able to play ... P–KN4.

Following are some examples from practical play. We also refer to V–*§12*, because the hybrid file is a factor of significance in the second stage of the Stonewall.

DENKER–FEUERSTEIN (Manhattan Chess Club championship 1956): *1* P–Q4, N–KB3; *2* N–KB3, P–KN3; *3* N–B3, P–Q4; *4* B–B4, B–N2; *5* P–K3, N–R4; *6* B–K5 (White is playing for the hybrid KR-file, but *6* Q–Q2, NxB; *7* PxN, which offers him the hybrid K-file, is preferable. Neither file has much attacking value, but the K-file renders better service in thwarting Black's intentions. Black is intent to play ... P–K4, but certainly not ... P–KR4.) 6 ..., P–KB3; 7 B–N3, NxB; 8 RPxN, P–B3; 9 P–K4, B–K3; 10 B–Q3 (Threatening 11 PxP, PxP; 12 RxP!) 10 ..., B–B2; 11 Q–K2, N–Q2; 12 PxP? (Unmotivated and weak. White should strive for the exchange of the front-twin, playing 12 P–KN4.) 12 ..., PxP; 13 0–0–0, 0–0; 14 R–R2, P–K4! (Threatening 15 ..., P–K5–which is a consequence of White's 12th move.) 15 PxP, PxP; 16 B–N5, P–K5; 17 NxQP (Hoping for 17 ..., PxN; 18 N–K7ch, K–R1; 19 RxPch, KxR; 20 R–R1ch, B–R3ch; 21 Q–K3.) 17 ..., N–N3!!; 18 QxP, NxN; 19 B–B4, Q–B3!, and Black won.

SHERWIN–PAVEY (Manhattan Chess Club championship 1955): 1 P–Q4, N–KB3; 2 P–QB4, P–KN3; 3 N–QB3, P–Q4; 4 N–B3, B–N2; 5 Q–N3, PxP; 6 QxBP, 0–0; 7 P–K4, B–N5; 8 B–K3, KN–Q2; 9 Q–N3, N–N3; 10 R–Q1, N–B3; 11 P–Q5, N–K4; 12 B–K2, NxNch; 13 PxN (This is a case where the hybrid file serves perfectly well thanks to the lever situation. The front-twin offers the advantage that White can proceed with P–B4–B5 and still rely on the important protection by PKB2. In changing the status of the KN-file from hybrid to half-open and finally to open, White obtains a winning attack.) 13 ..., B–R6; 14 R–KN1, Q–B1; 15 P–B4, B–Q2; 16 P–B5!, P–QB3; 17 P–Q6!, P–K3; 18 PxNP, BPxP; 19 P–KR4, B–K1; 20 P–R5, B–B2; 21 PxP, PxP; 22 P–K5!, BxP; 23 B–Q3, Q–K1; 24 Q–B2, B–N2; 25 BxP, BxB; 26 RxB, R–B4; 27 R–KN1, K–B1; 28 Q–K4, Q–B2; 29 Q–KR4, K–K1; 30 BxN!, B–B3; 31 P–Q7ch, QxP; 32 R–N8ch, and Black resigned.

SPIELMANN–LOKVENC (Vienna 1936): 1 P–Q4, P–Q4; 2 P–QB4, P–QB3; 3 N–KB3, N–B3; 4 N–B3, P–K3; 5 P–K3, QN–Q2; 6 N–K5, NxN; 7 PxN, N–Q2; 8 P–B4 (This is a situation of a very common type. The main feature of such positions is not the hybrid Q-file but the lever ... P–B3, which Black needs in order to gain space; he might otherwise succumb to a K-side attack in which the Rook lift plays part. However, ... P–B3 may favor either side; White must realize that before initiating the doubling, while Black must play ... P–B3 at the right time depending on tactical circumstances. The hybrid file usually changes its status after a few moves, becoming half-open or open.) 8 ..., R–B4; 9 P–QR3, Q–K2; 10 P–QN4, B–N3; 11 B–K2! (11 B–Q3?, PxP; 12 BxBP, NxP!) 11 ..., 0–0 (11 ..., PxP?; 12 0–0!) 12 0–0, P–B3!; 13 P–QB5, B–B2; 14 PxP, NxKBP; 15 P–N4, P–K4, with even chances.

CHAPTER VI

THE SEALER AND THE SWEEPER

An immobilized pawn may hamper its own pieces. We call such a pawn a *sealer*.

A dynamically immobilized pawn may self-sacrificially advance, thus vacating its square for the benefit of its pieces. We then call it a *sweeper*.

The elements of sealing and sweeping are often parts of the same action, for if the sacrificed pawn is captured by a pawn, the latter seals off a square to the detriment of its own pieces.

Let us now demonstrate this in detail.

VI–§1: The sealing

First an instructive composition.

DIAGRAM 137

W. E. Rudolph, La Stratégie 1912

White moves and draws

1 B–R4ch, KxB (Or *1* ... , K–B5; *2* B–N3ch with perpetual check.) *2* P–N3ch, K–N4; *3* P–B4ch, K–B3; *4* P–Q5ch, K–Q2;

5 P–K6ch, KxB; 6 P–B5, with a draw because Black, hampered by eight sealers, is unable to carry out a capture. This is the sealing ad absurdum.

Note that three of White's pawns could be replaced by minor pieces forming artificial rams, so to speak; e.g. BKB5; NKN4; NKR3 still with a draw.

The following example from practical play is just as absurd.

LAJOS ASZTALOS   BORIS KOSTICH

(From their game of the Bled 1931 tournament)

DIAGRAM 138

Self-sealing

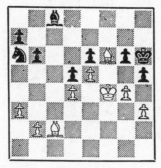

Monstrous

1 P–N5ch?? (A monstrous blunder, White sealing off KN5, the square he needs for the winning procedure. With 1 PxP he wins flatly, as is obvious.) 1 ..., K–R2; 2 B–R4, N–N1; 3 K–K3, B–Q2; 4 B–B2, N–B3; 5 P–N4, P–N4; 6 K–Q3, with a draw as the whole position is sealed off.

Of course, even the most loyal pawn must occupy a square. The detrimental effect of the sealing is likely to become perceptible, if not disturbing, in the measure that an unfree pawn loses in mobility as soon as it crosses the middle-line. The wisdom

of the advances P–Q5 and P–K5, for instance, is often difficult
to assess since it involves the question whether the critical
square should or should not be kept open for the pieces.

The following variation of the Queen's Gambit Accepted
offers a good example to the point:

1 P–Q4, P–Q4; *2* P–QB4, PxP; *3* N–KB3, N–KB3; *4* P–K3,
P–K3; *5* BxP, P–B4; *6* 0–0, P–QR3; *7* Q–K2, N–B3; *8* R–Q1,
P–QN4; *9* PxP, Q–B2; *10* B–Q3, BxP; *11* P–QR4, P–N5?!;
12 QN–Q2, 0–0.

DIAGRAM 139

Position after 12 . . . , 0–0

Black hampered by sealer . . . PQN5

In this position Black is hampered in several ways, for . . . QN5
is sealed off and the QN-file closed while White's Q-Knight has
excellent scope thanks to the squares QN3 and QB4. There is
danger that Black's QR-pawn and QN-pawn will become weak.

While it may be debatable to which degree the balance is
disturbed, disturbed it certainly is as the following two games
demonstrate.

ALEKHINE–FLOHR, Bled 1931 (*Diagram 139*): *13* N–N3, B–K2;
14 P–K4, N–Q2; *15* B–K3, KN–K4; *16* NxN, NxN; *17* QR–B1,
Q–N1; *18* B–B5, BxB; *19* NxB, Q–N3; *20* Q–R5, N–Q2; *21* B–K2,
P–N3; *22* Q–N5, NxN; *23* RxN, P–QR4; *24* P–R4, B–R3;

25 B–B3, P–B3; 26 Q–K3, QR–Q1; 27 RxR, RxR; 28 P–K5!, P–B4; 29 R–B8!, and Black resigned.

FLOHR–HOROWITZ, Radio match USSR-USA 1945 (*Diagram 139*): 13 P–QN3, N–K4; 14 N–K4!, NxB; 15 NxNch, PxN; 16 QxN, P–K4; 17 B–N2, B–K3 (17 ..., Q–K2 probably holds.); 18 BxP!, PxB; 19 N–N5, K–N2; 20 QxPch, K–B3; 21 N–K4ch, K–K2; 22 Q–R4ch, P–B3; 23 KR–QB1!, and White won.

The conclusion is that 11 ..., P–N5, a move which in positions of this type has always been played for many years, virtually causes trouble. Instead, avoiding the sealer with 11 ..., PxP offers Black a satisfactory game, as Flohr has pointed out.

VI–§2: The sweeping

The position of KKB5, RQN7, PKN6 vs KKR1, BQR8, given by von Guretzky-Cornitz, is a win for White thanks to sweeping: 1 P–N7ch, K–R2 (1 ..., BxP; 2 K–N6 and wins) 2 R–KB7 (2 R–N1 also wins according to Salvio and Berger) 2 ..., B–Q5 (2 ..., BxP; 3 K–N5, K–N1; 4 K–N6 and wins) 3 P–N8(Q)ch, KxQ; 4 K–N6, and White wins.

Following are two examples from practical play.

EMANUEL LASKER   CAPABLANCA

(From their decisive game of the St. Petersburg 1914 tournament)
(*See Diagram 140*)

White has a superior game but needs both activity for NQB3 and some remedy against ... N–B5–K4. A sweeper twist does the job.

1	P–K5!	QPxP
2	N–K4	....

The elements and consequences of this combination are typical. It starts with the self-sacrificial advance of a straggler; the sacrifice vacates K4 for White's pieces, at the same time sealing off ... K4 to Black's pieces; the half-open K-file changes hands.

White won quickly: *2 ...*, N–Q4; *3* N(6)–B5, B–B1; *4* NxR, BxN; *5* R–R7, R–B1; *6* R–R1, K–Q1; *7* R–R8ch, B–B1; *8* N–B5, and Black resigned.

DIAGRAM 140

A sweeper twist

Seals Black's fate

ALEXANDER ALEKHINE   HANS JOHNER

(From their game of the Zurich 1934 tournament)

DIAGRAM 141

Chain sweeping

Eruptive activation of the Bishop

White has a winning advantage but to win will be a hard job, it appears, since his Bishop is rather bad while the Knight may become very active on ... K4. These difficulties, however, White brushes away by a beautiful twist of chain sweeping:

1 P–K5!!, QPxP (Or *1* ..., BPxP; *2* P–B6!, QxP; *3* QxPch followed by *4* B–K4, also with an easy win.); *2* P–Q6!! (Preparing for the third sweeper shot: *3* P–B5!! with *4* B–N3ch to follow. Hence Black's desperate answer.) *2* ..., P–B4; *3* B–K4!, Q–Q2; *4* Q–R6!, and Black resigned.

These two examples also involve the element of sealing which, however, is obscured by the cataclysmic course of the events. Usually, both elements would show in milder cases.

VI–§3: Sweeping and sealing combined

Following are three examples of elaborate sweeper-sealer co-ordination.

ALEXANDER ALEKHINE   CAPABLANCA

(From the 24th game of their 1927 match)

DIAGRAM 142

Sweeper-sealer twist

Promising

White has a fine position but is handicapped by the backward-ness of PQ4, since Black is at the point of anchoring a Knight on

... Q4. Hence the following pawn sacrifice, which enables White to maintain the initiative.

1 P–Q5!	BPxP!
2 N(B)–K2	QR–B1
3 N–Q4	....

Everything in the pattern explained heretofore. A dangerous sacrifice on KB5 is now in the air.

3	N–N3
4 R–B5!	....

So this Rook would have horizontal activity after 4 ..., N–B5ch; 5 BxN, e.g. 5 ..., QPxB; 6 N(N)xPch, PxN; 7 NxPch, K–K3; 8 N–Q6, threatening among other things 9 P–B5ch, as Alekhine points out.

4	P–R5
5 B–B2	N–Q2

The complications after 5 ..., N–B5ch; 6 K–K2, NxNP; 7 R–QN1, P–R6; 8 N(N)xPch, PxN; 9 BxP would most likely also lead to a draw, according to Alekhine.

6 R–B3	....

With the strong threat of 7 BxBP.

6	P–N5
7 R–B6	....

But not 7 N–B6ch, BxN; 8 RxB because of the sweeper twist 8 ..., P–Q5ch!.

7	BxR
8 NxBch	K–K1
9 NxR	KxN
10 BxRP	....

The tension has subsided. After 10 ..., N–N3; 11 B–N3, N–R3; 12 N–K2, K–Q2; 13 R–Q4, R–B4; 14 K–Q2, R–B1 a draw was agreed.

SALO FLOHR   LUSTIG

(Played in Prague 1928)

RUY LOPEZ

1 P–K4, P–K4; *2* N–KB3, N–QB3; *3* B–N5, P–QR3; *4* B–R4,
N–B3; *5* Q–K2, B–K2; *6* P–B3, P–QN4; *7* B–N3, P–Q3; *8* P–KR3,
N–QR4; *9* B–B2, P–B4; *10* P–Q4, Q–B2; *11* 0–0, 0–0; *12* P–Q5,
P–B5; *13* B–K3, B–Q2; *14* N–K1, N–N2; *15* N–Q2, KR–K1;
16 P–KN4, P–N3; *17* P–B4!, PxP; *18* RxP, R–KB1; *19* R–B2, N–K1!;
20 KN–B3, N–Q1; *21* QR–KB1, P–B3; *22* B–R6, N–KN2.

This is a position of the type we call Spanish Benoni. The
basically weak P–KB4, cleverly played while Black was unpre-
pared to take advantage of the stopsquare . . . K4, has led to a
crucial situation.

DIAGRAM 143

Position after 22 . . . , N–KN2

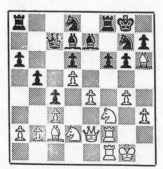

Powerful sweeper-sealer twist

23 P–K5!   . . . .

White gets rid of the hampering PK4, at the same time preventing . . . N–B2–K4. His attack now becomes very strong.

23 . . . .   QPxP

Or 23 ..., BPxP; 24 N–N5, N–N2; 25 QN–K4, RxR; 26 QxR, also with a winning attack (26 ..., R–KB1; 27 QxRch!).

24 N–K4	N–B2

Nor is 24 ..., P–B4 satisfactory because of 25 P–Q6!, BxP, 26 NxB, QxN; 27 BxN, KxB; 28 R–Q1, Q–K2; 29 NxP.

However, the consequences of the text move are worse.

25 BxN	KxB
26 N–R4!	....

A fascinating position. Black cannot escape the looming tornado of sacrifices.

26	N–Q3

Or 26 ..., P–B4; 27 NxNP!!, e.g. 27 ..., RPxN; 28 PxP, BxP; 29 RxB!, PxR; 30 Q–N2ch, K–R2; 31 RxP and wins (21 ..., R–KN1; 22 R–R5ch, N–R3; 23 N–B6ch).

27 NxBP!	BxN

27 ..., RxN fails against 28 QxKP, Q–Q1; 29 P–N5.

28 P–N5!	N–K1

If the attacked Bishop moves, 29 QxPch wins.

29 NxP!!	PxN
30 BxP!!	....

Fantastic—this process of stripping Black's King of protective pawns. Each pawn costs a piece, but it pays.

30	KxB
31 Q–K4ch	K–N2
32 Q–R4!	K–N1

Black is helpless, notwithstanding his enormous material advantage.

33 PxB	NxP
34 Q–N5ch	K–R1

Or 34 ..., K–B2; 35 RxNch, K–K2; 36 R–K6 mate.

35 RxN	Q–B4ch
36 K–R2	Resigns

EVFIM BOGOLYUBOV   RUDOLPH SPIELMANN

(From the eighth game of their 1932 match)

DIAGRAM 144

Sweeper-sealer twist

Decisive

This example is particularly striking. White has the edge, thanks to superiority in controlled space. With the following twist he obtains a number of more specific advantages which, taken as a whole, are strategically decisive.

1 P–Q5!   ....

Not a straggler does the sweeping, as in the preceding cases, but a healthy pawn.

1 ....   PxP

The alternatives are worse: 1 ..., R–B1; 2 N–Q4!; or 1 ..., P–QB4; 2 N–Q2!.

2 P–K5!   R(3)–Q2

There is the important point that the sweeper reply 2 ..., P–Q5, which is basically indicated, fails tactically against 3 PxR, PxR; 4 PxN with check.

3 N–Q4   ....

The pawn sacrifice has increased White's advantage in four ways in that (1) he has opened the QB-file and is controlling it (2) he has closed the file of Black's Rooks which are now inactive as a fleet would be in a harbor whose exit is closed to them by a scuttled ship (3) he has established a majority on the K-side in the powerful formation of the quart-grip (4) he has revealed a serious weakness of Black's Q-side formation consisting of the backwardness of ... PQN3.

These strategic advantages are decisive.

3	R–N1
4 P–B5	R(2)–Q1
5 R(1)–B2	....

Not 5 P–B6, PxP; 6 PxP, N–N1; 7 N–B6 because of 7 ..., NxP; 8 K–B3, N–K5; 9 R(3)–B2, N–B4 with a rather good game for Black. Such a liquidation is called "winning the exchange for two pawns," but that is a deceptive way of putting it; it should rather be "losing two pawns for the exchange."

5	R–K1
6 K–K3	R(N)–B1
7 N–N5??	....

Very superficial play.

Correct is 7 RxR, NxR (7 ..., RxR?; 8 P–B6!) 8 K–Q3 with a rather easy win.

7	RxRch
8 RxR	NxPch!

A saving stroke. Black gets many pawns for the piece.

The rest of the game is less interesting: 9 PxN, RxPch; 10 K–B4, R–K5ch; 11 K–N3, RxP; 12 P–B6 (12 R–B7 is a better try.) 12 ..., R–QB5!; 13 R–K3, R–K5!; 14 R–QB3, R–QB5, with a draw by repetition of moves.

VI–§4: The twin-lock

A double pawn may become a double sealer.

A double sealer may result from the bypassing of a rear-twin.

e.g. PK3, PK5, PKB3 vs PQ4, PK3, PKB4 when *1* P–K4 offers
Black the choice between *1* ..., QPxP; *2* PxP, P–B5, and *1* ...,
BPxP; *2* PxP, P–Q5. We call this type of reaction to a rear-twin's
lever action the *twin-lock*.

Following is an example.

EMANUEL LASKER   DR. BOGATYRTCHUK

(From their game of the Moscow 1935 tournament)

DIAGRAM 145

Winning advantage for White

But beware of the twin-lock

As Black is a pawn down and handicapped by his bad Bishop,
he must lose. However, White is also handicapped to some extent
owing to the backwardness of PQN4 as well as the twin, and he
therefore must proceed with care.

$$1 \text{ P–K4??} \qquad ....$$

A careless move ("criminal" as Lasker himself put it).

$$1 .... \qquad \text{P–Q5!!}$$

The twin-lock, which saves Black's game although the Q-pawn
must fall. White is unable to make any progress as the squares
K4 and K5 are definitely sealed off.

This is the rest of the game: 2 B–B4, B–N2; 3 K–N5, B–B1; 4 K–B4, K–Q2; 5 K–B3, B–N2; 6 K–K2, B–B1; 7 K–Q3, B–N2; 8 KxP, B–B1; 9 K–K3, B–N2, and the players agreed to a draw.

This is how White should have played, according to the tournament book:

1 K–N5, K–B2; 2 B–N6ch, K–K2; 3 K–N4, B–N2; 4 K–B3, K–B1; 5 K–K2, K–N2; 6 B–K8, K–B1; 7 B–R5, K–N2; 8 K–Q3, K–B1; 9 K–Q4, K–K2; 10 P–K4!

(1) 10 ..., PxP; 11 KxP, B–B1; 12 K–B4, B–N2; 13 K–N5, B–B1; 14 K–N6, B–N2; 15 K–N7, B–B1; 16 B–B3, B–N2; 17 B–K4!, B–R1 (If the King moves, 18 K–B6 wins.) 18 P–N5! (Only this combination makes the straggler tell.) 18 ..., RPxP; 19 P–R6, and White wins by *zugzwang*.

(2) 10 ..., K–Q2; 11 B–K2, K–K2; 12 PxP (So far given in the tournament book.) 12 ..., KPxP; 13 B–N4, K–Q1; 14 K–K3, K–K2; 15 K–B4, K–Q1; 16 K–N5 (Not 16 P–K6, K–K2; 17 K–K5 when PK6 works as a sealer allowing 17 ..., B–B1.) 16 ..., K–K2; 17 B–B5 and wins.

VI–§5: The Night attack

The formation PK5 vs PQ4, PK2, PKB2, if reached early in the opening, sometimes lends itself to the sacrificial thrust P–K6, e.g. 1 P–K4, N–KB3; 2 N–QB3, P–Q4; 3 P–K5, KN–Q2; 4 P–K6, PxP. Then, the twin sealer hampers Black's development while his King is imperiled owing to both the lack of protection by... PKB2 and the clearance of K5 for White's pieces.

Since the whole action is designed to catch the defender's forces, so to say, in their sleep, we call it the *Night attack*.

In the formation of PK5 vs PQ3, PK2, PKB2 the Night attack does not sweep open the square K5 and is consequently milder, but it may still be promising, e.g. 1 P–K4, N–KB3; 2 P–K5, N–Q4; 3 P–Q4, P–Q3; 4 N–KB3, N–QB3; 5 P–B4, N–N3; 6 P–K6, PxP.

With Black's Q-Bishop in action however, the Night attack does not work well, e.g. 1 P–K4, N–KB3; 2 P–K5, N–Q4;

3 P–QB4, N–N3; *4* P–Q4, P–Q3; *5* P–B4, PxP; *6* BPxP, N–B3; *7* B–K3, B–B4; *8* P–K6?, PxP!. This line has been tried repeatedly by Spielmann, but never with success.

But when Black's Q-Bishop is exchanged, and possibly his KN-pawn doubled, the Night attack might work particularly well, e.g. *1* P–K4, P–QB3; *2* P–Q4, P–Q4; *3* P–K5, B–B4; *4* B–Q3, B–N3??; *5* BxB, RPxB; *6* P–K6!, PxP; *7* Q–N4, with a winning advantage for White. Strangely enough a disaster of this type once occurred in a tournament game between two grandmasters: *1* P–K4, N–KB3; *2* P–K5, N–Q4; *3* N–KB3, P–Q3; *4* P–Q4, B–B4; *5* B–Q3, B–N3??; *6* P–B4, N–N3; *7* BxB, RPxB; *8* P–K6, and White won (Bogolyubov–Tarrasch, Breslau 1925).

Following is a magnificent example of the Night attack.

RUDOLPH SPIELMANN   MAX WALTER

(From the tournament at Trentschin-Teplitz 1928)

CARO-KANN DEFENSE

1 P–K4	P–QB3
2 N–QB3	P–Q4
3 N–B3	N–B3
4 P–K5	N–K5
5 Q–K2	....

A good move. White plays for the hybrid Q-file and is contemplating 0–0–0.

5	NxN
6 QPxN	P–QN3

Black would like to trade his slightly hampered Q-Bishop.

7 N–Q4!	....

Preventing 7 ..., B–R3 in view of 8 Q–B3, BxB (8 ..., P–K3; 9 NxBP!) 9 P–K6!, PxP; 10 Q–R5ch, K–Q2; 11 RxB with a superior game for White, e.g. 11 ..., P–B4; 12 NxP!!, KxN; 13 B–B4 and wins.

Besides, 8 P–K6 threatens.

7 ....   P–QB4?

An illusion. Correct is 7 ... , P–K3.

8 P–K6!   PxP?

Bad, as are 8 ... , B–R3? because of 9 QxB!, and 8 ... , PxN? because of 9 Q–N5ch, B–Q2; 10 QxQP (or PxPch).

The comparatively best is 8 ... , BxP; 9 NxB, PxN; 10 QxP, Q–Q3; 11 B–N5ch, K–Q1. Also 8 ... , P–QR3; 9 PxPch, KxP; 10 N–B3, N–B3 is preferable to the text move.

9 Q–R5ch!   ....

Much stronger than 9 NxP.

9 ....   K–Q2

After 9 ... , P–N3; 10 Q–K5, R–N1 White wins with 11 NxP, BxN; 12 QxB thanks to the double threat of 13 QxR and 13 B–N5ch.

10 N–B3   K–B2

It is impossible to prevent the centralization of White's Knight (10 ... , N–B3; 11 B–QN5!).

11 N–K5   ....

DIAGRAM 146

Position after 11 N–K5

The Night attack at its best

This position speaks for itself. White obviously has a winning advantage.

| 11 .... | B–Q2 |

The K-Rook is doomed, e.g. *11* ..., K–N2; *12* N–B7, Q–K1?; *13* N–Q6ch!; or *11* ..., N–Q2; *12* N–B7, Q–K1; *13* B–B4ch, P–K4; *14* BxPch, NxB; *15* QxNch, K–B3 when White has the choice between *16* NxR, and *16* B–N5ch, KxB; *17* N–Q6ch.

12 N–B7	Q–K1
13 Q–K5ch	K–N2
14 B–KB4!	P–B5

This enables White to proceed with his mating attack. After *14* ..., N–R3 he only wins the Rook.

| 15 Q–B7ch | K–R3 |
| 16 N–Q8! | N–B3 |

Or *16* ..., B–B3; *17* Q–B8ch, K–R4 (*17* ..., K–N4; *18* P–R4ch); *18* BxN, RxB; *19* P–N4ch and mate next move.

| 17 Q–N7ch | K–N4 |

Or *17* ..., K–R4; *18* NxNch, BxN; *19* P–N4ch and mate.

18 P–R4ch	K–B4
19 QxNch!!	BxQ
20 NxP mate	

A delightful finish.

In meeting the Night attack it is usually urgent to get rid of the two sealers by means of counter-sweeping, to be carried out by the self-sacrificial advance of the front-twin, so the rear-twin can move and the K-Bishop breathe.

Following is an example.

EVFIM BOGOLYUBOV   ALEXANDER ALEKHINE

(From their game of the Karlsbad 1923 tournament)

1	P–K4	N–KB3
2	N–QB3	P–Q4
3	P–K5	KN–Q2

Provocative, although not necessarily bad.
The safe line, which forestalls the Night attack, is 4 ..., P–Q5.

4	P–Q4	....

White hesitates.

4	....	P–QB4

And Black proceeds in a provocative manner instead of safely transposing to the French defense with 4 ..., P–K3.

5	B–QN5	....

Dubious, as is 5 NxP because of 5 ..., P–K3 followed by 6 ..., PxP.
Most reasonable is 5 P–K6, PxKP; 6 PxP.

5	....	N–QB3
6	N–B3	P–QR3

A good alternative is 6 ..., P–K3; 7 0–0, P–QR3—but not 7 ..., PxP; 8 KNxP, QNxP??; 9 R–K1, N–N3; 10 QNxP, P–QR3; 11 RxPch!, PxR; 12 NxP and wins (Romanenko–Baer, Washington, D.C. 1955).

7	BxN	PxB
8	P–K6	....

In this delayed form, and after the exchange of the K-Bishop which otherwise is very useful for threats on the K-side, the Night

attack offers only moderate chances. Even so however, White
has fair compensation for the pawn.

| 8 .... | PxKP |
| 9 O–O | P–K4! |

The counter-sweep. Getting rid of the sealers is much more
important than the extra pawn.

| 10 PxKP | P–K3 |

DIAGRAM 147

Position after 10 . . . , P–K3

After the counter-sweep

Black now has a steady position. While still facing some difficulty he has good counterplay.

And here comes a rarity of the first order.

DAVID BRONSTEIN, USSR   ROBERT BYRNE, USA

(Chess Olympics, Helsinki 1952)

QUEEN'S GAMBIT ACCEPTED

1 P–Q4	P–Q4
2 P–QB4	PxP
3 N–KB3	N–KB3
4 N–B3	. . .

Preparing for a dubious pawn sacrifice. The usual move is
4 P–K3.

4	P–QR3
5 P–K4	....

The sacrifice.

5 P–K3 now leads to a good game for Black after 5 ...,
P–QN4; 6 P–QR4, P–N5; 7 N–R2, P–K3; 8 BxP, B–N2.

A steady although unpretentious continuation is 5 P–QR4,
P–K3; 6 P–K3, P–B4; 7 BxP.

5	P–QN4
6 P–K5	N–Q4
7 P–QR4	....

This is at any rate more promising than 7 N–N5 (Bogolyubov
—Alekhine, Match 1934, 17th game).

7	NxN
8 PxN	B–N2

Very provocative, although probably good.

Much safer is 8 ..., P–QB3, intending 9 ..., P–K3 and
10 ...., B–N2.

9 P–K6!	....

The Night attack is strongly indicated as Black otherwise
consolidates his position with 9 ..., P–K3.

However, the circumstances are unusual, and the consequences
of the text move still more so.

9	P–KB3!

An exceptional reply, based on the exceptional fact that the
Q-file is not closed on Black's side. The dreadful PK6 must soon
fall as it is exposed to attack by ... Q–Q4 and, possibly, ...
N–B3–Q1. Indeed, Black loses time, but he is still better off than
after 9 ..., PxP when his two extra pawns are severely crippled.

DIAGRAM 148

Position after 9 ... , P–KB3!

Exceptional

10 P–N3?   ....

White has good chances for attack, but he must properly use the half-open K-file, and in that he fails.

The indicated line of play is *10 B–K2, Q–Q4; 11 0–0, QxKP; 12 R–K1,* possibly followed by *B–QR3.*

10	Q–Q4
11 B–KN2	QxPch
12 B–K3	....

White is now forced to put this Bishop on a square where it clogs a file and has no scope itself.

The rest of the game is marked by Black's steady progress towards utilization of his material advantage: *12 ... , P–B3; 13 0–0, Q–B1; 14 R–K1, K–B2; 15 PxP, RPxP; 16 RxR, BxR; 17 Q–K2, N–R3; 18 B–B4, P–N3; 19 N–Q2, P–R4; 20 P–R4, B–QN2; 21 K–R2, K–N2; 22 R–QR1, K–R2; 23 B–R3, Q–Q1; 24 N–K4, B–R3,* and Black won.

VI–§6: The Ram attack

Akin to the Night attack is the corresponding thrust of the Q-Pawn to Q6, which we call the *Ram attack* because the ram PQ6 vs PQ2, unlike the ram PK6 vs PK2, is an objective in itself, and even the ideal objective of this action. Other possible objectives of the Ram attack are the sacrifice of the Q-pawn for the purpose of sealing, and the exchange of the Q-pawn for the purpose of getting the half-open Q-file.

All three types of the Ram attack appear, for instance, in the Greco system of the Giuoco Piano:

1 P–K4, P–K4; *2* N–KB3, N–QB3; *3* B–B4, B–B4; *4* P–B3

(1) *4* ... , Q–K2; *5* P–Q4, B–N3; *6* P–Q5, N–N1 (or N–Q1) *7* P–Q6 (The Eisinger variation.) *7* ... , QxP; *8* QxQ, PxQ. This is the *sealer type* of the Ram attack. The line holds promise but is very rarely adopted.

(2) *4* ... , N–B3; *5* P–Q4, PxP; *6* PxP
   (2a) *6* ... , B–N3?; *7* P–Q5! (*7* P–K5, P–Q4!) *7* ... , N–K2; *8* P–K5, N–K5; *9* P–Q6!, and White has a winning advantage. This is the *ram type* of the attack, thus the Ram attack proper. The advanced ram, apart from having a sealing effect, offers White a 5:1 plus in rear-spans.
   (2b) *6* ... , B–N5ch; *7* N–B3, NxKP; *8* 0–0, BxN; *9* P–Q5, B–B3; *10* R–K1, N–K2; *11* RxN, 0–0; *12* P–Q6, PxP; *13* QxP, N–B4; *14* Q–Q5! (Preventing *14* ... , P–Q4.) *14* ... , N–K2; *15* Q–Q6! (Preventing *15* ... , P–Q4.) *15* N–B4 with a draw. This is the *lever type* of the Ram attack. The exchange of the pawn nets a span-plus on the Q-file, which in this particular case compensates for Black's extra pawn.

Following is a fine example of the Ram attack proper.

ANDRIJA FUDERER　　SAVIELLY TARTACOVER

(From the Bled 1950 tournament)

RUY LOPEZ

1 P–K4, P–K4; *2* N–KB3, N–QB3; *3* B–N5, P–QR3; *4* B–R4, B–N5?!; *5* 0–0, KN–K2; *6* P–B3, B–R4; *7* P–Q4, PxP; *8* P–QN4, B–N3; *9* PxP, 0–0?.

Positions of this type require the immediate destruction of White's duo. Hence 9 ..., P–Q4!. Should that fail, the blame would fall on 4 ..., B–N5?!.

10 P–Q5!	N–R2

As this hampers the K-Bishop, 10 ..., N–N1 is comparatively better (11 N–R3, P–Q3; 12 N–B4, B–R2!).

11 N–R3	P–QB4?

Very bad. It is necessary to play 11 ..., P–Q3 and, after 12 N–B4, to acquiesce to the outer-swap (13 NxB, PxN) as White's attack otherwise becomes too strong: 12 ..., P–QB3; 13 PxP, QNxP; 14 NxP, NxP; 15 B–N3.

12 P–Q6!	....

DIAGRAM 149

Position after 12 P–Q6!

The Ram attack full force

In establishing this ram, cutting Black's position in two, as it were, White has obtained a winning advantage.

12	N–N3
13 N–B4	PxP
14 B–KN5!!	....

Played with wonderful understanding. White obviously must play for a K-side attack; his Rooks must participate in the attack, but they need files, which in turn depend on levers. Hence this move; in provoking...P–B3 White procures a lever for his K-pawn.

14		P–B3
15 NxB		QxN
16 B–K3		Q–Q1
17 P–K5!		....

The lever action itself starts.

17		NxP

17 ..., PxP or *17* ..., P–B4 fails against *18* N–N5 with the threefold threat of *19* Q–R5, *19* NxP, and *19* B–N3ch.

Best under the circumstances is *17* ..., N–B3, but White still obtains an irresistible attack: *18* B–N3ch, K–R1; *19* PxP, QxP; *20* N–N5, P–R3; *21* P–B4!.

18 NxN		PxN
19 P–B4!!		....

Grandiose! The pawns themselves do not count; only the levers.

19		P–K5

Trying to gain time. After *19* ..., PxP; *20* Q–Q5ch, K–R1; *21* RxP White wins quickly.

20 P–B5!		....

But White would not waste time. He has a local majority on the K-side and is going to use it.

20		N–B3
21 Q–Q5ch		K–R1
22 P–B6!!		....

This third lever breaks all resistance.
White has wrought a true masterpiece.

22		PxP
23 B–N3		P–N4

If the Knight moves, White wins with 24 B–Q4.

24	R–B4	B–N2
25	R–R4	....

Threatening 26 RxPch and mate in two.

25	....	P–B4

Necessary on the one hand, but pernicious on the other as it opens the door to White's Q-Bishop.

26	R–R6	....

Threatening 27 B–Q4ch.

26	....	K–N2
27	R–KB1	R–B3
28	RxP!	RxR(3)
29	BxRch	K–R1

29 KxB fails against mate in three.

30	Q–B7	Q–N3ch

Mate is unavoidable.

31	K–R1	Q–Q5
32	Q–B8ch	Resigns

Chapter VII

THE CENTER AND THE FORK TRICK

The term *center* describes the squares Q4, K4 vs Q4, K4. It is also used in the sense of *pawn center*, meaning the pawn formation on these squares.

The squares Q3, K3 vs Q3, K3 are sometimes referred to respectively as White's and Black's *semi-center*.

The center including the surrounding squares is usually called the *central zone*.

The pawn formation in and around the center is fundamental for the character of the game and requires consideration from many angles. We have therefore deviated from the practice of discussing this item under just one heading but demonstrated its significance at many points in many ways, particularly in Chapter V.

By now it should be sufficiently clear how important the center is, and how the pieces depend on it to varying degrees: the Knights very much as they need squares in the central zone; equally the Bishops inasmuch as interference by center pawns is most harmful to them; the Rooks indirectly because center pawns would normally be the first to clash and produce levers; the almighty Queen not at all; and the vulnerable King only in the end-game for possible need of safe squares in the central zone.

However, there is one item concerning the center which we must discuss separately; it is a little combination of the pattern "sacrifice-fork-recovery," for instance *1* P–K4, P–K4; *2* N–KB3, N–QB3; *3* N–B3, B–B4; *4* NxP, NxN; *5* P–Q4.

We call this the *fork trick*.

The fork trick may occur in any part of the pawn realm, and in any stage of the game. It does occur however almost exclusively in the center, and in the opening stage of the game at that, for it is there and then that the opportunity most frequently arises.

An opportunity it is because the fork trick normally improves the position leading either from equality to a slight superiority, as it usually does if applied by White, or from a slight inferiority to equality, which it promises if applied by Black.

The regular characteristics of the fork trick are:

(1) it takes place in the opening;

(2) it starts with the temporary sacrifice of the K-Knight for the K-pawn on the fourth rank;

(3) it continues with the immediate acceptance of the sacrifice after which the Q-pawn forks Knight and Bishop;

(4) it nets improvement in the center leading, for instance, from the symmetrical formation PQ2, PK4 vs PQ2, PK4 to the jump formation of PK4 vs PQ3.

Deviations from this pattern may lead to irregular results.

However, the fork trick also depends on the kind of center formation it starts with. White, because of the aggressive attitude he is supposed to take in the center, is more often exposed to the fork trick than Black. For one thing the fork trick, like the fork lever, is apt to destroy a center duo, and it is usually White who faces this possibility. Normally, it is only in the symmetrical formation of PQ2, PK4 vs PQ2, PK4 that a chance for the fork trick may arise for either side.

Let us now turn to examples.

VII–§1: The fork trick re PQ2, PK4 vs PQ2, PK4

The following opening moves illustrate a number of common possibilities:

1	P–K4	P–K4
2	N–KB3	N–QB3
3	N–B3	....

3 B–B4, N–B3, the Two Knights' Defense, leads after 4 N–B3 to the same, but the main line is 4 N–N5. Then, the fancy fork

trick of 4 ..., NxP?, which in case of 5 NxN?, P–Q4 would serve well, fails two ways: (1) 5 NxP!, Q–R5; 6 0–0, B–B4; 7 P–Q4! (2) 5 BxPch!!, K–K2; 6 P–Q4!, P–KR3; 7 NxN, KxB; 8 P–Q5!.

3 ....   N–B3

Weak is 3 ..., B–B4? because of 4 NxP!, NxN (4 ..., BxPch? is worse.) 5 P–Q4 with a fine game for White. Black's comparatively best then is 5 ..., B–Q3. Instead, an off-hand game Réti–Dunkelblum went as follows: 5 ..., BxP?; 6 QxB, Q–B3; 7 N–N5!, K–Q1; 8 Q–B5!!, and Black resigned.

4 B–B4   ....

The Italian Four Knights' Game, which for its drawback of allowing the fork trick offers no promise.

Instead, the Spanish Four Knights' Game (4 B–N5) and the Scotch Four Knights' Game (4 P–Q4) offer White some initiative.

4 ....   NxP!
5 NxN   ....

The simple acceptance of the sacrifice constitutes the thematic reply to the fork trick.

Also thematic is the inferiority of 5 BxPch?, KxB; 6 NxN, P–Q4; this twist is usually possible, but it favors the opponent, whose powerful center and pair of Bishops overcompensate by far the loss of castling.

Other replies are unthematic but not necessarily weak.

No unthematic reply of significance is possible in this case.

5 ....   P–Q4
6 B–Q3   ....

Necessary, in order to restore the balance in the center.

The alternatives of 6 BxP?, QxB, and 6 B–N5?, PxN; 7 NxP, Q–N4! favor Black.

6 ....   PxN

The extension of the combination by means of 6 ..., P–B4;

7 N–B3, P–K5; 8 B–N5, PxN; 9 QxP also leads to equality, but it is less usual and characteristic.

7 BxP   ....

At the moment, the center formation of PQ2 vs PK4 favors Black. However, White threatens 8 BxNch and 9 NxP.

7 ....   B–Q3

The natural and usual protection of the pawn.

Some analysts recommend 7 ..., B–KN5; 8 P–KR3, BxN; 9 QxB, Q–Q2; 10 BxN, PxB. This line offers Black an advantage in the center (jump formation), but at the expense of doubling. There is some danger that the doubling would tell should White succeed to exchange ... P–K4 by means of P–KB4.

DIAGRAM 150

Position after 7 ..., B–Q3

Trade of PQ2 vs PK4 indicated

8 P–Q4!   ....

The correct way of doing it; White eliminates the two remaining center pawns thus establishing full equality.

Instead, 8 BxNch, PxB is promising for Black, his weakened pawn structure notwithstanding, for he then retains his center pawn, which in turn enhances the value of his Bishops (9 P–Q4, P–K5!; or 9 P–Q3, B–KN5!).

8 ....   NxP

The safe, although unpretentious continuation.

Much more enterprising, but at the same time double-edged is 8 ..., PxP, e.g.

(1) 9 NxP?!, 0–0! (a) *10* 0–0??, NxN! (b) *10* NxN?, Q–R5! (c) *10* BxN, PxB; *11* 0–0, P–QB4; *12* N–B3, B–N2, and Black has a fine game thanks to his Bishops;

(2) 9 BxNch!, PxB; *10* QxP!, 0–0; *11* 0–0, P–QB4; *12* Q–B3, B–N2; *13* P–QN3, Q–Q2, and it is questionable whether Black's pair of Bishops compensates for the weakness of his pawn structure.

9 NxN	PxN
10 QxP	....

This is a rather dull position, for there are no levers in sight while the open files only encourage the trade of the Rooks. A game *Tartacover–Szabo* (Groningen 1946) went on as follows: *10* ..., 0–0; *11* B–K3, Q–K2; *12* 0–0–0, B–K4; *13* Q–B4, Q–B3; *14* B–Q4, B–K3; *15* Q–B3, BxB; *16* QxB, Q–N4ch; *17* K–N1, QR–Q1!; *18* Q–B3!, P–QB3; *19* P–KN3, Q–N4; *20* P–N3, P–QR4; *21* P–QR4, Q–N3; *22* P–B4, B–N5; *23* B–B3, BxB; *24* QxB, Q–N5; *25* RxR, RxR; *26* R–Q1, and the game was soon given a draw.

The following example from the Vienna opening gives an idea to what undesired consequences the fork trick may lead to, owing to an unthematic answer.

1 P–K4	P–K4
2 N–QB3	N–KB3
3 B–B4	....

Most likely good.

| 3 .... | NxP |

Most likely bad. At any rate Black fails to achieve what he is virtually aiming at. The safe move is 3 ..., N–B3.

| 4 Q–R5! | .... |

The unthematic reply which spoils Black's intention.

The thematic *4* NxN, P–Q4 offers Black a slight edge as his K-pawn is not exposed to quick exchange.

After *4* BxPch?, KxB; *5* NxN, P–Q4 Black has a distinct advantage (*6* Q–R5ch?, P–KN3; *7* QxP?, B–R3! and wins).

4	N–Q3

A cumbersome retreat—but *4* ..., N–N4 is worse because of *5* P–Q4.

5 B–N3	....

5 QxKPch, Q–K2 leads to equality.

5	N–B3

Unless Black meekly returns the pawn (*5* ..., B–K2; *6* N–B3!) letting himself in for some trouble and thus admitting that his fork trick has partly failed, he must plunge into a great gamble.

6 N–N5	....

Still stronger is *6* P–Q4, according to Adams.

6	P–KN3
7 Q–B3	P–KB4

7 ..., N–B4 works badly because of *8* P–N4, P–QR3; *9* PxN, PxN; *10* PxP.

8 Q–Q5	Q–K2

Black must yield substantial material.

9 NxPch	K–Q1
10 NxR	P–N3

But now Black threatens to obtain a strong counterattack with *11* ..., B–QN2. This sacrificial line, suggested by S. R. Wolf, has kept the analysts busy for decades, and there are still differences of opinion about it.

11 N–K2	....

So as to give up the Queen for sufficient material if not better. This idea of late seems to put White in his right.

11	B–QN2
12 Q–B3	....

Also *12* P–QB3, N–Q5; *13* PxN has been successfully tried.

But the text move, suggested by W. W. Adams, seems to be the best way of carrying out White's idea.

12	N–Q5
13 NxN!	BxQ
14 NxB	....

This position still offers problems, but White has good chances, e.g.

14	P–K5
15 N–Q4	P–K6
16 QPxP	Q–K5
17 0–0	QxQN
18 R–Q1	....

One thing is sufficiently clear: the fork trick has failed to produce a smooth improvement of Black's game.

VII–§2: The fork trick re PQ4, PK4 vs PQ3, PK4

In this case only Black can operate with the fork trick. See the following example.

G. BROWN   SIR GEORGE A. THOMAS

(From the tournament at Southsea 1949)

HUNGARIAN DEFENSE

1	P–K4	P–K4
2	N–KB3	N–QB3
3	B–B4	B–K2
4	P–Q4	P–Q3

The characteristic situation. A struggle for and against White's center duo lies ahead. Aiming at the destruction of this duo in such a way that he would not emerge on the defensive side of the jump formation (PK4 vs PQ3) Black plans to operate with the fork trick and the pin of White's K-Knight, while the fork lever might come in as an outside chance.

5 N–B3   ....

There is something to say for anticipating both the pin and the fork trick with 5 P–KR3, N–B3; 6 B–QN5 (6 N–B3, NxKP!). However, 6 ..., NxKP! works satisfactorily because after 7 P–Q5, P–QR3; 8 B–Q3 Black escapes the loss of a piece with 8 ..., N–B3; 9 PxN, P–K5.

Poor is 5 P–Q5, but 5 PxP, PxP; 6 QxQch offers White a microscopic advantage.

5 ....   N–B3

Threatening both 6 ..., NxKP and 6 ..., B–N5.

5 ..., B–N5; 6 B–QN5!, BxN; 7 PxB favors White.

DIAGRAM 151

Position after 5 ..., N–B3

The fork trick a threat

6 P–KR3   ....

The book move, but not the best.

Indicated instead is 6 B–QN5!. In thus transposing to the Ruy Lopez White indeed loses a tempo, but this is well compensated by his reaching the Steinitz variation at its best, with the possibility of 0–0–0 still open that is.

6   0–0

Also the book move.

Preferable however is the fork trick: 6 ..., NxKP!; 7 NxN, P–Q4 with these possibilities:

(1) 8 B–Q3, PxN; 9 BxP, NxP; 10 NxP, B–KB4 with equality;

(2) 8 B–QN5, PxN; 9 NxP, Q–Q3 (or may be even 9 ..., B–Q2; 10 NxB, QxN; 11 P–Q5, 0–0–0; 12 P–QB4, Q–B4) with equal chances;

(3) 8 BxP, QxB; 9 N–B3, Q–Q3 with a comfortable game for Black (10 N–QN5?, Q–N5ch!);

(4) 8 NxP, NxN; 9 PxN, PxB; 10 QxQch, BxQ with equal chances (11 B–N5, B–B4!).

7 B–K3   ....

A dull continuation.

Correct is 7 0–0! when the fork trick becomes a highly dubious affair: 7 ..., NxKP?!; 8 NxN, P–Q4; 9 BxP!, QxB; 10 N–B3, Q–R4 (10 ..., Q–Q3?; 11 N–QN5!); 11 P–Q5, R–Q1; 12 N–Q2, N–N5; 13 N–N3, Q–N3; 14 P–R3, N–R3; 15 Q–R5, with a promising game for White.

7 ....   NxKP!

Under these circumstances a perfect equalizer.

8 NxN   P–Q4
9 NxP   ....

Rather convenient for Black, as is 9 BxP, QxB; 10 N–B3, Q–Q3 (11 N–QN5?, Q–N5ch!).

Correct is 9 B–Q3! with an even game.

9 ....   PxB!

Enterprising play. Avoiding both the inferior 9 ..., PxN; 10 NxN, PxN and the drawish 9 ..., NxN; 10 PxN, PxB, Black permits the trebling of his QB-pawn for the sake of attack.

10 NxN   PxN

Black has a fine game thanks to several circumstances; there is his pair of Bishops; there are the QN-file and the Q-file, both hybrid but still of positive value, for PQN2 and PQ4 are possible targets while ... Q4 is an excellent place for his Q-Bishop; there is the threat of ... P–KB4–B5, detrimental to White's development; and there is the fact that PQ4 hampers White's Bishop.

White fails to live up to the challenge losing quickly: *11* N–B5 (*11* Q–Q2!) *11* ..., P–B4; *12* Q–B3? (*12* Q–Q2!) *12* ..., P–B5!; *13* BxP, QxP; *14* B–K3, QxP; *15* Q–Q1, Q–N5ch; *16* P–QB3, QxPch; *17* K–B1, QxB, and White resigned.

VII–§3: The fork trick re PQ4, PK4 vs PQ3, PK2

This also is a formation where Black might operate with the fork trick and, possibly, with the fork-lever. However, since his K-pawn has not yet advanced to the center, these stratagems are not likely to have their full effect.

The following game offers a good example.

ALEKHINE   CARTIER–MARECHAL–WINFREY

(Exhibition game, Montreal 1923)

KING'S FIANCHETTO

1	P–K4	P–KN3
2	P–Q4	P–Q3
3	B–QB4	....

This move, while far from being faulty, has the slight drawback of unnecessarily bringing the fork trick into the picture.

In positions of this type White is best off by first of all castling on the Q-side, e.g. *3* N–QB3, N–KB3; *4* B–KN5, P–KR3; *5* B–R4, B–N2; *6* Q–Q2; he then has chances on the K-side as well as in the center.

3 ....   B–N2

3 ..., N–KB3 raises the question of how to protect PK4. There are these possibilities:

(1) *4* N–QB3, NxP (a) *5* BxPch—tolerable in view of the resulting center formation—*5* ..., KxB; *6* NxN, and White

has a playable game (b) 5 NxN, P–Q4; 6 B–Q3, PxN; 7 BxP, and White has the edge thanks to the pawn situation in the center;

(2) 4 Q–K2, P–Q4; 5 PxP, NxP; 6 N–KB3, and White has the edge; note that the fork lever, while also destroying the duo, offers basically less relief than the fork trick as it does not go along with the exchange of a piece;

(3) 4 Q–B3—preventing both the fork trick and the fork lever, but courting trouble in the way of development—(a) 4 ..., B–N2??; 5 P–K5! (b) 4 ..., B–N5?; 5 Q–QN3! (c) 4 ..., N–B3!; 5 N–K2, B–N2; 6 P–KR3, P–K4, with somewhat dubious consequences.

$$4 \text{ N–KB3} \qquad \text{N–KB3}$$
$$5 \text{ Q–K2} \qquad \text{....}$$

Anticipating the fork trick (5 N–B3, NxP!).

$$5 \text{ ....} \qquad \text{N–B3}$$

Threatening to put new pressure on White's duo with 6 ..., B–N5.

DIAGRAM 152

Position after 5 ..., N–B3

The duo under pressure

$$6 \text{ P–KR3} \qquad \text{....}$$

With an exclamation mark, according to Alekhine, who remarks that 6 N–B3 would still be premature.

Indeed 6 N–B3, which is much more desirable than 6 P–B3,
serves poorly because of 6 ..., B–N5 (7 B–K3, NxKP!; or
7 B–QN5, P–QR3!; or 7 Q–Q3, BxN!).

However, the text move involves a loss of time with regard
to the fork lever.

| 6 .... | 0–0? |

Inconsistent. Black now must hit the duo with the fork lever:
6 ..., P–Q4!; 7 PxP, NxP (8 0–0, N–N3!) leaving White with
only a slight edge.

Alekhine, in his notes, unfortunately ignores 6 ..., P–Q4,
so we have no inkling of what he had in mind.

| 7 N–B3 | .... |

Now that the fork trick and the fork lever are definitely precluded White has a fine game.

| 7 .... | P–K4 |

Indeed, this also destroys the duo, at the expense however of
locking in the fianchettoed Bishop and conceding White superior
chances along the Q-file.

| 8 PxP! | PxP |

8 ..., QNxP; 9 NxN, PxN leads to much the same.

| 9 B–K3 | Q–K2 |

Nor is 9 ..., N–Q5 satisfactory because of 10 Q–Q1!, NxNch;
11 QxN, P–B3; 12 P–QR4 (Alekhine).

| 10 0–0–0 | .... |

Whereby White has obtained a distinct advantage.

The game continued: 10 ..., B–K3; 11 N–KN5!, BxB; 12 QxB,
KR–Q1; 13 B–B5, Q–K1; 14 N–N5!, RxRch; 15 RxR, R–B1;
16 BxP!, and White won.

VII–§4: The fork trick re PQ4, PK4 vs PQ3

This formation is usually created by the elimination of White's
QB-pawn and Black's K-pawn. Consequently, the fork trick as

well as the fork lever constitute a minority attack in the center, which may become particularly effective as it leads to the isolation of White's Q-pawn.

We bring two examples both starting with the position of *Diagram 153*.

Giuoco Piano

1	P–K4	P–K4
2	N–KB3	N–QB3
3	B–B4	B–B4
4	P–B3	P–Q3

Known as inferior to *4 ...*, N–B3, but raising rather difficult questions.

5	P–Q4	PxP
6	PxP	B–N3

Diagram 153

Position after 6 ..., B–N3

Point of deviation

M. GOLDSTEIN   RENNIE

(From their game of the 1922 City of London championship)
(*See Diagram 153*)

7 N–B3   ....

The regular continuation.

7 ....   N–B3

Threatening to destroy the duo with 8 ..., NxKP or put it under heavy pressure with 8 ..., B–N5 (9 B–QN5, 0–0).

The immediate 7 ..., B–N5; 8 B–QN5 is inconvenient for Black as he is not yet ready to castle.

8 Q–Q3!   ....

This prevents the fork trick and takes the sting out of 8 ... B–N5.

8 ....   B–N5

An alternative aiming at the fork lever, interesting but not quite satisfactory, is 8 ..., N–QN5, e.g.

(1) 9 Q–Q1, N–B3 (9 ..., P–Q4?; 10 Q–R4ch!) with a possible repetition of moves;

(2) 9 Q–N1, P–Q4; 10 PxP, QNxQP; 11 NxN, NxN; 12 Q–K4ch, B–K3; 13 N–N5, Q–Q2 with approximate equality;

(3) 9 Q–K2, 0–0; 10 B–N3!, and White has favorably evaded the fork trick as well as the fork lever (10 ..., NxKP?; 11 NxN, R–K1; 12 KN–N5, P–Q4; 13 Q–R5!).

9 B–K3   0–0

Threatening 10 ..., N–N5 followed by 11 ..., P–Q4.

9 ..., N–N5 is ineffective because of 10 Q–Q1 when the counterthreat of 11 Q–R4ch prevents 10 ..., P–Q4 as well as 10 ..., NxKP.

10 P–QR3   R–K1

10 ..., BxN; 11 PxB only adds to White's advantage because of the mobility of the front twin.

11 N–Q2   ....

White now has definitely maintained his duo and obtained a superior game.

RUDOLPH SPIELMANN   DAVID JANOWSKI

(From the Karlsbad 1907 tournament)

See Diagram 153

7 P–KR3   ....

A fair continuation, but less consistent than 7 N–B3 as it leads to the isolation of White's Q-pawn.

7 ....   N–B3
8 0–0   ....

There is no direct protection to PK4 that would simultaneously prevent the fork trick and the fork lever (*10* N–B3, NxKP!; *11* Q–K2, 0–0; or *10* Q–Q3, P–Q4!).

8 ....   NxKP!

A fork trick of the irregular kind.
Also playable is *8* ..., 0–0, e.g.

(1) 9 N–B3, NxKP; *10* NxN, P–Q4; *11* B–KN5 (a) *11* ...,
P–B3?; *12* BxP!, PxB; *13* B–N3, with White for choice (b)
11 ..., Q–Q2!, with a satisfactory game for Black;

(2) 9 R–K1 (a) 9 ..., P–Q4 with a fair game (b) 9 ..., NxKP,
with transposition to the text.

9 R–K1   0–0

9 ..., P–Q4 is troublesome because of *10* B–KN5 followed by *11* BxQP.

10 RxN   P–Q4

By way of exception the fork hits R and N instead of B and N.

11 B–KN5   Q–Q3?

But here Black falters losing time and getting cramped.
Correct and satisfactory is *11* ..., P–B3, e.g. (1) *12* BxPch,
QxB; *13* N–B3, Q–R4 (2) *12* B–N3, PxB; *13* N–B3, B–KB4.

The game continued as follows: *12* BxP, QxB; *13* N–B3, Q–Q2; *14* P–Q5, P–B3; *15* B–K3!, N–Q1; *16* BxB, RPxB; *17* Q–K2, N–B2; *18* R–K7, Q–Q1; *19* P–Q6!! (A beautiful sweeper twist. White centralizes his Q-Knight thereby decisively strengthening his attack.) *19* ..., NxP; *20* N–Q5, R–B2; *21* R–K1, B–Q2; *22* N–R4, R–R4; *23* RxR, NxR; *24* N–B5!!, N–K4; *25* KN–K7ch, K–R1; *26* P–QN4, R–R1; *27* P–B4, N–N3; *28* NxNch, PxN; *29* N–K7, Q–K1; *30* Q–KB2!, P–KN4; *31* PxP, PxP; *32* Q–Q2, P–N4; *33* QxP, R–R3; *34* R–K4, R–R3; *35* N–B5!, Q–N3; *36* Q–Q8ch, K–R2; *37* QxB, R–R4; *38* R–N4, R–N4; *29* R–R4ch, and Black resigned.

VII–§5: The fork trick in the middle-game

In the middle-game (as well as in the end-game) the fork trick is a rarity. Following are two examples.

MAX EUWE　　PAUL KERES

(From one of their games
of the 1948 World Championship Tournament)

DIAGRAM 154

Devastating fork trick

Black to move

The position would be in the balance were it not for the fork trick.

$$1 \ldots\ldots \qquad\qquad \text{RxP!}$$

This unusual fork trick destroys White's position.

$$2 \text{ RxR} \qquad\qquad \text{P–Q4}$$

Irregularly the fork hits Q and R, so that capturing the forking pawn is out of question. Nor is it possible to recover the center pawn as the Bishop will be loose.

$$3 \text{ QxRP} \qquad\qquad \ldots\ldots$$

Sadly enough White must take this outsider for his center pawn.

$$3 \ldots\ldots \qquad\qquad \text{PxR}$$
$$4 \text{ B–K3} \qquad\qquad \text{Q–N5!}$$

The fork trick has netted Black a series of obvious advantages He now gets a winning attack.

$$5 \text{ Q–B4} \qquad\qquad \text{R–Q6!}$$
$$6 \text{ B–B1} \qquad\qquad \ldots\ldots$$

6 QxKP fails against 6 ..., Q–K7.

$$6 \ldots\ldots \qquad\qquad \text{N–R5!}$$
$$7 \text{ QxPch} \qquad\qquad \ldots\ldots$$

There is nothing better: 7 P–N3, RxPch!; or 7 R–B2, R–Q8ch!; or 7 Q–B2, P–KB4! with the irremediable threat of 8 ..., P–K6.

$$7 \ldots\ldots \qquad\qquad \text{P–KB4}$$
$$8 \text{ Q–N7} \qquad\qquad \ldots\ldots$$

Or 8 Q–B6, R–QB6 and wins.

$$8 \ldots\ldots \qquad\qquad \text{P–B3}$$

More accurate is 8 ..., R–QB6; 9 Q–Q5, P–B3.

$$9 \text{ QxP} \qquad\qquad \text{R–QB6}$$
$$10 \text{ Q–Q5} \qquad\qquad \text{R–B4!}$$

Not 10 ..., R–B7 because of 11 B–Q2.

11 Q–Q2 ....

Or 11 Q–N7, R–B7 and wins, e.g. 12 P–N3, Q–R6; 13 Q–R1, R–N7ch.

11 .... RxB!

Conclusive, as White obviously cannot recapture.
Black won.

SIEGBERT TARRASCH EMANUEL LASKER

(From the fourth game of their 1908 match)

DIAGRAM 155

A faulty fork trick

White to move

The position is in the balance but White commits an error.

1 N–N5? ....

Sacrificing an important pawn for the sake of the fork trick. This alone is strange reasoning.
Correct is 1 PxP.

1 .... PxP
2 RxP ....

The point to which White has committed himself. It seems that he recovers the pawn.

2	RxR
3 P–K5	RxKBP!!

Brilliantly refuting White's combination. In itself it is not very surprising that the extra Rook, being what Emanuel Lasker called a "desperado," would do some mischief before it goes. By the same token 3 ..., R–Q8ch; 4 QxR, Q–K2 offers an expedient most likely sufficient to hold the game.

4 NPxR	....

The choice is sad, e.g. 4 PxQ, RxQ; 5 RxR, R–Q4 and Black wins. White has irretrievably lost a pawn and also compromised his position.

4	Q–N3ch
5 K–R1	Q–QN8ch
6 K–N2	R–Q7ch
7 R–K2	QxP and Black won.

Part Three

PAWN POWER IN THE GAME

We have now arrived at the testing point. While the games given so far have served to exemplify separately one specific detail or another, the following collection of games must show how such details behave or work out in concert.

Convinced that positions of a more or less closed and static type would facilitate the study of pawn play, we have made our selection from a comparatively small number of openings with rather characteristic pawn formations. The examples, we decided, should be of a preponderantly strategic nature so that the plans under discussion would not be obscured by too many tactical questions.

These considerations led us to the Benoni type of opening play, which has become popular very recently and has rapidly produced a variety of clearly discernible sub-systems extending in nature from heavy positional entrenchment to lofty gambit play. There lay fine, untouched material, and we have availed ourselves of it freely. We also made a first attempt at assorting this material and labeling its components.

Games illustrating some formations other than Benoni are also included in this collection—not many in numbers but enough for the purpose involved. After all, the rules for acting in accordance with the pawn structure cover any position. We had grammar in mind, not a dictionary.

Chapter VIII

BENONI FORMATIONS

We start where we stopped under V-§13.
This is how we distinguish between Benoni formations:

(1) Full Benoni
   (1a) Benoni Major: PQB4, PQ5, PK4 vs PQB4, PQ3, PK4
   (1b) Benoni Minor: PQB2, PQ5, PK4 vs PQB4, PQ3, PK4
   (1c) Spanish Benoni: PQB3, PQ5, PK4 vs PQR3, PQN4, PQB4, PQ3, PK4

(2) Part Benoni
   (2a) Blitz Benoni: PQ5, PK4 vs PQB4, PQ3
   (2b) Wing Benoni: PQ5 vs PQB4, PQ3, PK2
   (2c) Gambit Benoni: PQR2, PQN2, PQ5, PK4 vs PQB4, PQ3, PK2
   (2d) Rex Benoni: PQ5 vs PQB2, PQ3, PK4.

The *Benoni Major* and the *Benoni Minor* differ by the square QB4 which in the latter formation is open offering White's pieces more scope. Therefore, Black usually avoids the Benoni Minor (*1* P–Q4, P–QB4) playing ... P–QB4 only in reaction to P–QB4. Thus *1* P–Q4, N–KB3; 2 P–QB4, P–B4.

The *Spanish Benoni* is a version of the Benoni Minor improved on Black's part through control of the square ... QB5.

The *Blitz Benoni*, of which *Diagram 120* gives an idea, is a half-closed formation with sharp tendencies owing to opposing majorities.

The *Wing Benoni* is designed to put White's Q-wing under converging pressure. Black therefore fianchettoes his K-Bishop and strives for the exchange of a pawn with ... P–QN4.

The *Gambit Benoni,* where Black sacrifices a pawn with . . .
P–QN4, constitutes an effort on his part to intensify the tendencies of the Wing Benoni.

The *Rex Benoni* differs from all other Benoni formations by
. . . PQB2 (instead of . . . PQB4). It is the most important of
the Part Benonis. Our term Rex is intended to hint at the King's
Indian defense from which this formation usually arises.

Any Benoni formation may conceivably occur with colors
reversed.

In referring to Benoni formations we distinguish between attacker and defender in accordance with the position of both
Q-pawns interpreting the crossing of the middle-line as a signal
for attack.

All Benoni formations favor the attacker with regard to space,
but the defender with regard to levers. The attacker, who should
strive for a duo with his Q-pawn, has difficulty in forming proper
levers, while the defender constantly faces the danger of being
either too early or too late with the exchange of a pawn. The
struggle is usually very difficult for both sides. Benoni formations, because of their intricacy and permanent tension, are the
heavy guns in present-day tournament chess.

VIII–§1: The Benoni jump

Before starting to discuss Benoni formations one by one, we
must deal with a typical tactical twist that may easily occur in
any of them. It consists in the sacrifice of a Knight on KB5
(. . . KB5). We call it the *Benoni jump.*

Benoni systems require the fianchetto of the K-Bishop on the
part of the defender. Hence . . . P–KN3, which also is a preparation for . . . P–KB4 and often induces White to play P–KN4.
This, then, is the pawn situation where N–KB5 may occur—
provided White is ready to use the KN-file for an assault on the
King.

Apart from the question of how the sacrifice would work out,
these four preliminary questions are essential for the assessment
of the Benoni jump: (1) Is . . . PxN forced? (2) Is . . . NxN or
. . . BxN forced? (3) If the Knight is ignored, can it make any

capture? (4) If the Knight is ignored and has nothing to capture either, does the Benoni jump still make sense?

Following are three examples.

ERICH ELISKASES   ERNST GRUENFELD

(From their game of the Maehrisch-Ostrau 1933 tournament)

DIAGRAM 156

Most effective Benoni jump

Forcing acceptance

This is a far advanced Benoni formation. White has prepared for the Benoni jump and now launches it most effectively.

$$1 \text{ N–B5!} \qquad \text{PxN}$$

Black must accept the sacrifice; otherwise he loses at least the exchange.

$$2 \text{ PxP} \qquad \dots$$

White's combination, apart from involving a sacrifice, has worked the same way as the queue method.

$$2 \dots \qquad \text{Q–K1}$$

The Queen must move so it would not interfere with the protection of the pinned Knight.

3 Q–KN2!   ....

But this wins as it forces Black's Queen to resume its interfering position.

3	....	Q–Q2
4	RxNch	RxR
5	BxR	QxB
6	Q–QB2!	N–N3
7	PxN	P–R3

White now holds a powerful extra pawn. He won.

MISS VERA MENCHIK   SIR GEORGE A. THOMAS

(From their game of the London 1932 tournament)

DIAGRAM 157

Effective Benoni jump

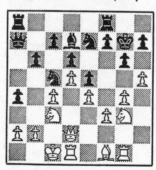

Forcing trade

This is a Benoni formation with a far advanced St. George attack. White has also prepared for the Benoni jump which now hits.

1 N–B5ch!   ....

Forcing Black to trade this Knight as he otherwise will be mated.

1 ....   NxN?

In parting with this useful Knight Black loses quickly. With 1 ..., BxN; 2 NPxB, N–Q2 he can prolong the struggle.

2 NPxN   P–R6

Nothing matters any more.

3 P–B6ch!   K–R1

Or 3 ..., KxP; 4 Q–N5ch, K–N2; 5 P–R6ch, K–N1; 6 Q–B6 and mate.

4 Q–R6   R–KN1
5 RPxP   BPxP
6 QxPch!   and mate

C. H. O'D. ALEXANDER   LUDEK PACHMAN

(From their game of the Zonal tournament at Hilversum 1947)

DIAGRAM 158

Useful Benoni jump

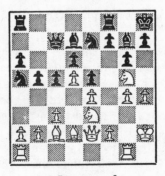

Offering trade

This is a Spanish Benoni with the Benoni jump in the air—
a very common situation. The game proceeded:

1 N–B5!　　　　　....

A good move, but far from decisive as Black is not forced to
capture the Knight.

1 ....　　　　　PxN?

But this loses.

Also bad is *1* ..., B–KB3? because of *2* NxRP!, KxN; *3* P–N5.

Correct is *1* ..., N–N1. However, the Benoni jump then still
works satisfactorily inasmuch as *2* NxB weakens Black's defenses.

2 NPxP　　　　　....

With the main threat of *3* NxRP!.

2 ....　　　　　P–B3

There is no reasonable defense (*2* ..., P–R3; *3* Q–R5!).

3 NxRP!　　　　　B–K1

Or *3* ..., KxN; *4* Q–R5ch, K–N1; *5* RxBch and wins.

4 RxB!	KxR
5 NxR	KxN
6 B–R6ch	K–B2
7 Q–R5ch	N–N3
8 PxNch	and White won

VIII–§2: The Benoni Major PQB4, PQ5, PK4 vs PQB4, PQ3, PK4

This formation may be reached either at the outset or later.
White normally holds a tiny edge. His indicated lever action is
P–QR3 and P–QN4—rarely P–KN3 and P–B4, as this might
weaken the position of his King. His very bad K-Bishop serves
best on Q3 where it helps guard against Black's lever moves ...
P–QN4 and ... P–B4. A little less effective is BK2, least effective
BKN2. In the latter case P–QR4 is often necessary as a measure
against ... P–QN4, but then White must give up the idea of
P–QN4 and rely on the somewhat dubious P–B4.

If the formation is reached early in the game, White may safely keep his King in the center, at least for some time; he then also has a chance for the St. George attack, provided Black has played ... P–KN3 as is usual; and he also can meet ... P–B4 more easily.

This ... P–B4 is Black's main trump. It normally requires ... P–KN3 so White will not gain the dominating square K4 by means of KPxBP. Also, ... P–B4 is likely to serve best after 0–0 as White then cannot use his home pawns for sharp lever play.

Since both K–Bishops are very bad, any exchange of a Bishop may have far-reaching consequences either way. For instance *1* P–Q4, P–K3; *2* P–QB4, B–N5ch; *3* B–Q2, BxBch; *4* NxB, P–Q3; *5* KN–B3, Q–K2; *6* P–K4, P–K4; *7* B–Q3, N–KB3; *8* 0–0, 0–0; *9* Q–B2, P–B4; *10* P–Q5. This is the beginning of the Becker –Przepiorka game, Prague 1931. White holds the regular plus in space and is ahead in development, too. But being left with his bad Bishop he has no advantage. As a matter of fact, Black lost the game, but only because of inaccuracies he committed later.

So much for generalities. Here are some illustrative games.

JULIUS PARTOS   V. HARRIS

(From the 1951 Colorado State championship)

1 P–Q4	P–QB4
2 P–Q5	P–K4
3 P–K4	P–Q3
4 P–QB4	....

The Benoni Major reached in the shortest way.

4 ....   P–B4?

A basic error. In prematurely forming this essential lever Black lands in a position of the *Diagram 128* type.

Almost any quiet continuation is better.

5 N–QB3   N–KB3

The attempt to seal off the position with 5 ..., P–B5 fails against 6 P–KN3!.

6 B–Q3   ....

White's otherwise bad Bishop becomes perfectly active. The consequences of 4 ..., P–B4? are beginning to show.

DIAGRAM 159

Position after 6 B–Q3

Consequences of 4 ..., P–B4? showing

6 ....   PxP

Conceding White the dominating square K4, the half-open K-file, and the open diagonal QN1–KR7.

However, the alternatives also have grave drawbacks:

(1) 6 ..., P–B5; 7 P–KN3!, P–KN4; 8 P–KR4!, PxNP; 9 RPxP!, PxPch; 10 KxP, N–N5ch; 11 K–K1 threatening 12 B–K2; White, thanks to the elimination of two pawns on the K-side, has a winning advantage;

(2) 6 ..., P–KN3; 7 Q–B2 (a) 7 ..., Q–Q2; 8 P–B4!, and the tension in the center is unbearable for Black (b) 7 ..., P–B5; 8 P–KN3!, with an even better effect than before (c) 7 ..., PxP; 8 NxP, similar to the game.

7 NxP   QN–Q2
8 N–QB3!   ....

Very good. White avoids both the unnecessary trade of a piece as well as the obscure consequences of 8 N–N5.

8	B–K2
9 KN–K2	0–0
10 N–N3	P–QR3
11 P–QR4	P–QN3
12 0–0	N–K1

The situation has the exact features of *Diagram 128*. White holds a great advantage. He won as follows:

13 Q–B2, QN–B3; *14* B–Q2, (*14* P–B4!) *14* ..., B–Q2; 15 B–B5 (*15* QR–K1! and P–B4!) *15* ..., N–B2; *16* P–N3, BxB; *17* NxB, Q–Q2; (Threatening *18* ..., N(3)xP.) *18* NxBch (Justified. White remains with the good Bishop against a Knight, which in Benoni positions usually constitutes an asset.) *18* ..., QxN; *19* QR–K1, P–QN4? (Recklessly leaving the Queen in the fire line of White's Rook. With *19* ..., Q–Q2; *20* P–B4, PxP; *21* BxP, QR–K1 Black can put up a much better resistance.) *20* P–B4, NPxBP; *21* NPxP, N–Q2; *22* N–K4! (Threatening *23* N–N5, P–N3; *24* N–B3.) *22* ..., N–K1 (Nor is *22* ..., P–R3 sufficient because of *23* B–B3, QR–K1; *24* N–N3, although Black then can resist much longer.) *23* N–N5, N(1)–B3; *24* B–B3, KR–B1; *25* N–K6, P–K5; *26* R–K3, K–B2; *27* P–N4!, NxNP; *28* R–N3, P–KR4; *29* P–R3, Q–R5; *30* Q–KN2, N(5)–B3; *31* RxPch, K–K1; *32* Q–N6 mate.

LASZLO SZABO   BORIS IVKOV

(From the 1955 Buenos Aires tournament)

1 P–Q4	N–KB3
2 P–QB4	P–KN3
3 N–QB3	B–N2
4 P–K4	P–Q3
5 P–B3	....

The Saemisch system of attack, which is a serious challenge to the King's Indian defense.

5	P–K4
6 P–Q5	....

The system requires a deadlock in the center on behalf of lever action on the K-side, more specifically the St. George attack. The text move creates the formation we call Rex Benoni.

6	P–B4

Black has many possibilities of meeting the Saemisch attack within the Rex Benoni, but none of them offers full satisfaction, according to present-day experience.

Hence this attempt of getting a better result by a switch to the Benoni Major. However, the switch works adversely as Black is exposed to brisk lever action on either wing.

7 B–N5	N–R3
8 B–Q3	N–B2
9 KN–K2	B–Q2
10 P–QR3!	....

Attack by P–QN4 is the best measure against the impending ... P–QN4, preferable by far to the purely defensive P–QR4.

10	P–KR3

In forming the duo ... PKN3, PKR3 before castling, Black anticipates the St. George attack. After 10 ..., 0–0; 11 Q–Q2 this attack is a threat, an important point being that 11 ..., P–KR3; 12 BxP, NxKP fails against 13 NxN!, Q–R5ch; 14 P–KN3, QxB; 15 QxQ, BxQ; 16 NxQP.

11 B–K3	0–0
12 P–QN4!	P–N3

12 ..., N–R3 leads after 13 R–QN1 to much the same; White would not free his Q-pawn at the heavy expense of parting

with his good Bishop and pre-empting ... Q3 for Black's pieces
(*13* PxP, NxP!; *14* BxN, PxB).

13	0–0	K–R1
14	R–N1	N–N1
15	Q–Q2	N–K1
16	R–N3	....

White is sustaining the lever PQN4 vs PQB4 as a means of
exercising pressure; he might play PxP any time, but not when
... QPxP would enable Black to make a good use of the square
... Q3.

16	....	P–B4

Black is duly afraid that stalling would increasingly imperil his
game, so he rather makes this bid for counterplay.

17	P–B4!!	....

Thanks to the exchangeability of PK4, which is no longer a
candidate for backwardness, White can play the text move with
impunity thus switching from pressure to attack. He threatens to
isolate ... PKB4 by means of *18* PxKP, BxP; *19* KPxP (*19* BxP,
BxPch!).

DIAGRAM 160

Position after 17 P–B4!!

Thanks to the exchangeability of PK4

17	....	P–KN4

There are three levers in the position, and Black cannot dissolve any of them without making a grave concession. This fourth lever is intended as a combination designed to alleviate the tension at the expense of a pawn, thus *18* PxNP, P–B5; *19* PxRP, NxP; *20* B–KB2, N–N5.

18 P–N3!	....

But White simply maintains all the tension, thereby keeping his advantage.

18	PxKP

Black is unable to wait.

19 NxP	B–R6

Another little combination, which also fails.

The alternative of *19* ..., KPxP; *20* PxKBP, P–N5; *21* QN–N3 is just as bad for Black.

20 R–B2	N(K)–B3
21 PxNP	N–N5
22 KN–B3!	....

Black was hoping for *22* RxR, QxR with some counterplay. The text move destroys his hope.

22	Q–Q2

After *22* ..., NxR; *23* NxN followed by *24* PxRP White has decisive compensation for the exchange.

23 N–N5!	....

Now the Q-pawn falls, and that is the end: *23* ..., NxR; *24* BxR, R–B6; *25* N(5)xQP, QR–KB1; *26* PxBP, PxBP; *27* R–N7, Q–Q1; *28* P–N6!, N–K2; *29* N–B7ch, R(6)xN; *30* PxR, and Black resigned.

SAMUEL RESHEVSKY   SVETOZAR GLIGORICH

(From their match in New York 1952)

1 P–Q4, N–KB3; *2* P–QB4, P–KN3; *3* N–QB3, B–N2; *4* P–K4,
P–Q3; *5* N–B3, 0–0; *6* B–K2, P–K4; *7* 0–0, QN–Q2; *8* R–K1,
P–B3; *9* B–B1, R–K1; *10* P–Q5, P–B4.

This is a well-known case of delayed transposition from the
Rex Benoni to the Benoni Major.

DIAGRAM 161

Position after 10 . . . , P–B4

Delayed Benoni Major

White's type of development requires action with P–QN4,
and counter-action with . . . P–KB4. Action the other way round
(P–B4 vs P–QN4) is precluded for the time being. The chances
are almost even. White has only the shade of an edge.

11 P–QR3   R–B1!

Back with the Rook, behind the lever-pawn. That is the right
way of doing it.

The only good alternative, amounting however to a mere
transposition of moves, is *11* . . . , P–KR3, a move that Black
usually needs so he can play . . . P–B4 without bothering about
N–KN5–K6.

Let us insert here a game where Black commits strikingly
instructive errors.

STAHLBERG–WADE (Staunton Memorial, England 1951): *11* ..., P–KR3; *12* P–R3, N–B1? (Hampering Black's indicated lever action.) *13* P–KN3, P–KN4?? (While *12* ..., N–B1? has hampered Black's indicated lever action, this move destroys his chance for getting in and maintaining the vital duo...PK4, PKB4.) *14* P–KR4!! (A very powerful lever action serving three basic purposes, namely the definite control of KN4, the exchange of the white-bound Bishops, and last but not least the opening of the KR-file.) *14* ..., KN–R2? (Black fails to put up strategic resistance. He must try *14* ..., P–N5.) *15* PxP, PxP; *16* N–KR2!, Q–B3; *17* B–K2, Q–R3; *18* B–N4!, N–Q2; *19* N–B3, N–N3; *20* BxB, KRxB; *21* Q–N3, B–B3; *22* N–KR4!, Q–B1; *23* N–B5, B–K2; *24* K–N2, R–B2; *25* N–N5, R–Q2; *26* R–R1!, N–B1; *27* Q–Q1!, B–Q1; *28* RxN!, KxR; *29* Q–R5ch, K–N1; *30* BxP, P–B3; *31* B–R6, Q–B2; *32* Q–N4ch, and Black resigned.

12 P–KN3	N–K1
13 P–QN4	Q–K2

Another game, showing imperfect play on White's part, may be quoted at this point.

CHRISTOFFEL–BOLESLAVSKY (Groningen 1946): *13* ..., P–KR3; *14* N–KR4, QN–B3; *15* PxP (Premature.) *15* ..., PxP; *16* P–QR4 (Threatening *17* B–K3, P–N3; *18* P–R5. However, PQR4 becomes a weakness. White should strive for P–B4 rather than operate on the Q-side.) *16* ..., P–QR4!; *17* R–N1, N–Q3!; *18* B–QR3 (Wasting time. Better *18* P–B3 or *18* B–Q3.) *18* ..., P–N3; *19* Q–N3, R–R3! (*19* ..., R–N1?; *20* BxP!) *20* Q–B2, N–R2; *21* N–N5? (B–B1!) *21* ..., N–N4 (...NxN!) *22* K–R1 (N–QB3!) *22* ..., NxN!; *23* BPxN (RPxN is the minor evil.) *23* ..., R–R2 (Black has the edge.) *24* B–QN2, Q–Q3; *25* Q–Q2, R–K2; *26* B–N2, B–R6!; *27* BxB, NxB; *28* N–N2? (28 P–B3!, P–B4; *29* R–KB1!) *28* ..., N–N4; *29* Q–Q1, P–B4! (After prolonged preparations, the basic lever comes in with decisive effect.) *30* PxP, PxP; *31* P–B4, N–K5!; *32* K–N1, P–B5!; *33* PxP, BxP; *34* BxB, RxB; *35* N–K3, N–B6; *36* Q–Q4, NxR; *37* RxN,

R–K5; *38* NxKBP, RxQ; *39* NxQ, P–B6!; *40* R–QB1, RxQP;
41 N–K4, R–Q5; *42* NxP, R–B1, and White resigned.

14 R–R2	N–B2
15 B–K3	P–N3
16 N–KR4	N–K1
17 Q–B1	N–B2

Both sides are biding their time, White with PxP, and Black
with . . . P–B4. They both would like to see the opponent commit
himself first. Their mutual attitude is one of due caution and
profound understanding. White has a slight, very slight edge.

18 B–N5	B–B3!

And not *18* . . . , P–B3, which is detrimental as it increases the
scope of White's K-Bishop, e.g. *19* B–K3, N–K1; *20* B–R3, N–B2;
21 QR–K2 with a fine game for White, the immediate threat
being *22* B–K6ch and *23* P–B4.

19 B–R6	B–N2
20 B–R3	....

White would not exchange his good Bishop and keep the
other one. In trading them both he maintains his slight initiative.

20	R–K1

Preparing for *21* . . . , B–B3 or *21* . . . , BxB; *22* QxB, Q–B1;
23 Q–N5, Q–K2. Black cannot play too passively; he must give
some thought to the fact that P–B4 might become strong if the
focal point . . . K4 is deprived of protection by minor pieces
owing to BxB and BxN.

21 BxB	KxB
22 Q–Q2	N–B1!

Black has the better Bishop, but he obviously lacks a reasonable way of keeping it.

23 BxB	KRxB

With this Rook, so there would be no traffic jam if it comes to defending the QN-file: ... KR–N1 and ... Q–Q1.

24 PxP   ....

The best moment for this exchange has come as Black can recapture neither with a piece nor with the Q-pawn.

24 ....   NPxP
25 R–N2   N–Q2!
26 N–R4   ....

26 R–N7 leads only to the exchange of this Rook because of 26 ..., N–N3 followed by 27 ..., KR–QN1.

26 ....   KR–QN1
27 KR–N1   Q–Q1
28 K–N2   ....

28 R–N7 offers no advantage because of 28 ..., N–N3. Nor does 28 Q–R5 because of 28 ..., RxR; 29 RxR, R–N1! (30 QxRP??, R–R1!).

Since White cannot prevent the exchange of the Rooks, his tiny advantage is evaporating.

The text move serves for a last try.

28 ....   P–KR3

A defensive measure, harmless indeed, but unnecessary.

Instead, Black can simply proceed with 28 ..., RxR; 29 RxR, R–N1; 30 RxR, QxR (30 ..., NxR?; 31 Q–R5!). Then, after 31 Q–N5 (the move that explains 28 K–N2 as well as 28 ..., P–KR3) Black holds his own perfectly with 31 ..., N–K1, e.g. 32 Q–K7, N(2)–B3.

29 Q–R5   N–N3?

Black gets scared. Correct is 29 ..., RxR; 30 RxR, R–N1 with equality (31 QxRP??, R–R1!).

The rest of the game is mainly a tactical affair.

30 NxN   PxN?

He should at least exchange a pair of Rooks for the sake of relief: 30 ..., RxN!; 31 RxR, PxR.

31 Q–B3   ....

Threatening 32 P–B4! (32 RxP?, RxR; 33 RxR, NxP!).

31 ....   K–N1

Better 31 ..., K–R2, although 32 P–B4!, PxP; 33 R–KB2! still favors White (not so 32 RxP because of 32 ..., RxR; 33 RxR, NxP; 34 Q–B3!, N–B3! with equality).

32 Q–Q2!   ....

Threatening both 33 QxP and 33 RxP, RxR; 34 RxR, NxP?; 35 QxN!.

32 ....   RxP?

The major evil; Black should protect his KR-pawn.

33 QxP	N–K1
34 P–B4!	PxP
35 R–KB2!	....

The point of the lever (with the further point of 35 ..., PxP; 36 NxP!).

| 35 .... | Q–K2 |
| 36 QxP | R–R5 |

Worse is 36 ..., P–KN4; 37 Q–N4! as well as 36 ..., K–N2; 37 R(1)–KB1, R–R2; 38 Q–N4!.

37 R(1)–KB1   R–N2

After 37 ..., RxP White maintains a winning attack with 38 QxPch, QxQ; 39 RxQ, e.g. 39 ..., RxP; 40 R–B8ch, K–R2; 41 R(1)–B7ch.

38 NxP!   ....

A decisive combination, although it does not win quickly.

| 38 .... | PxN |
| 39 Q–R6! | QxPch |

But this does lose quickly.

Correct is 39 ..., N–N2; 40 QxP, RxP with this plausible continuation: 41 R–B4, Q–K1; 42 QxQch, NxQ; 43 R–B8ch, K–N2; 44 RxN, R–Q5; 45 R–K6, P–N4; 46 RxP, RxKP; 47 R–QB6, P–B5; 48 P–Q6, R–K1; 49 R–KB5, R–Q1; 50 P–R4, and White must win.

40	K–N1	Q–Q5
41	K–N2	Q–K5ch
42	K–R3!	Resigns

VIII–§3: The Benoni Minor PQB2, PQ5, PK4 vs PQB4, PQ3, PK4⸱

The Benoni Minor, built of only two rams, offers the attacker better possibilities than the Benoni Major, yet the task of opening lines still remains a formidable one.

HANS KMOCH   ALEXANDER ALEKHINE

(From a tournament in Holland, 1937)

1	P–Q4	P–QB4
2	P–Q5	P–K4
3	P–K4	P–Q3
4	B–Q3	....

White's best, we believe.

Alternatives are:

(1) 4 P–KB4!?—a move which is bad in general (see *Diagram 175*) but characteristic for the Benoni Minor, inasmuch as it is playable at this point. For instance: 4 ..., PxP; 5 BxP (1a) 5 ..., Q–R5ch?!; 6 P–KN3, Q–K2; 7 N–QB3? (7 N–KB3!, QxPch?; 8 K–B2!) 7 ..., P–KN4!; 8 B–K3, N–Q2; 9 N–B3, P–KR3; 10 Q–Q2, KN–B3; 11 0–0–0, N–N5; 12 B–K2, B–N2, with a fine game for Black (Bogolyubov–Alekhine, ninth game of their 1934 match).

(1b) 5 ..., N–K2; 6 B–N5ch!, B–Q2; 7 BxBch, QxB;
8 N–KB3, N–N3; 9 B–N3, and White has a reasonably
good game, in spite of the backwardness of PK4.

(2) 4 N–QB3—the usually recommended move, which is somewhat innocent since it precludes lever action with P–QB3 and
P–QN4. For instance: 4 ..., N–K2!; 5 P–KN3, N–N3;
6 P–KR4, B–K2; 7 P–R5, N–B1; 8 B–N5ch, QN–Q2; 9 P–R4,
P–QR3; 10 B–K2, P–R3; 11 B–K3, B–N4!; 12 Q–Q2, N–R2;
13 N–B3, BxB; 14 QxB, 0–0; 15 N–Q2, P–QN3; 16 N–B4,
Q–B2; 17 P–B4, R–K1; 18 0–0, R–N1; 19 P–N3, P–B3, and
Black has a somewhat cramped but unshakable position
(Alekhine–Castillo, Buenos Aires 1939; there followed a
long period of harmless maneuvering until Black blundered
and lost).

$$4 \dots \qquad\qquad P–QR3$$

By exception, this move works out as a weakening of the
square ... QN3; Black should have omitted it and for the rest
continued as in the game, Alekhine declared later.

$$5 \ P–QR4 \qquad\qquad \dots$$

Necessary for the following development of the Q-Knight.

$$5 \dots \qquad\qquad N–K2$$
$$6 \ N–K2 \qquad\qquad \dots$$

It is useful to be ready for P–KB3 or P–KB4 at any time.

$$6 \dots \qquad\qquad N–N3$$
$$7 \ N–R3 \qquad\qquad B–K2$$
$$8 \ N–QB4 \qquad\qquad \dots$$

This fine position of the Knight makes the Benoni Minor very
attractive to White.

$$8 \dots \qquad\qquad 0–0$$
$$9 \ 0–0 \qquad\qquad N–Q2$$
$$10 \ B–Q2 \qquad\qquad \dots$$

Preventing 10 ..., N–N3, because of 11 B–R5, and threatening to paralyze Black's Q-side with 11 P–R5.

10	P–N3
11 P–QB3	R–N1
12 P–QN4!	....

A strong lever action, characteristic of this setup.
White has a fine game.

DIAGRAM 162

Position after 12 P–QN4!

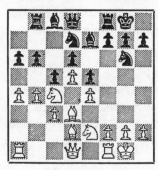

Characteristic

12	N–B3

Best, although it permits the following exchange; Black must develop his forces.

13 PxP	NPxP

Not 13 ..., QPxP, which under these circumstances is prohibitive because of 14 P–B4!.

14 R–N1	B–Q2
15 Q–B2	Q–B2
16 Q–R2	N–R4

Trying to get some counterplay on the K-side.

17 P–N3	....

Preventing 17 ..., QN–B5. White can afford this slight weakening thanks to the defensive duo PKB3, PKN3 which he has in mind.

17	B–R6
18 RxR	RxR
19 R–N1	RxRch
20 BxR!	....

So as to meet 20 ..., Q–Q2 with 21 P–B3.

After 20 QxR?, Q–Q2! White would lack a satisfactory defense to the double threat of 21 ..., QxP and 21 ..., Q–N5.

| 20 .... | B–N5 |

Preventing 21 P–B3.

| 21 K–B1 | .... |

Heading for P–B3.

| 21 .... | N–B3 |
| 22 N–N1 | P–KR4 |

Unable to forestall the said duo, Black is planning to destroy it.

| 23 Q–N3 | Q–B1 |
| 24 K–K1 | .... |

White plans to bring his King to QR3, removing it from the danger zone and charging it with the protection of PQR4 so that his Queen and Knight become available for penetration on QN6. A strong plan it is.

24	P–R5
25 B–Q3	B–Q2
26 P–B3	N–R4
27 N–K2	PxP
28 PxP	B–K1

Preparing for ... Q–R6.

| 29 K–Q1 | K–B1 |

Not 29 . . . , Q–R6 because of 30 Q–N8 followed by 31 NxQP. But now that his Q-Bishop is protected Black does threaten 30 . . . , Q–R6.

| | 30 P–N4 | . . . . |

The duo is no longer important. In giving it up this way White definitely stops all counterplay.

| 30 . . . . | N(4)–B5 |
| 31 NxN | PxN |

After 31 . . . , NxN; 32 BxN, PxB Black faces the additional danger of P–K5 (although the immediate 33 P–K5 is ineffective because of 33 . . . , Q–B2).

| 32 K–B2 | Q–Q1 |

So far the tough fight has gone well for White; he has a considerable advantage. However, he now abruptly loses owing to confusion in time pressure.

| 33 N–N6? | . . . . |

Senselessly deviating from the planned K–N2–R3.

| 33 . . . . | N–K4! |
| 34 BxRP?? | . . . . |

Leaving PKB3 en prise, which is disastrous.

Correct is 34 B–K2. Then the game is even as White cannot regain the favorable position of his Knight on QB4.

34	NxBP
35 BxP	B–N4!
36 B–N3	. . . .

With 36 BxB, QxB; 37 K–N2 White can resist longer.

36	N–Q7!
37 Q–N2	NxP
38 B–K1	N–B3
39 B–K2	Q–K2
40 K–Q1	NxQP!

White resigns

VIII–§4: The Spanish Benoni PQB3, PQ5, PK4 vs PQR3, PQN4, PQB4, PQ3, PK4

This is a formation which White would do better to avoid because it offers him too little chance for lever action; he had better leave his Q-pawn on Q4 or exchange it, as is usually done. Let us discuss this formation with the following game.

LARRY EVANS   NICHOLAS ROSSOLIMO

(U.S. Open championship 1955)

1 P–K4	P–K4
2 N–KB3	N–QB3
3 B–N5	P–QR3
4 B–R4	N–B3
5 0–0	B–K2
6 R–K1	P–QN4
7 B–N3	P–Q3
8 P–B3	0–0

Less commendable is *8* ..., N–QR4; *9* B–B2, P–B4 (the Tchigorin system accelerated) because of *10* P–Q4! when *10* ..., B–N5?; *11* PxKP! necessitates *11* ..., BxN, thus clearly favoring White.

9 P–KR3   ....

At this point *9* P–Q4, B–N5! is fully satisfactory for Black since *10* PxKP does not necessitate *10* ..., BxN.

9 ....   N–QR4

A remarkable alternative is Breyer's line: *9* ..., N–N1; *10* P–Q4, QN–Q2, followed by ... P–QB3.

10 B–B2   P–B4

This is the *regular Tchigorin system* of defense.
Remarkable is Lombardy's *10* ..., P–B3, which combines the

ideas of Tchigorin and Breyer; Black prepares for . . . Q–B2 and keeps . . . Q4 protected against invasion.

11 P–Q4   Q–B2

11 . . . , BPxP; *12* PxP, Q–B2, what might be called the *Exchange defense*, opens the QB-file, thereby creating an Open Benoni. In doing so, Black anticipates the *Exchange attack* consisting of QPxKP or QPxBP, when White opens the Q-file. There is no proof, however, that . . . BPxP was necessary.

12 QN–Q2   N–B3
13 P–Q5   . . . .

This completes the *Spanish Benoni* formation, which is of no promise for White.

More usual today is the Exchange attack, which offers White a slight initiative: *13* PxBP, PxP; *14* N–B1, possibly followed by N–K3–Q5; or *13* P–QR4, R–N1; *14* RPxP, RPxP; *15* PxBP, etc.

13 . . . .   N–Q1

This is the main version of the Spanish Benoni.

DIAGRAM 163

Position after 13 . . . N–Q1

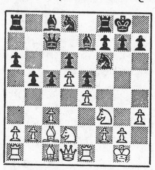

Spanish Benoni; main version

14 P–QR4   . . . .

The only sound lever White has at his disposal; it is his most reliable continuation.

14	R–N1

The square QB4 is more important than the QR-file.

After *14* ..., P–N5?; *15* N–B4, P–QR4 White has the edge, his best continuation being *16* B–K3 and *17* KN–Q2, according to Alekhine, but not *16* KNxP, B–R3; *17* B–N3, PxN; *18* P–Q6, BxP; *19* QxB, QxQ; *20* NxQ (Capablanca—Vidmar, New York 1927) when Black gets a satisfactory game with *20* ..., R–N1.

15 P–B4	....

Should White thus close the Q-side or rather open the QR-file? The answer depends on one's assessment of White's chances on the K-side. We consider these chances slightly inferior and believe, therefore, that White should open the file. Thus *15* PxP, PxP; *16* P–B4!, P–N5!; *17* N–B1, N–K1; *18* P–N4, P–N3, e.g.

(1) *19* B–R6!?, N–KN2; *20* N–K3, P–B3; *21* K–N2, N–B2!; *22* BxN, KxB; *23* N–Q2, R–KR1!; *24* N(2)–B1, P–R4! with a good game for Black (Bogolyubov—Rubinstein, Berlin 1926; compare Ivkov—Bisguier);

(2) *19* N–N3, N–N2; *20* K–R1, P–B3; *21* N–R2, N–B2; *22* R–KN1, B–Q2; *23* B–K3, R–R1; *24* Q–Q2, RxR! with equality (Nilsson—Gruenfeld, game by mail, 1937).

15	P–N5!
16 K–R2	N–K1
17 P–N4	P–N3
18 R–KN1	P–B3
19 N–B1	N–B2
20 N–N3	....

The game Bogolyubov—Rubinstein, Breslau 1925, proceeded with *20* N–K3, K–R1; *21* P–N3, R–N1; *22* B–N2, B–B1; *23* P–R4, Q–K2; *24* R–N2, B–R3; it took a similar course except that ... P–B4 was played much later.

20	N–N2

The situation is of a type where the Benoni jump might work, having the effect of a lever. Black must be careful.

21 P–N3   B–Q2

The game Keres–Vidmar, Bad Nauheim 1936, went on with 21 ..., R–N2; 22 B–Q2, K–R1; 23 Q–K2, B–Q1; 24 R–N2, Q–Q2; 25 R–R1, Q–K1. Black's play in this case is not exactly faulty but it lacks the logical aiming at the lever thrust... P–B4. Small wonder that White finally won.

22 B–K3	K–R1
23 Q–Q2	QR–K1
24 R–N2	Q–B1
25 R–R1	....

There is nothing exceptional in White's play; he has followed conventional lines.

Exceptional however is the consistency and economy with which Black has been striving for his basic lever thrust. He now strikes.

DIAGRAM 164

Position after 25 R–R1

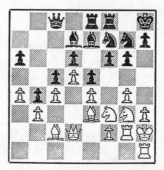

Black strikes

25 ....   P–B4!

This logical move, logically prepared, demonstrates the draw-backs of White's setup. Black obtains a slight edge.

26	NPxP	PxP
27	PxP	NxP
28	NxN	BxN
29	R(R)-KN1	....

A little trap: 29 ..., BxP??; 30 Q-Q3! and White wins.

29	....	R-N1

For the sake of ..., P-B4 Black has even refrained from making this move earlier, as is usually done.

30	N-N5	NxN
31	BxN	KBxB
32	RxB	BxB
33	QxB	RxR
34	RxR	....

This position is even, the backwardness of White's KB-pawn notwithstanding, for the reduced material offers Black no chances for attack. Nor has White such a chance, but in the game itself he did proceed aggressively and lost.

BORIS IVKOV   ARTHUR BISGUIER

Yugoslavia   United States

(From the 1950 team match by radio)

1 P-K4, P-K4; 2 N-KB3, N-QB3; 3 B-N5, P-QR3; 4 B-R4, N-B3; 5 0-0, B-K2; 6 P-Q3, P-Q3; 7 P-B3, 0-0; 8 R-K1, K-R1; 9 P-Q4, P-QN4; 10 B-B2, B-N5; 11 P-Q5, N-QR4; 12 QN-Q2, P-B4; 13 N-B1 (A typical Spanish Benoni. Instead, 13 PxP e.p. transposes to a line very similar to the Sicilian ram system.) 13 ..., N-N2; 14 P-KR3, B-Q2; 15 P-KN4, Q-B1; 16 N-N3, P-N3; 17 K-N2, N-K1; 18 B-R6, N-N2; 19 Q-K2, P-B3;

20 N–Q2, N–Q1; 21 N(2)–B1, N–B2 (By and large everything according to pattern.) 22 BxNch? (A typical error. White would rarely fare well in parting with his good Bishop this way. Correct is 22 B–Q2. Then, 22 ..., P–B4 is premature because of 23 KPxP, PxP; 24 P–KB4! when 24 ..., PxNP?? fails against 25 Q–K4!.) 22 ..., KxB; 23 N–K3, P–B5; 24 R–R1, B–Q1; 25 P–QR4? (The opening of the QR-file favors Black under the circumstances.) 25 ..., B–N3; 26 R–QR2, R–QN1; 27 PxP, PxP; 28 KR–R1, R–KR1!

Here we come to the purpose of this example. Black is aiming at lever action with ... P–R4.

However, he does not threaten 29 ..., P–R4 because of 30 PxP, BxPch; 31 K–N1 when the inevitable elimination of ... PKN3 nets White the dominating square KB5.

29 R–KN1?   ....

But this unfortunate move paves the way for Black's action.

DIAGRAM 165

Position after 29 R–KN1?

Lever attack with ..., P–KR4

29 ....   P–R4!

Perfect and decisive as White cannot gain control of KB5.

30 P–B3   ....

After *30* PxP, BxPch; *31* K–R2 (*31* K–B3, N–N4 mate)
31 ..., BxN; *32* QxB, B–N5 Black wins the R-pawn while maintaining his KN-pawn in its vital position (*33* B–Q1, N–N4!).

30	PxP
31 RPxP	....

Or *31* BPxP, N–N4; *32* R–KR1, R–R5, and the R-pawn falls.

The game has become a rather simple affair: *31* ..., Q–B4;
32 N(N)–B1, N–N4; *33* R–KR1, RxR; *34* KxR, R–R1ch;
35 K–N2, R–R6; *36* R–R1, Q–B1! (Even stronger than *36* ...,
RxP.) *37* N–R2, RxNch! (...Q–KR1!!) *38* KxR, Q–R1ch;
39 K–N2, N–R6!; *40* K–N3, N–B5; *41* Q–R2 (Desperation.)
41 ..., QxQch; *42* KxQ, BxN and Black won.

VIII–§5: The Blitz Benoni PQ5, PK4 vs PQB4, PQ3

This is a Part Benoni formation which normally arises as
follows: *1* P–Q4, N–KB3; *2* P–QB4, P–B4; *3* P–Q5, P–K3;
4 N–QB3, PxP; *5* PxP, P–Q3; *6* P–K4. Characterized by opposing majorities it usually leads to very sharp play focused at the
duo-move P–K5. Appropriate measures on behalf of this move
or against it are of paramount importance.

Most consistent on White's part is the extension of his pawn
front to PQ5, PK4, PKB4—a classical concept, recently re-ana-
lyzed and strongly recommended by Al Horowitz. However,
this concept is also a very committing one, and there is the
warning example of Euwe's Blitz formation (*Diagram 120*) at
the far end of it.

A question of major importance is the development of both
K-Bishops. Black obviously must rely on ... B–KN2, for he
would otherwise have no chance to prevent P–K5 for long. But
White's B–KN2, although frequently adopted, is poorly moti-
vated; it costs an extra tempo, thereby reducing the chance for
P–K5, and this while the Bishop's activity depends exclusively
on P–K5; and it facilitates Black's key move ... P–QN4.

The following examples need little further comment.

AKIBA RUBINSTEIN   JACQUES MIESES

(From the tournament at Bad Kissingen 1928)

1	P–Q4	P–QB4
2	P–Q5	P–Q3
3	P–QB4	....

Skipping the strong Benoni Minor.

3	....	P–KN3
4	P–KN3	....

Rather harmless. Black now should strive for the Major (...P–K4), Blitz (...P–K3) or Wing Benoni (...N–QR3).

4	....	B–N2
5	B–N2	N–KB3
6	P–K4	0–0
7	N–K2	QN–Q2?

But Black pins down his K-pawn rather than moving it, thus losing precious time.

8	P–B4	N–N3
9	Q–B2	....

More accurate is 9 Q–Q3.

9	....	P–K3
10	0–0	PxP

Better 10 ..., R–K1, as White then cannot proceed with 11 QN–B3.

11	BPxP	....

A typical Blitz Benoni—badly misplayed by Black so that White holds a clear advantage, in spite of his fianchetto.

DIAGRAM 166

Position after 11 BPxP

Misplayed by Black

| | 11 .... | R–K1 |

More urgent is *11 ...*, QN–Q2 so this Knight would no longer interfere with Black's majority.

| | 12 QN–B3 | B–N5 |

Starting a suicidal action.

	13 P–KR3	BxN
	14 NxB!	Q–K2
	15 N–B3	N–R4
	16 K–R2	BxN
	17 PxB	N–B3
	18 P–B4!	NxKP

Black thinks he has won a pawn while he virtually has indulged in disastrous pawn snatching.

| | 19 B–N2 | P–KR3 |

Or *19 ...*, N–B3; *20* Q–B3!, QN–Q2; *21* QR–K1, Q–Q1; *22* P–N4, and White wins.

| | 20 QR–K1 | P–B4 |
| | 21 P–N4! | .... |

A murderous lever.

21	K–R2
22 PxP	PxP
23 R–KN1	R–KN1
24 BxN	Resigns

ISAAC KASHDAN SVETOZAR GLIGORICH

(From a tournament in Hollywood, 1952)

1 P–Q4	N–KB3
2 P–QB4	P–KN3
3 N–KB3	B–N2
4 P–KN3	P–B4
5 B–N2	0–0
6 0–0	P–Q3
7 N–B3	N–B3
8 P–Q5	....

More modest but steady is 8 P–K3, while 8 PxP is safe and dull.

| 8 .... | N–QR4 |

A rather new line of Yugoslav origin. The Knight is well placed, contrary to appearance.

| 9 N–Q2 | P–QR3 |
| 10 Q–B2? | .... |

A loss of time. Correct is 10 P–QR3, although Black has the satisfactory replies of either 10 ..., Q–B2 or 10 ..., P–N3.

10	P–K3
11 P–K4	PxP
12 BPxP	....

12 KPxP leads to an Open Benoni with Black for choice (12 ..., B–B4!). Note how the Benoni ram hampers White's K-Bishop.

| 12 .... | P–QN4 |

Another typical Blitz Benoni—but this one is misplayed by White, whose ineffective B–N2 and weak Q–B2 together amount

to as much as a serious error. Black has a clear advantage thanks
to his advanced majority and preparedness against P–K5.

DIAGRAM 167

Position after 12 ..., P–QN4

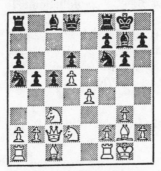

Misplayed by White

13 R–K1   ....

The more desirable *13* P–N3 fails against *13* ..., P–N5. The
same at White's next turn.

13	R–K1
14 N–B1	R–R2!
15 P–B3	QR–K2
16 B–K3	N–B5

Black obviously has a winning position.

17 B–B2   ....

Losing by force. Only *17* N–Q1 holds for the moment.

17	NxNP!!
18 QxN	P–N5
19 N–Q1	NxKP!
20 Q–B1	....

White should rather try 20 QxBch and 21 PxN.

20	....	NxB!
21	RxR	QxR
22	NxN	B–Q5!!

The last point of Black's combination. He threatens 23 ...,
Q–K7.

23	K–R1	BxN
24	R–N1	B–B4
25	R–N3	B–Q5

White resigns

MARK TAIMANOV   PETAR TRIFUNOVICH

USSR   Yugoslavia

(Team match 1957)

1	P–Q4	N–KB3
2	P–QB4	P–B4
3	P–Q5	P–K3
4	N–QB3	PxP

The system White adopts in this game raises the question of
whether the text move can be postponed until White has moved
his K-Bishop, so that B–N5ch is eliminated. For instance 4 ...,
P–Q3; 5 P–K4, P–KN3; 6 P–B4, B–N2; 7 N–B3, 0–0; 8 B–Q3,
PxP; 9 BPxP, Q–N3, which transposes to *Diagram 120*.

However, this is not the place for a closer investigation of this
opening problem.

5	PxP	P–Q3
6	P–K4	....

Also 6 N–B3, P–KN3; 7 P–K4, B–N2; 8 B–Q3 (Evans–Lombardy, New York 1955) is a good continuation, definitely preferable to the fianchetto of White's K-Bishop.

However, the text move has more immediate significance. For one thing, White's K-Bishop is ready for action.

                6 ....   P–KN3

The conventional continuation. There is strong indication, however, that ... P–QR3 must be interpolated either here or at Black's next turn. No time is lost with ... P–QR3, since the threat of ... P–QN4 necessitates P–QR4.

                7 P–B4   ....

This is White's most energetic line of play. It holds promise, but is risky, too. Adopted in this sequence of moves it has hardly been tested so far.

                7 ....   B–N2?

At this point the interpolation of 7 ..., P–QR3 is strictly necessary. After 8 P–QR4, B–N2 Black is definitely better off than in the game, no matter what else happens. The same after 8 P–K5, N–R4.

                8 B–N5ch!   ....

This check causes disorder in Black's ranks.

DIAGRAM 168

Position after 8 B–N5ch!

Disorder in Black's ranks

                8 ....   KN–Q2

Otherwise 9 P–K5 is too strong, e.g. 8 ..., QN–Q2; 9 P–K5, N–R4; 10 P–K6, Q–R5ch; 11 K–B1, N–N6ch; 12 PxN and White wins; or 8 ..., B–Q2; 9 P–K5, N–R4; 10 N–B3 with a decisive advantage for White, the main point being that Black, after the exchange of his Q-Bishop, has too much trouble in preventing P–KN4.

$$9 \text{ B–Q3!} \qquad \ldots$$

The immediate retreat of the Bishop is important, for White wants to meet 9 ..., P–QR3 with 10 P–QR4.

$$9 \ldots \qquad 0–0$$

The damage suffered by Black amounts at least to the loss of one move which in this tense situation is of great significance. White's pawn center becomes a dominant factor. We do not believe that essential improvements for Black can be found in the rest of the game.

10 N–B3, N–R3; 11 0–0, N–B2; 12 N–Q2, N–B3; 13 P–KR3, R–K1; 14 Q–B3, R–N1; 15 P–QR4, N–R3; 16 N–B4, N–QN5; 17 B–N1, P–QR3; 18 P–R5, B–B1; 19 P–B5!, B–K2; 20 PxP, BPxP; 21 P–K5!, PxP; 22 P–Q6!, BxQP; 23 NxB, QxN; 24 N–K4!, and Black resigned.

VIII–§6: The Wing Benoni PQ5 vs PQN4, PQB4, PQ3, PK2

This is another Part Benoni formation. Its design is to converge pressure against White's Q-side for which purpose Black fianchettoes his K-Bishop and plays ... P–QN4 thus normally getting the half-open QN-file.

Since B–KN2 facilitates ... P–QN4, the Wing Benoni can be considered as a typical reaction to the fianchetto of White's K-Bishop, although it does not necessarily depend on it.

Black's K-pawn moves only one square if at all.

Since the moves ... P–QN4 and ... P–K3 also appear in the Blitz Benoni, it is necessary to realize the difference between the two systems. In the Wing Benoni Black does not create opposing majorities as he does in the Blitz Benoni; he plays

... P–QN4 for the purpose of creating a lever; and he would not move his K-pawn unless later developments may indicate ... P–K3.

For instance: *1* P–Q4, N–KB3; *2* P–QB4, P–KN3; *3* P–KN3, B–N2; *4* B–N2, 0–0; *5* N–QB3, P–Q3; *6* N–B3, P–B4; *7* P–Q5, N–R3; *8* N–Q2, N–B2; *9* Q–B2, R–N1; *10* P–N3, P–QN4, with about even chances (Reshevsky–Gligorich, Switzerland 1953).

The following game is a typical Wing Benoni.

OLAF BARDA   BORIS SPASSKY

(From the Bucharest 1953 tournament)

1 P–Q4	N–KB3
2 N–KB3	P–B4
3 P–Q5	....

This might be called the Semi-Indian type of the Benoni. It offers White a little more choice than the Indian type (*2* P–QB4) but a little less than the Benoni proper (*1* ..., P–QB4).

3	P–KN3
4 P–KN3	....

The fianchetto is harmless. More commendable is *4* N–B3, leading to a version of the Benoni Minor, or at least *4* P–B4.

4	B–N2
5 B–N2	0–0
6 0–0	P–Q3
7 P–KR3	....

A waste of time. Indicated under the circumstances is *7* P–B4.

7	P–QN4!

An indirect lever action. Intending to attack the Q-pawn, Black anticipates P–QB4 so that ... P–K3 must become very effec-

tive. Consequently, efforts on White's part to destroy the duo
... PQN4, PQB4 can be expected. And in this way the text move
provokes the lever that the Wing Benoni requires.

8 P–QR4   ....

A little better is 8 P–B4, B–N2; 9 KN–Q2, although Black
still obtains strong counterplay: 9 ..., N–R3!; 10 P–K4 (10 PxP,
N–B2!); 10 ..., N–B2; 11 N–QB3, B–QR3; 12 Q–K2, R–N1.

8	B–N2
9 N–R2	....

There is no convenient protection to the Q-pawn.

The alternative of 9 P–B4, PxBP; 10 N–B3, P–K3; 11 P–K4,
when White threatens to obtain a fine game with N–Q2xP, leads
after 11 ..., NxKP!; 12 NxN, BxP to the opposite, Black holding
ample compensation for the piece.

9	P–QR3
10 PxP	PxP

The Wing Benoni is completed. By way of exception the exchange of pawns has opened the QR-file instead of the QN-file.
But that is rather an improvement for Black inasmuch as his
pressure is focused on QR1, the square that White needs for contesting the vertical.

11 RxR	BxR
12 N–R3	Q–Q2
13 P–N3	....

After 13 P–QB4, PxP; 14 NxP, Q–N4 White is handicapped
by the backwardness of his QN-pawn.

13	N–R3
14 B–N2	N–B2
15 P–K4	B–N2
16 Q–K2	R–R1

Threatening to win a pawn with *17* ..., KNxQP!; *18* BxB, KxB; *19* PxN, RxN. Black has the edge, holding all the assets which the Wing Benoni has to offer.

DIAGRAM 169

Position after 16 ..., *R–R1*

The assets of the Wing Benoni

17 B–B1	R–R2
18 P–KB4	....

White would like to get in P–B4 and P–K5.

18	P–K3!
19 P–B4	P–N5
20 N–B2	PxP!

This exchange destroys White's lever chance in the center.

21 KPxP	....

Not *21* BPxP because of *21* ..., B–QR3.

21	R–R7!

With a strong threat.

22 P–N4?	....

Overlooking the threat. White has a bad game, indeed, but 22 R–B2 holds for the time being (22 ..., KNxQP?; 23 Q–Q3!!).

| 22 .... | KNxQP!! |
| 23 PxN | .... |

There is nothing better (23 Q–Q3, B–QR3!).

23	B–QR3
24 Q–Q1	BxR
25 BxB	....

Preventing the powerful 25 ..., N–N4, at the expense of another pawn though. Black won as follows:

25 ..., NxP!; 26 QxN, RxN; 27 B–K3, Q–K3!; 28 Q–R8ch, B–B1; 29 B–B2, QxP; 30 P–N5, R–B8!; 31 K–N2, Q–R6; 32 Q–Q5, R–R8!; 33 N–N4, Q–R1!; 34 B–B4, B–N2; 35 QxQch, RxQ; 36 N–B6ch, BxN; 37 PxB, R–R6; 38 B–K1, P–N6; 39 B–B3, R–R7ch; 40 K–B3, R–B7, and White resigned.

VIII–§7: The Gambit Benoni PQR2, PQN2, PQ5, PK4 vs PQB4, PQ3, PK2

Although our discussions are limited to materially balanced formations, in dealing with Benoni formations we must also mention this gambit. The following game demonstrates Black's idea.

T. D. VAN SCHELTINGA   KAREL OPOCENSKY

(From the team tournament at Buenos Aires 1939)

1 P–Q4	N–KB3
2 P–QB4	P–KN3
3 N–QB3	P–B4
4 P–Q5	P–Q3
5 P–K4	P–QN4

The key move of the Gambit Benoni.

6	PxP	B–KN2
7	N–B3	0–0
8	B–K2	P–QR3

The necessary follow-up of the gambit move. Black must eliminate PQN5.

9	0–0	PxP
10	BxP	Q–N3
11	N–Q2	B–QR3
12	N–B4	Q–N2
13	BxB	QxB

This position is typical of the Gambit Benoni. In controlling the void QR-file and the half-open QN-file Black holds considerable compensation for the pawn. We believe however that White's material advantage must tell in the long run.

(A somewhat similar position was reached by accident in the famous Nimzovich–Capablanca game of St. Petersburg 1914; Black won.)

DIAGRAM 170

Position after 13 ..., QxB

Typical of the Gambit Benoni

14 Q–K2   ....

Not a good idea, for White protects the Knight but pins it at the same time. He should proceed with *14 N–K3*.

14	QN–Q2
15 B–K3	....

Much more urgent is *15 R–K1* as a preparation for *16 N–K3* (*15 N–K3?*, QxQ; *16* NxQ, NxKP!).

15	KR–N1

Black has a perfectly developed game. He now threatens *16 ...*, N–N3; *17* NxN, QxQ; *18* NxQ, RxN, recovering the pawn favorably.

16 QR–N1?	....

White again misses *16 KR–K1*, and falls into serious trouble.

16	N–K1!

Threatening even to win the pinned Knight.

17 KR–K1?	....

Too late now, as it fails to parry the main threat. White must try *17 B–Q2*.

17	BxN!
18 PxB	RxR

White resigns (in view of *19* RxR, N–K4).

VIII–§8: The Rex Benoni PQB4, PQ5, PK4 vs PQB2, PQ3, PK4

This Part Benoni formation is the most important member of the Benoni family. It is distinctly featured by the state of the square...QB4; open as this square is it invites Black to ...N–QB4, and White to P–QB5. Indeed, the latter move would not easily occur but, still, more easily than in any other Benoni formation.

We distinguish between the plain Rex Benoni (... PKN2) and the extended Rex Benoni (... PKN3).

The extended Rex Benoni occurs most frequently. White's best chance for lever action then is the St. George attack; the threat of P–KR4–R5 usually leads to other levers, depending on Black's counterplay, which normally is based on ... P–KB4. For the rest, particularly in the plain Rex Benoni, White must aim at P–QB5, a good chance for P–B4 being rather exceptional.

The Rex Benoni often leads to the Benoni Major (after ... P–QB4) and sometimes to an open Benoni (after the elimination of PQB4 vs PQB2 resulting from either ... P–QB3 or P–QB5).

Following are some examples.

SALO FLOHR   EVFIM BOGOLYUBOV

(From the tournament at Sliac 1932)

1 P–Q4, N–KB3; *2* P–QB4, P–KN3; *3* N–QB3, B–N2; *4* P–K4, P–Q3; *5* N–B3, 0–0; *6* B–K2, QN–Q2; *7* 0–0, P–K4; *8* P–Q5, N–B4; *9* N–Q2, P–QR4; *10* Q–B2.

Diagram 171

Position after 10 Q–B2

Extended Rex Benoni—Conservative

This is the conservative line of play for both sides.

Given the time White would slowly make progress on the Q-side playing P–QN3, P–QR3, P–QN4 and P–QB5. He would then find targets in . . . PQB2 and/or . . . PQ3, and might even get a chance of taking the K-side under fire via the seventh rank.

However, the fighting rarely takes this course as the indicated counter-thrust . . . P–KB4 creates sharp complications on the K-side; only if the tension there somehow dies down may White resume his activities on the Q-side.

10	B–N5

Trading the white-bound Bishops is not as unfavorable as it may seem, for Black envisages the ensuing change of the pawn formation with its repercussions on the relative value of the Bishops.

Other possibilities are:

(1) *10* . . . , KN–Q2?!; *11* N–N3, P–B4; *12* PxP!

    (1a) *12* . . . , RxP?;   *13* B–K3!,   P–N3   (*13* . . . , NxN; *14* PxN!) *14* B–N4!, R–B1; *15* NxN, NxN; *16* BxB, QxB; *17* BxN, NPxB; *18* N–K4, and Black suffers from grave leucopenia (M. Luckis–D. Byrne, radio match La Plata–Manhattan Chess Club 1947);

    (1b) *12* . . . , PxP; *13* P–B4, and Black is more cramped than in the text line;

(2) *10* . . . , P–R5 (A remarkable idea of Euwe's; Black provokes P–QN4, at the same time weakening its effect.) *11* R–N1;

    (2a) *11* . . . , N–K1?; *12* P–QN4, PxP e.p.; *13* PxP, B–Q2; *14* P–QN4, N–R5; *15* NxN, BxN; *16* Q–B3, B–Q2; *17* P–B5, P–B4; *18* P–B3, and White has the edge (Euwe–Christoffel, Zaandam 1946);

    (2b) *11* . . . , B–R3!; this puts pressure on PK4 thus keeping the chances approximately in the balance; after *12* P–QN4, PxP e.p.; *13* PxP, B–Q2; *14* P–QN4, N–R5; *15* NxN, BxN; *16* Q–Q3, B–Q2; *17* P–B5, R–R7 the QR-file is rather an asset for Black.

11 N–N3	BxB
12 QxB	QN–Q2

Or *12* ..., NxN; *13* PxN, N–Q2; *14* B–K3, with a slight edge
for White.

13	B–K3	P–R3
14	N–B1	N–R2
15	N–Q3	....

As usual in a Benoni formation, the Knight is well placed on
Q3, for it controls the duo-squares QN4, QB5, K5 and KB4.

15	....	P–KB4

The indicated lever.

16	PxP	....

The normally indicated reply.

Instead, *16* P–B3, P–B5 is a pattern of play which usually
favors Black thanks to lever attack with ... P–KN4–N5. Compare
Szabo–Spassky.

16	....	PxP

It is vital to deny White the square K4.

17	P–B4	....

A strong move, typical of the Rex Benoni.

17	....	P–K5

Black cannot allow *18* PxP, as he then remains either with the
isolated ... PKB4 or with a highly vulnerable duo, to say nothing
of the majority he faces on the Q-side.

The text move however concedes to White the dominating
square Q4 (which would not be the case in any other Benoni
formation).

18	N–B2	BxN??

A very weak move which fatally compromises the position of
Black's King.

A. Becker recommends *18 . . . , N–B4; 19 P–KN4, Q–K2; 20 PxP, QR–K1; 21 BxN, PxB; 22 QNxP, B–Q5*, which offers Black strong counterplay.

Also *18 . . . , K–R1; 19 P–KN4, PxP* is a reasonable continuation, e.g. *20 QxP??, BxN!;* or *20 NxNP, Q–R5; 21 NxKP?!, QR–K1;* or *20 QN(KN)xKP, QN–B3.*

What now follows is slaughter: *19 PxB, KN–B3; 20 P–KN4, K–R1; 21 P–N5, N–KN1; 22 K–R1, Q–K1; 23 R–KN1, Q–N3; 24 PxP, QxP; 25 R–N3, KN–B3; 26 R–R3*, and Black resigned.

LASZLO SZABO   BORIS SPASSKY

(From the tournament at Bucharest 1953)

1	P–Q4	N–KB3
2	P–QB4	P–Q3
3	N–KB3	P–KN3
4	N–B3	B–N2
5	P–K4	0–0
6	B–K2	P–K4

So as to proceed with *7 . . . , N–B3*, which offers Black more scope than the conservative . . . QN–Q2 (see Flohr–Bogolyubov).
6 . . . , N–B3 at once is inaccurate because of *7 P–Q5.*

7 0–0   . . . .

After *7 P–Q5* Black has a choice; he can proceed conservatively with *7 . . . , QN–Q2*, or satisfactorily transpose to the Benoni Major with *7 . . . , P–B4 (8 PxP e.p.?!, PxP!).*
7 PxP is of no promise because of the portentous weakness of the square Q4.

7	. . . .	N–B3
8	P–Q5	. . . .

Reshevsky, in three games against Najdorf, proceeded with *8 B–K3*. In the first and second of these (match 1953) White

got the edge after 8 ..., N–KN5; 9 B–N5, P–B3; 10 B–B1. In
the third game however (Zurich 1953) Black found the reply
that radically equalizes: 8 ..., R–K1!; 9 P–Q5, N–Q5!; 10 NxN,
PxN; 11 BxP, NxKP; 12 BxB, KxB; 13 NxN, RxN; 14 Q–B2,
R–K1, and a draw was agreed upon.

8	N–K2
9 N–K1	N–Q2

Black uses his Knights more economically and effectively
than in the conservative line (Flohr–Bogolyubov).

10 B–K3   ....

With a popular but unfortunate idea.

Two remarkable ideas have been adopted in two games of
the 1954 USA–USSR match: 10 N–Q3, P–KB4;

(1) 11 PxP!, PxP; 12 P–B4, P–K5; 13 N–B2 (Evans–Taimanov);
the same line of play as in Flohr–Bogolyubov, probably a
little less effective, owing to Black's more economical setup,
but still very reasonable; indeed, White obtained a satisfactory game, but he lost, owing to the unnecessary acceptance
of a sacrifice;

(2) 11 P–B3, P–B5; 12 B–Q2, P–KN4; 13 R–B1, R–B3;
14 P–B5!?, NxBP; 15 NxN, PxN; 16 N–R4, P–N3; 17 P–QN4,
PxP; 18 BxNP, B–B1 (Taimanov–Evans); White has a rather
good compensation for his positional pawn sacrifice, but he
lost owing to a faulty combination: 19 RxP?, N–B4!!.

10	P–KB4
11 P–B3	P–B5
12 B–B2	P–KN4
13 P–QN4?	....

Both sides are striving for their respective head-duo: PQB5,
PQ5 vs PKB5, PKN5. However, this pattern of play spells trouble
for White as it gravely imperils his King. There is plenty of ex-

perience to the point, the most recent example being Reshevsky–
Lombardy, U.S. championship 1958.

Bad as the outlook for White may be, *13* N–Q3 serves at any
rate better than the unnecessary text move; e.g. *13* ..., R–B3;
14 P–B5, R–N3; *15* PxP, PxP; *16* N–N5; or *13* ..., N–KB3;
14 P–B5, N–N3; *15* R–B1, R–B2; *16* PxP, PxP; *17* N–N5. In
these cases White has a fair chance to hold his own.

13	R–B3
14 N–Q3	R–N3
15 P–B5	N–KB3
16 Q–N3	K–R1
17 KR–B1	P–N5!

This superior duo-lever decides the issue. Black has a winning
attack.

DIAGRAM 172

Position after 17 ..., P–N5!

The superior duo-lever

18 PxNP	BxP
19 B–B1	....

Slightly better is *19* Q–Q1.

19	B–B6!
20 Q–B4	BxP!

A little combination to the effect of another lever. Black opens the KN-file.

21	BxB	P–B6
22	N–K1	....

White can better try 22 B–N3, PxB; 23 R–B2.

22	....	PxB
23	NxP	B–R3
24	R–B2	Q–KN1
25	B–N3	....

An attempt at stemming the tide with a plug.

25	....	RxB!
26	PxP	PxP
27	Q–B7	....

After 27 PxR, QxP White is helpless against 28 ..., N–N5.

27	....	R–N2
28	QxQP	N–N5
29	K–R1	R–Q1

White resigned

AARON NIMZOVICH   SAVIELLY TARTACOVER

(From the Karlsbad 1929 tournament)

1 P–Q4, N–KB3; 2 P–QB4, P–KN3; 3 P–B3, B–N2; 4 P–K4, P–Q3; 5 N–B3, 0–0; 6 B–K3, QN–Q2; 7 N–R3!, P–K4; 8 P–Q5, P–QR4; 9 N–B2, P–N3; 10 Q–Q2, N–B4; 11 B–N5, B–Q2; 12 P–KN4, Q–B1; 13 P–KR4!, K–R1; 14 P–R5!

These moves give an elementary idea of how dangerous the St. George attack is in the extended Rex Benoni. White has a winning position, and this while Black has committed no particular errors except that he followed the conservative line of play.

The only basic improvement of Black's play, usually adopted today, consists in an early ... P–KB4. However, no convincing results have been achieved so far, and the St. George attack stands as enemy number one of the extended Rex Benoni.

DIAGRAM 173

Position after 14 P–R5!

St. George attack beats Rex Benoni

14	PxP

Sad, but hardly worse than *14* ..., N–N1.

15 BxN	....

Still stronger is *15* 0–0–0, as suggested by Nimzovich.

15	BxB
16 RxP	....

Another winning line, suggested by Emanuel Lasker, is *16* Q–R6, B–N2; *17* QxRP.

16	B–N2
17 N–R1	P–KB3
18 Q–R2	P–R3
19 N–N3	and White won

The rest of the game is less instructive.

JAMES SHERWIN   SAMUEL RESHEVSKY

(U.S. Championship 1957-8)

1	P–Q4	N–KB3
2	P–QB4	P–KN3
3	N–QB3	B–N2
4	P–K4	P–Q3
5	P–B3	....

This is the Saemisch system in the regular sequence of moves. Its main purpose is the St. George attack, the assumption being that Black must castle on the K-side.

$$5 ....   0–0$$

The move that Black invariably makes very early so as to proceed with ... P–KB4, when the Rook belongs behind the lever pawn. Although it is dangerous to have the King on the K-side, Black may rely on ... 0–0 for the sake of counterplay.

The alternatives lead by and large to the same type of play. For instance:

(1) 5 ..., P–K4; 6 P–Q5 (a) 6 ..., 0–0 which transposes to the text (b) 6 ..., KN–Q2, so as to proceed with 7 ..., B–R3; 8 BxB, Q–R5ch and, possibly, postpone or avoid ... 0–0; this line of play, suggested by Pachman, deserves testing.

(2) 5 ..., P–B3, with the general idea of meeting P–Q5 with ... BPxQP, giving White no chance for QPxBP; some experts believe that Black is better off if he aims at the opening of the QB-file in this way.

$$6 B–K3   P–K4$$

Black can also try to solve his lever problem with ... P–QN4, which is the stratagem of the Wing Benoni. The idea of adopting this stratagem in the Rex Benoni has been introduced by Panno.

However, the results are somewhat discouraging for Black. For instance 6 ..., P–QR3; 7 B–Q3, N–B3; 8 KN–K2, R–N1; 9 P–QR3, N–Q2; 10 B–QN1, N–R2; 11 B–R2, P–QN4; 12 PxP, PxP; 13 P–QN4, and White has the edge (Botvinnik–Smyslov, match 1958, second game).

7 P–Q5   ....

Consistent with respect to the St. George attack.

A reasonable alternative is 7 KN–K2, P–B3; 8 Q–Q2. Then, if Black transposes to the Boleslavsky wall with 8 ..., PxP, his Q-pawn becomes very weak.

7 ....   N–R4

7 ..., P–B4 transposes unfavorably to the Benoni Major. See Szabo–Ivkov, VIII-§2.

8 Q–Q2   P–QR3

In playing for ... P–QN4 as well as ... P–KB4 Black only loses time.

The usual 8 ..., P–KB4 is preferable, although it leads to a good game for White two ways (a) 9 0–0–0, P–B5; 10 B–B2, B–B3; 11 KN–K2, B–R5; 12 B–N1, e.g. Geller–Gligorich, Switzerland 1953; this is a slow line of play; White must mainly rely on P–QB5 (b) 9 PxP, PxP; 10 0–0–0; this is the line usually adopted today; Black has several better moves than 10 ..., P–QR3, which leads to the text.

9 0–0–0   P–KB4

Or 9 ..., P–QN4; 10 P–B5!, with a fine game for White.

10 PxP!   PxP

Black has avoided the St. George attack, but his King is obviously still in danger.

DIAGRAM 174

Position after 10 ... , PxP

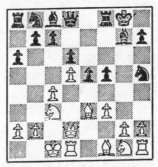

St. George attack avoided; danger remains

11	B–Q3	Q–K1
12	KN–K2	N–Q2
13	QR–K1!	K–R1
14	B–QB2	N–B4
15	P–B4!	....

White has obtained a great advantage.

$$15 .... \qquad Q–K2?$$

This loses outright. Black must try 15 ... , P–K5; 16 P–KR3, N–B3, although he then faces the dangerous P–KN4 (probably even 16 P–KN4, PxP; 17 N–N3).

$$16 \ N–N3! \qquad NxN$$

Otherwise Black loses a pawn. However, to open the KR-file for White is just as bad.

The rest is easy: 17 PxN, B–Q2; 18 P–KN4!, QR–K1; 19 PxBP, Q–B3 (Or 19 ... , BxP; 20 BxB, RxB; 21 P–KN4, KR–B1; 22 BxN, PxB; 23 P–B5! and wins.) 20 BxN, PxB; 21 N–K4, Q–QN3; (21 ... , QxP, 22 NxP!) 22 P–B6!, RxP; (The best there is.) 23 NxR, QxN; 24 PxP, RxP; 25 RxR, QxR; 26 BxP, B–KB3; 27 K–N1!, and White won.

SAVIELLY TARTACOVER   EMANUEL LASKER

(From the New York 1924 tournament)

1 P–QB4, P–K4; *2* P–QR3, N–KB3; *3* P–K3, B–K2; *4* Q–B2, 0–0; *5* N–QB3, P–Q3; *6* N–B3, R–K1; *7* B–K2, B–B1; *8* 0–0, N–B3; *9* P–Q4, B–N5; *10* P–Q5, N–K2; *11* P–R3, B–Q2; *12* N–KR2, Q–B1; *13* P–K4, N–N3.

This is a plain Rex Benoni where P–QB5 is White's clearly indicated objective. However, White now makes a basic error of which Black takes advantage in a truly classical way—the reason why we give this example.

DIAGRAM 175

Position after 13 ..., N–N3

The trouble with P–KB4??

14 P–B4??   ....

The lever move which is rarely playable with impunity in a Benoni position. (For exceptions see Flohr–Lustig, *Diagram 143;* also *4* P–KB4 in the Benoni Minor, *VIII-§3.*)

14	PxP
15 BxP	NxB

White's faulty lever action has the added drawback of permitting the elimination of his good Bishop.

16 RxN   ....

Now the issue is the stopsquare of White's backward K-pawn. Black should bring his Knight there, at the same time avoiding dangerous tacticalities as well as the strategic concession of locking in his bad K-Bishop with . . . P–KB3. Lasker solves these problems with captivating lucidity.

16	B–K2

Anticipating a possible RxN.

17 QR–KB1	R–B1

Providing extra protection for . . . PKB2, and vacating . . . K1 for the Bishop.

18 Q–Q3	B–K1

Vacating . . . Q2 for the Knight.

19 Q–KN3	Q–Q1

Parrying the threat of 20 RxN, at the same time covering the squares which the K-Bishop might need for going into action.

20 N–Q1	N–Q2

Thwarting the threatened N–K3–B5.

21 N–K3	. . . .

Losing the exchange—while White probably thought of it as a sacrifice. He has a very bad game, anyhow.

21	B–N4!
22 R–N4	. . . .

The Rook is trapped (22 R–B5, B–R5; 23 Q–N4, N–K4; 24 Q–R5, P–KN3 or 24 Q–B4, P–KN4).

22	P–KB3

Threatening 23 . . . , P–KR4 (not 23 . . . , B–R4 because of 24 RxB).

23 Q–B2	P–KR4
24 R–N3	P–R5!

After 24 ..., B–R5?; 25 RxPch!, which White probably expected, the loss of the exchange would indeed turn out as a promising sacrifice.

25 R–N4   B–R4

But not 25 ..., N–K4 because of 26 RxB.

26 N–B5   BxR
27 NxB   Q–K1
28 B–B3   N–K4, and Black won

J. H. VAN DEN BOSCH   HANS KMOCH

(Played 1941 in a tournament at Baarn, Holland)

1 P–K4, P–K4; 2 N–KB3, N–QB3; 3 B–N5, P–QR3; 4 B–R4, N–B3; 5 0–0, P–Q3; 6 P–B3, B–Q2; 7 P–Q4, B–K2; 8 P–Q5, N–N1; 9 B–B2, 0–0; 10 P–B4, B–N5; 11 N–B3, QN–Q2; 12 P–KR3, B–R4; 13 P–KN4, B–N3; 14 Q–K2.

This is a plain Rex Benoni where the situation on the K-side offers Black an extra lever. It is the same lever as in the Ivkov–Bisguier example (*Diagram 165*) but the position as a whole constitutes a type in itself, and so does the indicated procedure.

DIAGRAM 176

Position after 14 Q–K2

A type in itself

This position also occurred in the Alekhine–Johner game of the Zurich 1934 tournament. Black proceeded with *14 ...*, N–K1; *15* B–Q2, P–R3, failed to obtain a satisfactory game and lost (see *Diagram 141*).

14 ....   P–KR4!

Starting with this lever move Black obtains strong counterplay.

15 N–R4   PxP
16 PxP   N–R2

Black is going to utilize the square ... KN4, which has become a safe spot for his pieces thanks to the elimination of White's KR-pawn.

17 N–B5   B–N4

Typical for Benoni formations. Circumstances permitting, this trade of the black-bound Bishops constitutes a partial success for Black.

The move itself is not necessarily good, nor is Black's entire action. Let us exemplify that:

1 P–K4, P–K4; *2* N–KB3, N–QB3; *3* B–N5, P–Q3; *4* P–B3, B–N5; *5* P–Q3, B–K2; *6* QN–Q2, N–B3; *7* 0–0, 0–0; *8* R–K1, P–KR3; *9* N–B1, N–R2; *10* N–K3, B–R4; *11* P–KN4, B–N3; *12* N–B5, P–KR4; *13* P–KR3, PxP; *14* PxP, B–N4; *15* NxB, NxN; *16* K–N2, with a winning position for White (Capablanca–Marshall, sixth game of their 1909 match). Note these essential points all counting against Black (1) White plays QN–B5, not KN–B5 (2) Black plays ... P–KR3–R4, not ... P–KR4 at once (3) Black's intention of getting in ... KBxQB is thwarted by NxKB (4) nor is this a Benoni formation with its sharp distinction between good and bad Bishops as White's Q-pawn is placed on Q3.

18 K–N2   ....

Or *18* B–K3, B–B5!, and Black still gets the square ... KN4 for his Queen.

18 ....   BxB
19 QRxB   Q–N4
20 R–KR1?   ....

White does not have a good game, anyhow, and this move makes it worse. He should play 20 N–N3 or 20 N–K3.

| 20 .... | BxN! |
| 21 KPxN | P–KN3! |

A little move of great importance serving mainly as an aggressive lever.

| 22 P–B4 | .... |

A combination, dictated by the necessity of starting some action before it is too late.

| 22 .... | KPxP |

But not 22 ..., QxP(5) when White obtains excellent chances indeed with 23 QR–B1.

| 23 N–N4 | QR–K1 |
| 24 Q–B3 | .... |

24 NxQ, RxQch; 25 K–B3 loses because of 25 ..., RxB!.

| 24 .... | RxN |

Necessary, but at the same time powerful.

25 BxR	KN–B3
26 Q–R3	K–N2
27 B–B3	N–K4

Threatening ... PxP followed by ... PxP.

27 ..., PxP at once is premature because of 28 Q–R4!; Black is then in trouble as he cannot get connected passers (28 ..., Q–N3; 29 P–N5!).

| 28 Q–R4 | .... |

Losing both K-side pawns. A little better, although still insufficient, is 28 PxP.

28	QxQ
29 RxQ	P–KN4!
30 KR–R1	KNxNP, and Black won

Chapter IX

A VARIETY OF FORMATIONS

Formations other than Benoni require other moves but no other principles. Ram, duo, lever, and stop always have their due significance, monochromy remains a vital factor, and everything ultimately depends on the proper exchange of pawns.

The following examples illustrate some formations of major importance.

IX–§1: The two Wyvill formations

The Wyvill formation, mentioned with *Diagram 40,* may occur with the square ... QB4 open or sealed off: PQB3, PQB4, PQ4 vs PQB2, PQ3, PK4 or PQB3, PQB4, PQ4 vs PQB4, PQ3, PK4.

The difference is the same as that between the Rex formation and some other Benoni formation. We accordingly distinguish between the Rex-Wyvill (... PQB2) and the Benoni-Wyvill (... PQB4). Following is an example of each of them. We start with the more important Benoni-Wyvill.

ROBERT BYRNE   ALEXANDER KOTOV

(From the USA–USSR team match in 1954)

1	P–Q4	N–KB3
2	P–QB4	P–K3
3	N–QB3	B–N5

This is the Nimzo-Indian defense, called after its brilliant promoter Aaron Nimzovich.

It should be mentioned, however, that the Hungarian master
Dr. Joseph Noa (1856-1903) used to play this system as well as
its relative, the Queen's Indian defense, much earlier. Let us
quote, for instance, three games of the Frankfurt 1887 tournament (1) Englisch—Noa: *1* P-Q4, P-K3; *2* P-QB4, N-KB3;
3 N-QB3, B-N5; *4* N-B3, P-QN3. (2) Blackburne—Noa:
1 P-Q4, P-K3; *2* N-KB3, N-KB3; *3* P-QB4, P-QN3. (3) Zuker-
tort—Noa: *1* P-Q4, P-K3; *2* P-QB4, N-KB3; *3* P-QR3.

This latter game is particularly remarkable, for White obviously
plays *3* P-QR3 in order to prevent Noa's pet move *3* ..., B-N5.
It is the first compliment ever paid to the Nimzo-Indian defense.

Dr. Noa's experiments have been forgotten because he lacked
the strength to excel among the masters of his time. Yet, he deserves credit for his ideas.

4 P-K3	P-B4
5 B-Q3	0-0
6 P-QR3	BxNch
7 PxB	....

The QB-pawn is doubled, but the formation is not yet definite;
it depends on whether or not Black plays ... P-Q4.

7	N-B3
8 N-K2	....

Better than 8 N-B3. White is aiming at the extension of his
center with P-K4, for which purpose he may need P-B3.

8	P-QN3

Allowing 9 P-K4, which indicates Black's intention of adopting the Wyvill formation. It is indeed his best.

After 8 ..., P-Q4; 9 PxQP! Black is in trouble. He must recapture with a piece, dangerous as this is, so he can use the half-
open Q-file; only then has he a reasonable chance for counterplay. Bad is 9 ..., KPxP, because White then obtains a strong
attack on the K-side with 0-0, N-N3, P-B3, and finally P-K4;

Black's only dim chance of adequately meeting this plan consists in ... PxQP followed by a resolute use of the open QB-file.

> 9 P–K4 ....

Intending 10 B–N5, which is a strong threat, as Black would have great difficulty in shaking off the pin.

> 9 .... N–K1

Important—and not entirely passive, as this Knight might take PQB4 under fire (... N–Q3).

> 10 B–K3 ....

No good is 10 P–K5 as it offers Black the strong levers ... P–Q3 and ... P–B3.

As for P–Q5, White should postpone this advance as long as possible.

> 10 .... P–Q3

The Benoni-Wyvill formation is reached.

> 11 0–0 B–R3
> 12 N–N3 ....

Preparing for Q–K2. It is important to have available this protection of the front-twin. Protection by Q–QR4 is unreliable as it might lead to the exchange of Queens after ... Q–Q2 or ... Q–K1. In the end game White is handicapped owing to lack of chances for a K-side attack.

> 12 .... N–R4
> 13 Q–K2 R–B1

Threatening to win the front-twin.

> 14 P–Q5 ....

Necessary, as 14 QR–B1 fails against 14 ..., Q–Q2 followed by ... Q–R5.

> 14 .... Q–Q2

Again threatening to win the front-twin (15 ..., Q–R5).

> 15 P–QR4 ....

Forced, but not detrimental. Indeed, this pawn will now require care, for the time being however White is safe on the Q-side and thus ready to start action on the K-side.

15 ....   P–K4

Whereby the Benoni-Wyvill formation is completed.

DIAGRAM 177

Position after 15 ..., P–K4

Benoni-Wyvill completed

The situation is reminiscent of the Benoni Major, but there are essential differences caused by the double pawn as well as the kind and position of the minor pieces. A period of passivity lies ahead for Black as he has only very remote chances for a lever.

16 P–B4!   ....

The move which in Benoni positions usually fails (compare Diagram 175) is justified in this case.

16 ....   P–B3!

It is a wise policy to omit 16 ..., PxP. Being unable to utilize the square ... K4 quickly, Black would drift into a situation similar to Diagram 143.

17 P–B5   ....

White's only chance of making headway; he must strive for the lever-duo PKB5, PKN5. Bad is *17* PxP because of *17* ..., QPxP!, threatening *18* ..., N–Q3.

17 ....   K–B2!

Well played. Black is going to bring his King to the other wing thus frustrating White's plan.

18 R–B3!   ....

Realizing that his intended lever would work adversely under the circumstances, and that he has no other lever at his disposal, White immediately changes his plan. From now on he concentrates on the anticipation of any lever action on Black's part. For this defensive purpose his K-Rook serves better in front of the pawns.

The next part of the game is a slow motion picture.

18 ..., K–K2; *19* N–B1, K–Q1; *20* R–KR3, R–KR1; *21* P–N4, K–B2; *22* N–N3, K–N1; *23* K–B2, N–B2; *24* Q–R2, QR–N1; *25* R–KN1, Q–K2; *26* B–K2, B–B1; *27* N–B1, B–Q2; *28* N–Q2, P–KN4; *29* N–B1, B–K1; *30* N–N3, P–KR3; *31* N–R5 (Eliminating a possible ... P–KR4.) *31* ..., BxN; *32* PxB (With PKR2 exchangeable the KR-pawn is not definitely doubled.) *32* ..., N–K1; *33* B–N4 (So that ... P–KN5 would never disturb White's peace.) *33* ..., N–KN2; *34* K–K2, K–B2; *35* K–Q3, R–R1 (Black now starts preparing for the lever thrust ... P–N4.) *36* R–N1, KR–QN1; *37* R–N2, P–R3; *38* K–B2, Q–Q2; *39* R–KN3, Q–K1; *40* B–Q2, R–R2 (*40* ..., NxRP; *41* R–R3 favors White.) *41* R–R3, P–N4! (A strong forklever. Black obtains a dangerous initiative.) *42* RPxP, PxP; *43* PxP, RxP; *44* RxR, QxR; *45* P–B4!! (A brilliant saving action.) *45* ..., QxPch; *46* QxQ, NxQ; *47* BxP!! (The point.) *47* ..., NxBP! (Best. Bad for Black is *47* ..., RPxB?; *48* P–R6! as well as *47* ..., BPxB?; *48* P–B6!) *48* PxN, BPxB!; *49* P–B6, P–K5!; *50* P–B7, R–R1; *51* R–QB3!, N–K4; *52* R–QR3!, R–KB1; *53* B–K6, K–N3; *54* R–N3ch, K–B2; *55* R–QR3, and the players agreed to a draw.

EVFIM BOGOLYUBOV   MARIO MONTICELLI

(From the tournament at San Remo 1930)

1	P–Q4	N–KB3
2	P–QB4	P–K3
3	N–QB3	B–N5
4	N–B3	....

Not in harmony with the Wyvill formation, but sound at this point since *4* ..., BxNch; *5* PxB, P–B4; *6* N–Q2!, N–B3; *7* N–N3 prevents Black from taking the front-twin under fire with ... N–QR4. But even if ... N–QR4 does come in first, somehow, White can conveniently dislodge this Knight with N–QN3 relying on possible recapture with his QR-pawn.

As a rule, White is better off if he can get the Wyvill formation without playing P–QR3, which costs a tempo and weakens the square QN3.

4	....	P–QN3
5	B–N5	....

But this is double-edged. A safe and steady alternative is *5* Q–N3 (Englisch–Noa, Frankfort 1887).

5	....	BxNch

Now justified, thanks to the position of White's Q-Bishop.

6	PxB	B–N2

The setup with ... N–QR4 and ... B–R3 is less effective in the Rex-Wyvill than in the Benoni-Wyvill, for the front-twin is neither fully immobilized (so that White may play P–QB5) nor exposed to vertical pressure (so that White can avoid P–Q5).

Besides, any effective ... N–QR4 is ruled out as long as PQR2 has not moved.

7	P–K3	....

Or *7* N–Q2, P–KR3; *8* B–R4, P–Q3; *9* P–B3, QN–Q2; *10* P–K4, Q–K2; *11* B–Q3, P–KN4; *12* B–KB2, N- R4, with a good game for Black.

The single-step of the K-pawn is preferable to the double-step, for it keeps the formation more flexible.

7	....	P–Q3
8	B–Q3	QN–Q2
9	0–0	Q–K2
10	N–Q2	P–KR3
11	B–R4	....

The pawns have not yet made any contact, and the formation is of the immature type. Nevertheless the double pawn causes a distinction between White's Bishops, making his Q-Bishop more valuable. Consequently, the dubious nature of White's fifth move begins to show at this point, inasmuch as 11 BxN involves one slight concession, and the text move another.

11 ....   P–KN4!

As usual, this chase of the Q-Bishop is strong if (1) Black's pawn center firmly barricades the diagonal KR2–QN8 (2) White has castled on the K-side (3) Black has not castled on the K-side.

The chase then compels White to move one of his home-pawns, thereby enabling Black to start lever action against the King.

12 B–N3   0–0–0?!

The key move of Black's setup, but made at this point it is premature and very risky.

Desirable but not good is 12 ..., P–K4? because of the hole it creates on ... KB4. Had White played P–K4, this hole would not be accessible to White's K-Bishop and have little or no significance.

Best is 12 ..., P–KR4!; Black should make some headway on the K-side before committing himself with ... 0–0–0.

13 P–QR4   P–QR4

A weakening of the King position, but inevitable, as the lever 14 P–R5 must be prevented.

14 R–N1   QR–N1

This is a Rex-Wyvill position in the state of immaturity—actually a hybrid formation (compare *Diagram 101*). Essential contact between the pawns is in the air, though. White has a typical chance.

DIAGRAM 178

Position after 14 ..., QR–N1

Immature Rex-Wyvill

15 P–B3?   ....

But White makes a typical error instead.

Correct, strong, and of basic significance for positions of this type is the sweeper twist 15 P–B5!, which obviously offers fine attacking chances. For instance 15 ..., QPxP; 16 Q–K2, P–R4; 17 B–R6, P–R5; 18 BxBch, KxB; 19 N–B4. Starting this line with 15 Q–K2, as suggested by Panov, allows 15 ..., P–B4!. This transposition to the Benoni-Wyvill, dangerous as it may look, serves rather well, as White remains hampered by his front-twin.

15	P–R4
16 P–K4	P–R5
17 B–K1	P–K4

Black now has a fine game. His position has greatly gained in steadiness thanks to the central ram. There is only one reason for some concern: White's Knight may appear on KB5.

18 P–R3   ....

Let us parenthetically glance at *18* P–Q5??. This advance is often all right in the Benoni-Wyvill but in the Rex-Benoni it amounts to positional suicide, as Black is conceded the square ... QB4. But if White is able to seal off this square, he may consider P–Q5. For instance, if Black had a Knight on QB3 instead of on Q2, there would be sense in *18* P–Q5 because of the following sweeper-sealer twist *19* P–QB5.

18	N–R4
19 P–B5?	....

This is the sweeper-sealer twist we just mentioned, only in the other sequence of moves. However, while basically reasonable, it works poorly under the circumstances.

White should rather play *19* R–B2 and try to bring his Knight on KB5, possibly via QN3–QR1–QB2.

19	QPxP
20 P–Q5	N–B5
21 N–B4	....

Threatening *22* P–Q6, thus winning the exchange, but at the high cost of two pawns.

21	R–R3!
22 R–B2	P–B4!

A fine, intricate combination of positional tendencies.

23 P–Q6	....

White does not even try to create problems. Of course, *23* PxP, BxP favors Black even more.

The move leading to complications is *23* N–K3. We then like the following continuation, given by A. Becker: *23* ..., PxP; *24* N–B5, Q–B1; *25* NxR, PxB!; *26* NxR, P–B5!. Black is both exchanges down, but he has excellent compensation in pawns and position.

After the text move Black won as follows:

23 ..., RxP!; *24* NxRch, QxN; *25* B–B4, R–B1; *26* PxP, RxP; *27* R–Q2 (Or *27* QxQ, PxQ, and Black wins in the end-game.)

27 ..., Q–K2; *28* Q–N3, R–B1; *29* B–Q3, P–K5!; *30* BxKP, BxB; *31* PxB, QxP; (Threatening *32* ..., P–N5; *33* PxP, P–R6; *34* PxP, N–K4.) *32* Q–B2, Q–B3; *33* P–B4, P–N5; *34* BxP, PxP; *35* P–N3, N–K4!; *36* R–N3, N–K7ch!; *37* RxN, R–B8ch!; *38* KxR, Q–R8ch; *39* K–B2, N–N5 mate.

IX–§2: The Orthodox Exchange formation

This example illustrates the item we have discussed in general with *Diagrams 106-110.*

ROBERT BYRNE   ERICH ELISKASES

(From the Chess Olympics at Helsinki 1952)

1 P–Q4, P–Q4; *2* P–QB4, P–K3; *3* N–QB3, N–KB3; *4* PxP, PxP; *5* B–N5, B–K2; *6* P–K3, P–B3 (The pawn formation of *Diagram 106.*) *7* Q–B2, QN–Q2; *8* B–Q3, N–R4; *9* BxB, QxB; *10* KN–K2, N–N3; *11* 0–0, P–KN3; *12* N–R4!, NxN; *13* QxN, 0–0; *14* P–QN4, P–QR3; *15* Q–N3 (*15* P–N5?, BPxP; *16* BxQNP??, B–B4!) *15* ..., B–K3; *16* P–QR4, KR–B1; *17* Q–N2, N–N2; *18* P–N5, RPxP; *19* PxP, B–B4 (We prefer *19* ..., P–QB4. See *Diagram 109.*) *20* N–B4, BxB; *21* NxB, N–B4; *22* RxR, RxR; *23* PxP, PxP; *24* R–B1.

DIAGRAM 179

Position after 24 R–B1

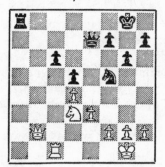

Orthodox Exchange formation

A position typical for the result of the so-called minority attack. Black's pawn formation is inferior because of dispersion into two groups and the backwardness of the QB-pawn. The disadvantage is serious but not necessarily decisive.

24 ....   N–R5

So as to meet 25 RxP with 25 ..., NxP.

25 Q–K2   R–R6

With the same intention.

26 P–N3   Q–K5
27 N–K1   N–B4
28 Q–B2!   ....

Forcing the exchange of Queens, thereby reducing Black to complete passivity.

28 ....   QxQ
29 RxQ   N–K2
30 K–B1   ....

In itself the pawn formation indicates 30 P–N4 so that Black's R-pawn would remain a target without pawn protection (30 ..., P–R4; 31 PxP!). However, there is some reason to distrust the consequences of 30 ..., R–R8.

30 ....   P–B3

The thus created duo is useful but not urgent. Urgent is 30 ..., P–R4! so this outside pawn would become the protected spearhead of a chain instead of the too remote and thus vulnerable base of a chain it is.

31 K–K2   K–B2

Again missing 31 ..., P–R4!.

32 N–Q3   ....

Threatening 33 N–N4.

32	....	K–K3
33	R–N2	R–R2

Since Black cannot hold his second rank for long, he would still be better off by playing 33 ..., P–R4.

34 P–N4!   ....

Making Black's R-pawn a permanent target. From now on Black suffers from the extra drawback that the two weak bases of his pawn formation, namely the QB-pawn and the R-pawn, are too distant from each other for proper protection by the King.

34 ....   P–N4

With the idea, it seems, of trading the R-pawn by means of ... K–B2–N3 and ... P–R4. But that requires too much effort.

35	R–N8	K–B2
36	R–KR8	K–N2

Or 36 ..., K–N3; 37 P–R3, e.g. 37 ..., R–B2; 38 K–Q2, R–B1; 39 RxR, NxR; 40 K–B3 and White wins.

37 R–Q8   R–B2

Or 37 ..., K–N3; 38 R–Q6, when 38 ..., P–R4 is prevented.

38	N–B5	K–B2
39	K–B3	N–N3
40	K–N3	R–R2
41	R–Q6	R–B2

41 ..., N–K2 loses a pawn because of 42 N–Q7, N–N1; 43 N–N8.

42	N–R6	R–B1
43	R–Q7ch	N–K2
44	N–B5	R–QR1
45	R–Q6	R–R8

A sortie that fails. However, continued passivity offers no chance against White's impending lever attack with P–R4, P–B3, and P–K4.

46 N–Q7	P–KB4
47 N–K5ch	K–N2
48 P–R3	....

Threatening (besides 49 NxP) 49 R–K6, R–R2, 50 PxP, NxPch; 51 K–N4.

| 48 .... | PxP |
| 49 PxP | R–QB8 |

Nor is 49 ..., R–R3 sufficient because of 50 R–K6, K–B1; 51 N–B3.

| 50 R–K6 | N–N3 |

Or 50 ..., K–B1; 51 N–B3. Black loses a pawn in any case.

| 51 RxP | and White won. |

IX–§3: The Sicilian ram system

Following are two examples illustrating the formation of *Diagram 111.*

SIEGBERT TARRASCH   LOUIS PAULSEN

(From the tournament at Breslau 1889)

1 P–K4	P–QB4
2 N–KB3	N–QB3
3 N–B3	N–B3
4 P–Q4	PxP
5 NxP	P–Q3
6 B–K2	....

Also worth quoting is Noa–L. Paulsen, Frankfort 1887: 6 B–K3, P–K4.

| 6 .... | P–K4 |

The Ram system—one of the fine weapons that Hephaistos Paulsen has contributed to present-day chess. His revolutionary view on the backward Q-pawn has since been accepted in general. Formations thus featured are no longer looked upon as implicitly weak and, consequently, more frequently adopted. See e.g. these two opening lines:

(1) *1* P–K4, P–K4; *2* N–KB3, N–QB3; *3* B–N5, P–QR3; *4* B–R4, N–B3; *5* 0–0, B–K2; *6* Q–K2, P–QN4; *7* B–N3, P–Q3; *8* P–B3, 0–0; *9* P–Q4, B–N5; *10* P–Q5, N–QR4; *11* B–B2, P–B4; *12* PxP e.p., NxBP, with a satisfactory game for Black (Réti—Rubinstein, Vienna 1922);

(2) *1* N–KB3, P–Q4; *2* P–B4, P–Q5; *3* P–K3, N–QB3; *4* PxP, NxP; *5* NxN, QxN; *6* N–B3, P–QB3; *7* P–Q3, P–K4; *8* B–K3, Q–Q1; *9* B–K2, N–B3; *10* 0–0, with a satisfactory game for White (Botvinnik—Flohr, USSR championship, 1944).

7 N–B3   ....

Better 7 N–N3, as is usually played today. White should be ready for P–KB3 or P–KB4.

7 ....   P–KR3!

A measure on behalf of the square ... Q4; Black prevents 8 B–KN5 in order to keep his K-Knight.

8 0–0   ....

8 B–QB4?, B–K2; *9* Q–K2, 0–0; *10* P–KR3, B–K3; *11* 0–0, R–B1; *12* B–N3, N–QR4; *13* R–Q1, Q–B2; *14* P–N4, NxB; *15* RPxN, P–R3; *16* K–R1, P–QN4; *17* P–N4, Q–B5 favors Black (Stoltz—Boleslavsky, Groningen 1946).

8 ....   B–K3
9 R–K1   ....

Another playable but harmless continuation is 9 P–QN3 (Znosko—Borovsky—H. Kramer, Zaandam 1946).

9 ....   B–K2

Not 9 ..., P–Q4 because of *10* PxP, NxP; *11* NxN, BxN; *12* NxP, NxN; *13* B–N5ch.

10 B–K3 ....

The game is in the balance, according to present-day views, but Tarrasch claimed that White had the edge and could maintain it with B–QN5–R4–N3. This maneuver however virtually leads to the Stoltz–Boleslavsky game quoted in the note under White's eighth move.

10 0–0

Now the straggler is ready to advance with impunity.

11 Q–Q2 ....

White is unable to prevent the impending lever thrust.

Diagram 180

Position after 11 Q–Q2

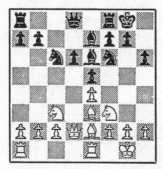

Lever thrust ... P–Q4 unpreventable

11 .... N–KN5

Paulsen yields to his exaggerated predilection for Bishops and now makes this extra effort for the sake of the exchange which he just before has prevented with ... P–KR3. Owing to this inconsistency, the backward Q-pawn really becomes a burden, but it also offers Paulsen the opportunity to display his virtuosity in handling such positions.

However, having selected this game only for the purpose of documenting Paulsen's authorship on the system, we give the rest in brief:

12 QR–Q1, NxB; *13* QxN, Q–R4; *14* P–QR3, Q–B4; *15* Q–Q2, P–R3; *16* P–QN4, Q–R2; *17* N–Q5, B–Q1!; *18* P–B4, R–B1; *19* Q–K3, P–QN3; *20* Q–Q2, Q–N2; *21* P–R3, N–K2! (So as to seal off the critical stop.); *22* N–K3, B–B2; *23* B–Q3, N–N3; *24* N–Q5, B–Q1 (*24* ..., BxN; *25* BPxB favors White.); *25* K–R2, Q–Q2 (Preventing *26* P–N3.); *26* Q–K3? (Time pressure. Correct is *26* B–B1.) *26* ..., BxN!; *27* KPxB (Conceding Black the majority on the K-side, which is dangerous. However, *27* BPxB is worse because of *27* ..., R–B6.) *27* ..., P–B4!; *28* B–B1, Q–R5 (Also time pressure. Tarrasch recommends *28* ..., N–R1 and ... P–KN4.) *29* R–N1, Q–K1??; *30* N–Q4!, N–B5; *31* N–B6? (*31* P–N3! should win.) *31* ..., B–B2; *32* Q–KB3, Q–B2; *33* P–N3, N–N3; *34* P–QR4, N–K2; *35* P–N5, P–QR4; *36* B–K2, NxN; *37* NPxN!, P–K5; *38* Q–R5, Q–B3; *39* B–B1, QR–K1; *40* B–N2, Q–Q5; *41* Q–K2, R–K2; *42* QR–Q1, Q–B3; *43* Q–Q2, KR–K1; *44* R–K2, R–K4; *45* QR–K1, P–N4; *46* K–N1, P–R4; *47* Q–Q4, P–N5; *48* P–R4, K–N2, with a draw.

BRACLAV RABAR   GEDEON BARCZA

(From the Chess Olympics at Helsinki 1952)

1	P–K4	P–QB4
2	N–KB3	N–QB3
3	P–Q4	PxP
4	NxP	N–B3
5	N–QB3	P–Q3
6	B–K2	P–K4
7	N–N3	....

The usual and best retreat.

7	....	B–K3

Or 7 ..., B–K2, when 8 B–KN5 offers no advantage because of 8 ..., NxP; 9 NxN, BxB; 10 NxPch, K–K2. This twist would fail in case of 7 N–B3, a reason why 7 ..., P–KR3 is then useful.

8 B–KN5 ....

The first step towards improvement in span control.

8 .... B–K2
9 0–0 0–0

Not 9 ..., NxP because of 10 NxN, BxB; 11 NxPch, K–K2; 12 NxNP, as Rabar points out.

10 BxN BxB
11 N–Q5 BxN

Needlessly parting with the good Bishop. The threat of 12 NxBch, QxN; 13 QxP should be parried with 11 ..., B–N4!; Black then has a satisfactory game, e.g. 12 P–QB3, N–K2!, or 12 P–KB4, PxP; 13 NxP, BxN; 14 RxB, P–Q4!.

12 QxB Q–B2
13 P–QB3 ....

Now the span control is even, and White has the edge. The backward pawn has become a liability, partly because it hampers Black's Bishop.

DIAGRAM 181

Position after 13 P–QB3

The straggler a liability

13 .... KR–Q1

Threatening to exchange the straggler with *14* ..., N–K2 and *15* ..., P–Q4.

14 B–B4	QR–B1

So as to obtain approximate equality with *15* ..., N–N5; *16* QxPch, QxQ; *17* BxQch, KxB; *18* PxN, R–B5; *19* P–B3, RxNP; *20* QR–B1, R–Q2.

15 N–Q2	N–R4
16 B–N3	P–QR3

16 ..., NxB would leave Black with the bad Bishop against a Knight.

17 KR–Q1	R–Q2

Rabar correctly remarks that *17* ..., P–QN4, possibly followed by ... B–N4 and ... N–B5, offers a better chance for counterplay.

18 P–KN3	N–B3
19 N–B1	R–B1

A preparation for *20* ..., N–K2.

20 Q–Q3	....

Creating the possibility of N–K3–Q5. However, White must avoid the exchange of the Knights so that the neutralizing effect of the Bishops of opposite color would not become prevalent.

20	B–N4

Relying on *21* N–K3, BxN (although White then still holds the edge, his Bishop being stronger than the Knight).

21 P–KR4!	B–R3

Not ideal, but the alternatives are worse (1) *21* ..., B–B3; *22* N–K3, N–K2; *23* N–N4! (2) *21* ..., B–Q1; *22* N–K3, N–K2; *23* N–B4! (3) *21* ..., B–K2; *22* N–K3.

22 N–R2!	....

Threatening to double Black's KR-pawn with 23 N–N4.

22 ....   P–KN3

A necessity of portentous significance, for it exposes Black to the St. George attack.

23 N–N4   K–N2

The choice is difficult. Black also is in dire straits after 23 ..., B–N2; 24 K–N2!, P–KR4; 25 N–K3, N–K2; 26 P–N4, PxP; 27 R–R1.

24 K–N2   R(2)–Q1

24 ..., P–B4 fails against 25 PxP, PxP; 26 NxB, KxN; 27 B–K6, as pointed out by Rabar.

25 NxB	KxN
26 Q–Q2ch	K–N2
27 P–R5!	Q–K2
28 PxP	RPxP
29 R–R1	R–KR1
30 QR–Q1!	....

The St. George attack is in full swing. White threatens 31 RxR, winning either the Q-pawn (31 ..., RxR; 32 QxP) or the KN-pawn (31 ..., KxR; 32 Q–R6ch, K–N1; 33 QxPch).

30	RxR
31 RxR	Q–B3

It is necessary to concede White the open file (31 ..., R–KR1?; 32 RxR, KxR; 33 Q–R6ch, K–N1; 34 QxPch).

32 Q–R6ch	K–N1
33 B–Q5	R–Q2
34 Q–R3	R–B2
35 Q–R7ch	K–B1
36 Q–R6ch	K–K2

Black has escaped, it seems.

37 Q–K3!   ....

But this fine move keeps the attack going. In threatening
38 Q–N6, K–Q2; 39 BxNch, White wins time for a full-scale
penetration along the KR-file.

37	N–Q1
38 R–R7	K–Q2
39 Q–R6	K–B1
40 Q–B8	....

Only now White's advantage has become decisive.

40	R–Q2
41 Q–R8!	....

White can also win with 41 R–R8!, followed by pawn action
against the King, according to Rabar.

41	QxQ
42 RxQ	R–K2
43 K–B3!	....

The final action is left to the King. White won as follows:

43 ..., K–Q2; 44 K–N4, R–K1; 45 RxR, KxR; 46 K–N5, K–K2;
47 P–N3, P–N3 (Or 47 ..., N–B3; 48 P–QN4. Black is in a
squeeze.) 48 P–QB4, P–R4; 49 P–R3, N–K3ch (Otherwise Black
must allow 50 K–B6, which is just as bad.) 50 BxN, KxB;
51 K–R6, K–B3; 52 P–B3, K–K3; 53 P–QN4, PxP; 54 PxP, K–B3;
55 P–N4, K–K3; 56 K–N7, K–K2; 57 P–KN5, K–K1 (Or 57 ...,
K–K3; 58 K–B8, P–B3; 59 K–N7!.) 58 K–B6, K–B1; 59 P–B5!,
QPxP; 60 PxP, PxP; 61 KxKP, P–B3ch (A last try.); 62 PxP!,
K–B2; 63 K–Q6! (The short way. After 63 K–Q5, KxP White
still wins with 64 P–B4! while 64 KxP? only draws: 64 ...,
K–K4; 65 K–B4, P–N4; 66 K–Q3, K–B5; 67 K–K2, P–N5!; 68 PxP,
KxKP!) 63 ..., P–B5; 64 P–K5, P–B6; 65 P–K6ch, KxBP;
66 P–K7, P–B7; 67 P–K8(Q), P–B8(Q); 68 Q–K7ch, and mate
next move.

IX–§: The Boleslavsky wall

Here follows an example illustrating the pawn formation of *Diagram 124* as characterized by PQB4, PK4 vs PQB3, PQ3.

ROBERT BYRNE   ALEXANDER KOTOV

(From the 1954 team match USA—USSR)

1 P–Q4, N–KB3; *2* P–QB4, P–KN3; *3* P–KN3, B–N2; *4* B–N2, 0–0; *5* N–QB3, P–Q3; *6* N–B3, QN–Q2; *7* 0–0, P–K4; *8* P–K4, P–B3; *9* P–KR3, R–K1; *10* R–K1, P–QR4; *11* B–K3, PxP; *12* NxP.

This is the most usual form of the Boleslavsky wall, its fianchetto type.

DIAGRAM 182

Position after 12 NxP

Boleslavsky wall, fianchetto type

There is no basic difference between the positions of *Diagram 124* and this one.

| 12 .... | N–B4 |
| 13 Q–B2 | P–R5 |

A preparation for ... Q–R4 and, possibly, a later ... P–QR6.

| 14 QR–Q1 | .... |

White sometimes fares well by meeting ... Q–R4 with QR–N1 and P–QN4, provided he can do it without losing time. And time he would lose in this case. The text move, threatening *15* NxBP, is too strongly indicated to be replaced by something like *14* K–R2.

$$14 \ldots \ldots \qquad\qquad Q–R4$$

There is no hurry with this sortie.

More usual for the sake of a convenient protection of the Q-pawn is *14* ..., KN–Q2, e.g.

(1) *15* B–B4, N–K4, with about even chances;

(2) *15* KN–K2, Q–R4!
   (2a) *16* RxP, Q–N5!, and Black recovers the pawn with a good game;
   (2b) *16* B–KB1, N–K4 (*16* ..., Q–N5?; *17* P–QR3!, QxBP??; *18* N–Q4!) *17* N–Q4, P–R6; *18* P–B4, KN–Q2; *19* P–N3, N–R3; *20* B–B2, KN–B4; *21* R–K3, N–N5; *22* Q–K2, B–Q2, with a good game for Black (Reshevsky–Bronstein, Zurich 1953);

(3) *15* P–B4, Q–R4; *16* B–B2, N–N3, with sharp play and approximately even chances (Stahlberg–Boleslavsky, Zurich 1953).

$$15 \ P–B4 \qquad\qquad \ldots \ldots$$

Best, according to Robert Byrne.

A good alternative is *15* B–B4, e.g. *15* ..., B–B1; *16* N–B3, B–K3; *17* BxP, BxBP; *18* BxB, KxB; *19* P–K5, N–Q4; *20* R–Q4, P–QN4; *21* Q–Q2, K–N1; *22* Q–R6, P–B3; *23* PxP, NxP; *24* Q–N5, with a superior game for White (Reshevsky–Najdorf, match 1952, 14th game).

Not commendable is *15* P–R3, e.g. *15* ..., KN–Q2; *16* B–KB1, R–K2; *17* P–B4, N–B3; *18* B–B2, B–Q2, with a good game for Black (Botvinnik–Geller, Budapest 1952).

$$15 \ldots \ldots \qquad\qquad B–Q2$$

Black is going to double his Rooks on the K-file, which is tactically faulty.

He should proceed with *15* KN–Q2 transposing to Stahlberg–
Boleslavsky (see above).

16	B–B2	R–K2
17	P–KN4	QR–K1
18	P–B5!	....

Tactically decisive as Black's pieces seriously hamper each
other. White threatens to win a piece with *19* P–N5, and this
while ... NKB3 has no move. Another strong threat is *19* B–N3.

18	....	PxP

The only other move is *18* ..., P–R3, but then White obtains
a winning advantage with *19* B–N3, Q–B2; *20* PxP, PxP;
21 P–K5, PxP; *22* QxNP.

19	NxKBP!	BxN
20	KPxB	RxRch
21	RxR	....

White has a great advantage thanks to his advanced majority
and pair of Bishops. He still threatens P–N5.

21	....	P–R6

A clever combination which prevents P–N5 for the moment.

22	P–N5?	....

White fails to see the point and falls into trouble. Simply
22 P–N3 (or even *22* PxP) keeps the advantage.

22	....	PxP!!
23	PxN	RxRch
24	BxR	BxP
25	QxP	....

There is no way of keeping the piece, for White faces too many threats (25 ..., N–R5; 25 ..., BxN, and 25 ..., P–N8(Q)).

25	N–Q6
26 Q–K2	NxB
27 QxN	B–Q5ch
28 K–R1	K–B1
29 Q–Q2	QxN
30 QxQ	BxQ

Black has emerged with an extra pawn and some winning chances, Bishops of opposite color notwithstanding. Indeed not a very logical result. However, the way it went gives at least an idea of the highly tactical nature of the Boleslavsky wall.

Following is the rest of the game in brief:

31 B–B3, K–K2; *32* K–N2, K–B3; *33* B–R5, KxP; *34* BxP, K–K5; *35* K–B2 (P–KR4–R5 draws, as pointed out by Bondarevsky, for it finally leads to KQ3, PKR5 vs KQ4, BQN3, PKR3. Byrne sensed such a possibility but was too short of time to analyse the details.) *35* ..., K–Q6; *36* B–K6, P–R3; *37* K–B3, B–K4; *38* K–B2, B–B3; *39* K–B3, B–N4; *40* K–B2, B–R5ch; *41* K–B3, B–N4; *42* K–B2 (Missing his last chance. After *42* K–N4! he still gets in P–KR4–R5). *42* ..., P–R4!; *43* K–N3, P–R5ch! (Decisive, for it finally leads to KQ3, PKR3 vs KQ4, BQB3, PKR5.) *44* K–N4, B–Q1; *45* P–R4, K–Q5; *46* P–R5, P–Q4!; *47* PxP, P–B4!; *48* B–B8, P–B5; *49* K–B3, BxP; *50* K–K2, P–N4; *51* P–Q6, P–N5; *52* K–Q1, P–N6; *53* K–B1, K–B6; *54* B–B5, B–Q1; *55* K–N1, B–N4; *56* P–Q7, K–N5; *57* B–N4, P–B6; *58* B–B5, K–B4, and White resigned.

INDEX OF GAMES

Alphabetical, according to the players with White. The columns "Full," "Part," and "Text" refer to whole games, excerpts, and briefly mentioned games respectively.